Ancient Rhetoric and the Style of Paul's Letters

"Decades into the renewed study of Paul's rhetoric, a satisfying evaluation of his style remains elusive. Brookins's thorough and thoughtfully crafted inventory of stylistic features gathers the raw material in an accessible and illuminating format. With a judicious introduction surveying the scholarly terrain, this book will be a valuable companion for readers seeking a richer appreciation of the stylistic texture of Paul's letters."

—**Ryan S. Schellenberg**, Methodist Theological School in Ohio

"Drawing on his deep knowledge of ancient rhetoric, Timothy Brookins has produced a most useful book on the rhetorical style of Paul's letters. Every student interested in the ways the Apostle makes his arguments will want this well-organized reference work always close at hand. All of us interested in the literary shape of Paul's argument are indebted to Brookins for this model of 'lucid brevity'!"

—**Mikeal C. Parsons**, Baylor University

"Paul and rhetoric continues to be a hot topic. Some see Paul as a full-blown orator and others downplay his level of rhetorical knowledge. However, one factor that most scholars engaging in the Paul and rhetoric debate accept is that Paul uses elements of Greek style. Paul doesn't just use these for superficial display; he uses them with purpose. Brookins provides the examples, and now it is up to Pauline interpreters to explain their exegetical importance."

—**Stanley E. Porter**, McMaster Divinity College

"An outstanding and much needed resource! Attention to Paul's style has dwindled in an era preoccupied with Paul's invention and arrangement, but there is much to be learned from the kind of meticulous analysis of Paul's style provided herein. Brookins rightly claims that attention to Paul's style is relevant to such topics as Paul's education, theology, epistolary types, letter distinctives, Pauline authorship, and interpretive clarity. Highly recommended!"

—**Mark D. Given**, Missouri State University

"*Ancient Rhetoric and the Style of Paul's Letters* is a helpful tool for both the study of Pauline letters and the study of rhetoric. . . . Brookins gives concrete examples from the Pauline corpus of how Paul used the smaller figures of style to achieve their persuasive ends in these New Testament letters. Brookins does so with a complete lack of tendentiousness or partisanship. I commend this careful and comprehensive work."

—**Frank W. Hughes**, co-author of *The Corinthian Correspondence: Redaction, Rhetoric, and History*

Ancient Rhetoric and the Style of Paul's Letters

—— *A Reference Book* ——

Timothy A. Brookins

CASCADE *Books* • Eugene, Oregon

ANCIENT RHETORIC AND THE STYLE OF PAUL'S LETTERS
A Reference Book

Copyright © 2022 Timothy A. Brookins. All rights reserved. Except for brief quotations in critical publications or reviews, no part of this book may be reproduced in any manner without prior written permission from the publisher. Write: Permissions, Wipf and Stock Publishers, 199 W. 8th Ave., Suite 3, Eugene, OR 97401.

Cascade Books
An Imprint of Wipf and Stock Publishers
199 W. 8th Ave., Suite 3
Eugene, OR 97401

www.wipfandstock.com

PAPERBACK ISBN: 978-1-5326-9895-8
HARDCOVER ISBN: 978-1-5326-9896-5
EBOOK ISBN: 978-1-5326-9897-2

Cataloguing-in-Publication data:

Names: Brookins, Timothy A., author.

Title: Ancient rhetoric and the style of Paul's letters : a reference book / by Timothy A. Brookins.

Description: Eugene, OR: Cascade Books, 2022 | Includes bibliographical references and index.

Identifiers: ISBN 978-1-5326-9895-8 (paperback) | ISBN 978-1-5326-9896-5 (hardcover) | ISBN 978-1-5326-9897-2 (ebook)

Subjects: LCSH: Bible. Epistles of Paul—Language, style. | Bible. Epistles of Paul—Socio-rhetorical criticism. | Rhetoric in the Bible | Rhetoric, Ancient | Greek language—Style

Classification: BS2655.L3 B76 2022 (print) | BS2655.L3 (ebook)

10/12/22

To
Mikeal Parsons

CONTENTS

Acknowledgments | ix

Introduction | 1
Style in Paul's Letters | 28
   1. Correctness (Lausberg, §463–527)   28
      1.1. Barbarisms (Lausberg, §479–95)   29
      1.2. Solecisms (Lausberg, §496–527)   29
         1.2.1. By addition (Lausberg, §502–503)   29
         1.2.2. By subtraction (Lausberg, §504)   30
         1.2.3. By transposition (Lausberg, §505)   38
         1.2.4. By substitution (Lausberg, §506–527)   41
   2. Clarity (Lausberg, §528–537)   44
   3. Ornament (Lausberg, §538–1054)   47
      3.1. In Single Words   48
         3.1.1. Archaisms (Lausberg §546)   48
         3.1.2. Neologisms (Lausberg §547–51)   48
         3.1.3. Tropes (Lausberg §552–98)   49
      3.2. In the Conjunction of Words   93
         3.2.1. Figures (§600–910)   93
         3.2.2. Composition (Lausberg, §911–1054)   194

Bibliography | 201
Author Index | 207
Subject Index | 209
Scripture Index | 213

ACKNOWLEDGMENTS

Many people have contributed to the completion of this book. This work would not have been possible without the gracious understanding of my wife, Mary Mac, and my children, Adam, Ryan, and Caitlin, as I spent time on breaks, and here and there between classes and other responsibilities, slowly gathering my research over the course of several years. I am grateful to Houston Baptist University for my sabbatical during the Spring 2021 semester, during which I completed no small portion of the manuscript. I owe thanks to one of our graduate students, Keith Idol, for consulting many commentaries for me. I thank Douglas Estes, Mark Given, Frank Hughes, Mikeal Parsons, Peter Reynolds, and Ryan Schellenberg for their feedback at various stages in the process. I owe special thanks to Ryan Schellenberg for engaging thoughtfully with the project and for offering helpful critical feedback. Mike Parsons acted as a consultant at many points throughout the writing process. It was Mike, too, who first introduced me to rhetorical criticism of the New Testament, during my first semester at Baylor University in Fall 2008. I am grateful to Mike not only for what I learned from him in seminar, but also for the patience he showed toward me as an underprepared and overconfident graduate student, and for his efforts to validate me, not to the extent that I was worthy of it, but so that I might become worthy of it. If I may adapt Vergil: "*I was able because I was seen to be able.*" It is to Mike that I dedicate this book.

Introduction

This book is a reference work dedicated to the examination of "style" in Paul's letters. The subject is style specifically in the rhetorical sense of the term,[1] that is, in the *ancient Greco-Roman* rhetorical sense, style as *elocutio* or λέξις, the third "part" of ancient rhetorical theory.[2]

Important as the *content* of Paul's theology has been to his interpreters, the subject of his *style of address* has never been far from concern. For many interpreters across history, the character of Paul's style has been held to have essential relevance to the question of the efficacy of his message. Did his success as a preacher depend upon his formal training as an orator? Did the persuasive power of the gospel reside in rhetorical skill and the manipulative tactics of the human agent of proclamation? While the interpreter has no way of answering such questions through the methods of academic inquiry, the pertinent concerns illustrate how important traditional interpreters have regarded the matter of style in Paul's letters. In recent decades, interest in rhetorical analysis of his letters has only grown, and exponentially so. The concerns of older interpreters remain, though recent rhetorical analysis has also been motivated by other interests, as we discuss below.

The main part of this book is essentially an inventory of stylistic devices that appear in Paul's letters, as defined and systematized by ancient Greco-Roman theorists. Prefatory to this examination of style, it will be necessary first to discuss the place of "style" within ancient rhetorical theory; the history of rhetorical analysis of the NT and the letters

---

1. As Botha ("Style in the New Testament," 71–87) observes, modern interpreters have used the term "style" to describe "virtually anything related to language and language usage," from grammar and syntax, to dialect (especially "Semitic" versus "Hellenistic"), idiolect (i.e., "Pauline" style), and the use of rhetorical figures.

2. On the five "parts" (*partes*) of rhetoric, see Cicero, *Or.* 1.142; Quintilian, *Inst.* 3.3.11; elsewhere called the five "duties" (*officia*): Ps.-Cicero, *Rhet. Her.* 2.1.1; or "functions" (*opera*): Quintilian, *Inst.* 3.3.11.

of Paul; and questions of method in analysis of the kind undertaken here. Introduction concludes with a precis of the present volume, explaining its format, scope, and purpose.

Ancient Rhetorical Theory and Style

Naturally, ancient "rhetoric" (ῥητορική) predated its theorization. Centuries before rhetoric became a "theory," Homer extolled the virtue of eloquence in the person of his legendary characters, most of all the eloquent Nestor (*Il.* 1.249). By the fifth century BCE, rhetoric had become a matter of "analytic" interest. Originating in the schools of the Greek sophists, the analytic approach to rhetoric gave rise to the first theoretical handbooks, of which the earliest extant examples are Pseudo-Aristotle's *Rhetoric to Alexander* and Aristotle's *On Rhetoric*, both dating to the fourth century BCE.[3]

The handbook tradition reached its most systematic form during the Roman period (beginning in the first-century BCE). This period saw the production of Cicero's works *On Invention* and *On the Orator*, as well as a work now assigned to Ps.-Cicero entitled *Rhetoric for Herennius*, and most comprehensive in its treatment, Quintilian's *Institutes of Oratory*.

For the Roman theorists, oratory entailed five "parts": invention (*inventio*), arrangement (*dispositio*), style (*elocutio*), memory (*memoria*), and delivery (*pronuntiatio*).[4] While this fivefold division is not found in works prior to the Roman theorists, all five parts receive functional treatment in the earlier handbooks. Among the earlier handbooks, style (φράσις or λέξις in Greek),[5] receives treatment in both Pseudo-Aristotle's *Rhetoric* and book 3 of Aristotle's *Rhetoric*. The earliest complete treatise on style is that attributed traditionally to Demetrius of Phaleron, *On Style*; although the attribution is no longer regarded as correct, the work is commonly dated between the third and first centuries BCE. More than a dozen extant treatises written between the first century BC and second century CE treat style in part or in whole, including among them the Latin works by Cicero, Pseudo-Cicero, and Quintilian cited above.[6]

---

3. See a lengthy history of Greco-Roman rhetoric in Litfin, *St. Paul's Theology of Proclamation*, 21–134; and a briefer history in Mack, *Rhetoric and the New Testament*, 25–31.

4. "Parts" (*partes*): Quintilian, *Inst.* 3.3.11; cf. Cicero, *Or.* 1.142; alternatively, "duties" (*officia*): Ps.-Cicero, *Rhet. Her.* 2.1.1; "functions" (*opera*): Quintilian, *Inst.* 3.3.11.

5. For the terminology, see Quintilian, *Inst.* 8.1.1.

6. Other notable works on style include: Ps.-Aristotle, *Rhetoric to Alexander* (fourth

INTRODUCTION

As the most extensive and systematic extant treatise on style, Quintilian's *Institutes of Oratory* provides a useful summary of what ancient theorists commonly included under this part of rhetoric. Style, or *elocutio*, occupies parts 8.1—11.1 out of the twelve books in the treatise. Here Quintilian arranges the sections according to the primary "virtues" (*virtutes*) of style. Included are the virtues of correctness (*Latinitas*), clarity (*perspicuitas*), and as the most distinguishing virtue, ornament (*ornatus*). To these Quintilian adds a fourth virtue, that of propriety (*aptum*), though as he says, theorists commonly subsume this virtue under the heading of ornament.[7]

In discussing each of the virtues, Quintilian arranges the matter according to a recurring division between what is expressed "in single words" (*in singulis verbis*) and what is expressed "in conjoined words" (*in coniunctis verbis*, or *in pluribus verbis*).[8] Quintilian leaves his lengthiest treatment to the virtue of ornament (*Inst.* 8.3—10.7), dividing discussion, again, into ornament *in singulis verbis* (8.3.15–39) and ornament *in coniunctis verbis* (8.3.40–89). Under the former heading he puts tropes (τρόποι, *tropoi*)—including metaphor, metonymy, and synecdoche, among other tropes (8.6). Under ornament *in coniunctis verbis* are included figures (*figurae*), which divide into figures of thought (9.2) and figures of speech (9.3). Last of all Quintilian discusses "composition" (*compositio*), which concerns linguistic aspects of expression like syntactic-formation, word order, and rhythm (9.4).

---

century BCE); Theophrastus, *On Style* (fourth/third century BCE); Caecilius, *On Figures* (first century BCE); Dionysius of Halicarnassus, *On Composition* (first century BCE).

7. Quintilian, *Inst.* 1.5.1; cf. 11.1. Other ancient theorists enumerated the virtues differently, though the standards remained substantially consistent. Aristotle describes "excellence of style," or "virtue of style" (ἀρετὴ τῆς λέξεως), as being clear (σαφής), fitting (πρέπουσα), and correct (τὸ ἑλληνίζειν), and though he does not speak explicitly of "ornament," he describes throughout *Rhet.* 3.2.6—3.12.4 the ornamental devices that Quintilian includes under this heading. Cicero's *De Oratore* describes four virtues of style (3.37), namely those of correctness (*Latine*), clarity (*plane*), ornament (*ornate*), and appropriateness (*congruenter*). In *De Officiis* (1.2), he mentions all but the first of these (one should speak *apte, distincte*, and *ornate*). The Stoics are said to have added a fifth virtue (Diogenes Laertius, *Vit. phil.* 7.59), that of brevity (συντομία). The author of *Rhetorica ad Herennium* says that style should have the qualities of elegance (*elegantia*), artistic composition (*compositio*), and distinction (*dignitas*).

8. Quintilian, *Inst.* 1.5.2; 8.1.1; 8.3.15.

History of Research

Before Modern Rhetorical Criticism

It is hardly a simplification to say that Greco-Roman education was primarily education in the "art of speaking well."[9] Rhetorical training constituted the final stage in the ancient school curriculum and, in a world where most people lacked competence in even basic literacy, served not only as a measure of one's educational achievement, but also of one's social status.[10]

Hence, it is not surprising that Paul's manner of speech so frequently attracted the attention of his earliest interpreters. Among the Church Fathers many remarked that Paul's writings lacked the elegance characteristic of the great Greco-Roman orators of the time.[11] On the other hand, St. Augustine's (354–430 CE) assessment reveals that a low estimation of Paul's rhetorical abilities among Christian writers may have been at least partially theologically motivated. In Augustine's view Paul's letters indeed exemplified the same stylistic features as those taught by secular rhetoric. The difference was that Paul's eloquence derived from the moving of the Spirit, not the taught rules of rhetoric per se.[12]

An interest in Paul's style continued beyond antiquity. From Bede (673–735 CE) to the Reformers to early modern interpreters Paul's many readers continued to analyze his letters according to the stylistic standards of rhetorical theory.[13] The late seventeenth century saw the production of Keach's *Tropologia* (1682), and the nineteenth century Howson's collection *The Metaphors of St. Paul* (1868) and Bullinger's lengthy inventory *Figures of Speech Used in the Bible* (1898), which prominently featured Paul's letters.[14] Through the early and mid-twentieth century, scholarly

---

9. This (*ars bene dicendi*) is Quintilian's definition of "rhetoric (*rhetorice*)" (Quintilian, *Inst.* 2.17.37); also, the "science of speaking well (*bene dicendi scientia*)" (Quintilian, *Inst.* 2.16.11; 2.18.38).

10. Morgan, *Literate Education*, esp. 190–239.

11. Irenaeus, *Haer.* 3.7.1–2; Origen, *Comm. Jo.* 4.2; John Chrysostom, *Laud. Paul.* 4.10.

12. Augustine, *Doctr. chr.* 4.6.9—4.7.11. Augustine (*Doctr. chr.* 4.7.11) observes Paul's use of climax, followed by a periodic sentence, in Rom 5:3–5. Origen (*Comm. Jo.* 4.2) attributed the power of Paul's speech to the Spirit and the truthfulness of the message.

13. See a brief history in Watson and Hauser, *Rhetorical Criticism of the Bible*, 102–3; on Phillip Melanchthon see especially Classen, "St. Paul's Epistles," esp. 325–31.

14. Keach, Τροποσχημαλογία. *Tropes and Figures*; Howson, *Metaphors of St. Paul*; Bullinger, *Figures of Speech*.

articles and books considered tropes and specific figures of speech in Paul's letters along with the other NT documents.[15] Most Greek grammars of this period touched upon or included sections that discussed style of composition and figures of speech used by the biblical writers.[16] Many commentaries also commented on style.[17]

Modern Rhetorical Criticism

Whatever interest earlier interpreters had in the rhetoric of the NT, in the final third of the twentieth century, interest in rhetorical analysis reached a new and sudden high. A narrative quickly arose to explain this explosion of interest.[18] According to the standard version, interpreters historically were disinclined to apply rhetorical standards to the NT writings, since rhetoric was a *mere* matter of style and style, inflated by the ornamental devices taught by rhetorical theory, was beneath the dignity of the gospel message. Classical rhetoric, however, was about more than mere *style*; it was about *persuasion*. Therefore, even if the NT writings lacked the *stylistic* features recommended by rhetorical theory, rhetorical theory is still relevant to the NT since its writings follow the standards of rhetorical theory in other departments.[19]

This acclaimed rediscovery of ancient rhetoric as more-than-mere-style owed its impetus to several sources: James Muilenburg's 1968 Society

---

15. Tropes: Heylen, "Les Métaphores et les Métonymies"; irony: Reumann, "St. Paul's Use of Irony"; chiasmus: Jeremias, "Chiasmus in den Paulusbriefen." Judge ("Paul's Boasting") treats the question of Paul's education on the basis of his style; antithesis: Schneider, *Die rhetorische Eigenart*.

16. Of note is Turner, *Grammar of New Testament Greek*. Robertson (*Grammar of the Greek New Testament*) discusses sentence composition (390–445) and figures of speech (1194–208) at length; see also Blass et al., *Greek Grammar of the New Testament*, §458–71.

17. E.g., Weiss, "Beiträge zur paulinischen Rhetoric"; Robinson and Plummer, *First Epistle of St. Paul to the Corinthians*.

18. A story told many times over: Kennedy, *New Testament Interpretation through Rhetorical Criticism*, 8–12; Watson, "New Testament and Greco-Roman Rhetoric," esp. 465; Mack, *Rhetoric and the New Testament*, 14–21; Classen, "St. Paul's Epistles and Ancient Greek and Roman Rhetoric," 319–21; Watson and Hauser, *Rhetorical Criticism of the Bible*, 107–9; Fairweather, "Epistle to the Galatians and Classical Rhetoric," esp. 2; Olbricht, "Flowering of Rhetorical Criticism"; Sampley and Lampe, *Paul and Rhetoric*, 3–5.

19. Repeated in Kennedy, *New Testament Interpretation through Rhetorical Criticism*, 11–12; Mack, *Rhetoric and the New Testament*, 14–16, 19–21; Watson and Hauser, *Rhetorical Criticism of the Bible*, 105.

of Biblical Literature presidential address, which called for a move "beyond form criticism" to "literary and rhetorical criticism"; a 1976 article by Wilhelm Wuellner; H. D. Betz's 1979 commentary on Galatians; and the publications of George Kennedy (especially 1984).[20]

The originality of modern rhetorical criticism could be questioned.[21] Yet, the new interest in rhetorical analysis in this era differed from what came earlier in several ways. First was the precipitous gain in popularity of this approach and the sheer level of enthusiasm with which interpreters pursued it. A full-blown movement was underway by the 1980s. In 1988 Duane Watson published a bibliography on "The New Testament and Greco-Roman Rhetoric" containing nearly one hundred publications that specifically treated the NT, about half of which treated the letters of Paul. In 1990 Watson published a follow-up bibliography that contained more than two hundred additional publications, with more than fifty of these treating the Pauline letters.[22] The next two decades produced, among many other publications, a series of essay collections on rhetorical analysis of the NT, in which the lion's share of essays treated the letters of Paul.[23]

Taking seriously the realization that ancient rhetoric was about more than "mere style," most studies during this period directed their attention to the "parts" (*partes*) of rhetoric that ancient theorists referred to as "invention" (*inventio*) and "arrangement" (*dispositio*).[24] The latter was of particular interest in the analysis of Paul's letters, which interpreters regarded essentially as "speeches," arranged by Paul according to the same parts of

20. James Muilenburg's address, published as "Form Criticism and Beyond"; Wuellner, "Paul's Rhetoric of Argumentation"; Betz, *Galatians*; Kennedy, *New Testament Interpretation through Rhetorical Criticism*.

21. As Classen has shown ("St. Paul's Epistles and Ancient Greek and Roman Rhetoric," esp. 321–33), Phillip Melanchthon paid extensive attention to non-stylistic aspects of Paul's rhetoric. Classen discusses this point in response to Wuellner's 1976 article and reviews, for demonstration, Melanchthon's examination of Galatians.

22. Watson, "New Testament and Greco-Roman Rhetoric"; Watson, "New Testament and Greco-Roman Rhetoric: A Bibliographical Update." A vast majority of these publications date to the 1970s and 80s. See also Watson and Hauser, *Rhetorical Criticism of the Bible*, which Watson describes as a "comprehensive bibliography" of rhetorical criticism of the bible (treating the NT in 126–206, and Paul in 178–202).

23. Watson, *Persuasive Artistry*; Porter and Olbricht, *Rhetoric and the New Testament*; Porter and Olbricht, *Rhetorical Analysis of Scripture*; Porter and Stamps, *Rhetorical Interpretation of Scripture*; Porter, *Handbook of Classical Rhetoric*; Sampley and Lampe, *Paul and Rhetoric*.

24. This is the focus of several essays in Porter and Olbricht, *Rhetoric and the New Testament*.

a speech prescribed by rhetorical theorists.²⁵ Interest in *inventio* picked up in the 1990s as interest in *dispositio* somewhat waned.²⁶ In this vein interpreters looked closely at the speech "situation" (rhetorical *status*), the "kind" (*genus*) of speech that such a situation demanded (forensic, deliberative, or epideictic), and the argumentative strategies that Paul utilized to carry out the needed ends (his use of proofs, topoi, exempla, etc.).²⁷ In some instances, studies considered the elements of *inventio* and *dispositio* together; style (or *elocutio*) was sometimes included, though generally with less serious attention.²⁸

Despite the turn to matters of *inventio* and *dispositio* in the new era, stylistic aspects of Paul's letters have continued to receive some attention on their own²⁹—with some studies examining the various devices used in specific passages;³⁰ others concentrating on specific stylistic devices;³¹ and others examining style of composition.³² The general feeling reflected in literature of this period, however, is that observations about style are of little value on their own. In a 2010 collection, Watson observed that scholarship

---

25. This became the standard approach to outlining Paul's letters in commentaries in the 1980s and early 90s; e.g., Betz, *Galatians*; Jewett, *Thessalonian Correspondence*, 72–76; Wanamaker, *Epistles to the Thessalonians*, 48–52. An essay by Olbricht ("Rhetorical Criticism in Biblical Commentaries") summarizes the place of rhetorical analysis in the commentaries of the time. Several essays in Watson, *Persuasive Artistry* take this approach; so also essays in Porter and Olbricht, *Rhetorical Analysis of Scripture*. Most recently, see Hughes and Jewett, *Corinthian Correspondence*.

26. So Eriksson, "Special Topics in 1 Corinthians 8–10," esp. 273.

27. E.g., Sampley, "Paul, His Opponents in 2 Corinthians 10–13"; numerous essays in Porter and Olbricht, *Rhetoric and the New Testament*; Novenson, "'God Is Witness'"; and recently Schmeller, "Dissimulatio artis?"

28. E.g., Olbricht, "Aristotelian Rhetorical Analysis"; Given, "Paul and Rhetoric."

29. In addition to the studies listed below, see Duane Watson's letter-by-letter catalog of publications, in Watson, "Role of Style in the Pauline Letters," esp. 124–33.

30. Romans 5: Cosby, "Paul's Persuasive Language in Romans 5"; Rom 8:31–39: Snyman, "Style and Meaning in Romans 8:31–9"; Rom 12:9–16: Black, "Pauline Love Command"; 1 Cor 1:17—2:10: Levison, "Did the Spirit Inspire Rhetoric?"; 2 Cor 11:16—12:13: Spencer, "Wise Fool (and the Foolish Wise)"; Galatians 1–2: Classen, "St. Paul's Epistles," 334–39.

31. Prosopopoeia and sermocinatio: Stowers, "Romans 7:7–25 as a Speech-in-Character (προσοποποιία)"; Witherington, *New Testament Rhetoric*, 132–52; King, *Speech-in-Character*, 163–293; irony: Spencer, "Wise Fool (and the Foolish Wise)"; Holland, "Paul's Use of Irony."

32. Robbins, "Composition of Eph 1:3–14"; Jewett, "Rhetorical Function"; Holloway, "Paul's Pointed Prose."

has moved away from the mere *identification* of stylistic features to discussion of their rhetorical *function*,[33] since, as both he and others observe, the identification of devices adds little benefit to interpreters apart from the light they shed on Paul's purposes and meaning.[34]

In sum, the post-Muilenburg era of rhetorical criticism has seen a major surge of interest in the matters of *inventio* and *dispositio*, resulting in less emphasis on style than was seen in previous centuries. Indeed, the inception of rhetorical criticism as a *response* to traditional interpreters' conception of rhetoric as "mere style" inevitably meant that style would not be a major part of the new agenda. Moreover, studies have often warned about the "mere identification" of stylistic devices, characterizing this activity as something that scholarship has "moved beyond." With regard to style, these are somewhat unfortunate trends, since in fact no one to date has attempted anything approximating an extensive inventory (or "identification") of devices in Paul's letters, much less the other NT documents.[35] While attention to the function of these devices would surely help elucidate the meaning of the text, a comprehensive inventory would, as we suggest below, offer benefits of its own.

Method

Epistolary and Rhetorical Theory

By the early 1990s an increasing number of scholars were challenging the validity of rhetorical criticism as an approach to *letters*, for one simple reason: the ancient theory of letter-writing—or epistolography—existed as a separate branch of literary study and one that theorists did not integrate with rhetorical theory until Late Antiquity and the Middle Ages.[36]

33. Watson, "Role of Style in the Pauline Letters," 120.

34. Cf. Spencer, "Wise Fool (and the Foolish Wise)"; Snyman, "Style and Meaning in Romans 8:31–9," 94; Black, "Pauline Love Command," 4.

35. Porter, "Paul of Tarsus and His Letters" (Porter, *Handbook of Classical Rhetoric*, 533–86) includes an inventory of stylistic devices on 578–83; at the same time, Porter himself declares that "rhetorical labeling in and of itself is not a viable way of interpreting the meaning of those texts as discourses" (*Linguistic Analysis of the Greek New Testament*, 104–5). In the same volume, the article "Style" (Porter, *Handbook of Classical Rhetoric*, 121–58), by Rowe, gathers some of its examples of specific figures of speech/thought from Paul's letters. For an extensive compilation of stylistic devices without extensive commentary, one must see Bullinger's old work *Figures of Speech Used in the Bible*.

36. Note the objections of: Classen, "St. Paul's Epistles and Ancient Greek and Roman

INTRODUCTION

According to epistolographical theory, letters had a proper style of their own. Letters are not speeches (Cicero, *Fam.* 9.21.1; Quintilian, *Inst.* 9.4.19-20; Ps.-Demetrius, *Style* 225); they should not contain long periods (Ps.-Demetrius, *Style* 229) or extensive ornamental features (Gregory of Nazianzus, *Ep.* 51.5-7); they should exhibit a mix of the "elegant" and "plain" style (Ps.-Demetrius, *Style* 235; cf. 190); and the writer should write as they would speak in casual conversation (Cicero, *Quint.* 1.1.45-46; *Fam.* 9.21.1; *Att.* 9.10.1; Seneca, *Ep.* 75.2). Hence, whereas "ornament" (*ornatus*) was the crowning virtue of good oratorical style, the chief virtues of letter-writing were "clarity" and "appropriateness," that is, appropriateness of style to the correspondents' relationship and the occasion of writing (Cicero, *Fam.* 15.21.4; Ps.-Libanius, *Epistolary Styles* 48-49; Gregory of Nazianzus, *Ep.* 51.4).[37]

Proponents of rhetorical analysis of ancient letters have responded with counter considerations. First, while ancient theorists never explicitly integrated rhetorical and epistolographical theory, letter-writers expected the letters' recipients to read aloud; hence, it is argued, letters are analogous to speeches.[38] Second, while letters typically exhibited a personal character and less formal style, there were exceptions. Jeffrey Reed cites, among many examples, letters written as self-apologies from exile (Demosthenes, *Ep.* 1-4) and letters that functioned as moral treatises (Plutarch, *Ep.* 6.464; 13.1012). Diplomatic and pseudonymous letters also tended to deploy a more elevated style.[39]

More recent discussions have asserted that there is validity in the application of both epistolographical and rhetorical theory in the analysis of letters.[40] This conclusion is predicated, more controversially, on the view that the principles of arrangement prescribed for speeches—even if they do not

---

Rhetoric," 342-43; Murphy-O'Connor, *Paul the Letter-Writer*, 79-83; Porter, "Paul as Epistolographer *and* Rhetorician?" (Porter and Stamps, *Rhetorical Interpretation of Scripture*, 222-48), esp. 230-34; Klauck, *Ancient Letters and the New Testament*, 224-25; that the two came together over time: Klauck, *Ancient Letters and the New Testament*, 210.

37. For a long discussion of ancient epistolary theory, see Klauck, *Ancient Letters and the New Testament*, 183-211.

38. Kennedy, *New Testament Interpretation through Rhetorical Criticism*, 141; Watson, *Rhetorical Criticism of the Bible*, 120-25; Witherington, *New Testament Rhetoric*, 3-8; cf. Hughes, "Rhetoric of Letters."

39. Reed, "Epistle," esp. 182-90.

40. Lampe, "Rhetorical Analysis of Pauline Texts," esp. 13-17; Martin, "Invention and Arrangement," esp. 51-62; Given, "Paul and Rhetoric."

apply perfectly to letters—can still be legitimately applied if regarded more flexibly. In a less controversial way, the conclusion that both theoretical systems apply is grounded in the difference between the various departments of rhetorical theory. Specifically, those who object to the application of rhetorical theory to Paul's letters object primarily to its application in the area of arrangement (*dispositio*), since letters are not in the end the same as speeches. These scholars consistently emphasize that rhetorical theory is still quite applicable, on the other hand, in the areas of invention and style.[41]

Ancient and Modern Rhetoric

Quintilian's arrangement of the rhetorical system as summarized above ("Rhetorical Theory and Style") has served as the basis for Heinrich Lausberg's massive modern *Handbuch der literarischen Rhetorik*. First published in 1960, Lausberg's handbook offers a systematic summary of ancient rhetorical theory, including in its coverage of the "parts" of rhetoric an exhaustive summary of stylistic devices. Lausberg's second edition, published in 1973, has now been translated into English (*Handbook of Literary Rhetoric*, 1998).[42] Despite criticisms in matters of detail, Lausberg's volume remains the most complete and systematic work of its kind.[43]

While Lausberg's work is rooted in Greco-Roman rhetorical theory, the handbook aims to describe, *through* ancient theory, the kind of "rhetoric" that he believes appears in literature throughout history, from antiquity, through the Middle Ages and Renaissance, and into the modern period. In this sense, Lausberg presents the standards of rhetoric as *enshrined* in Greco-Roman theory as being equally applicable in

---

41. Classen, "St. Paul's Epistles and Ancient Greek and Roman Rhetoric," 342–43; Reed, "Epistle," 182; Porter, "Paul of Tarsus and His Letters" (Porter, *Handbook of Classical Rhetoric*, 533–86), esp. 578, 585. And cf. Aristotle, *Rhet.* 3.1–12; Theon, *Prog.* 70; Quintilian, *Inst.* 12.10.49–51.

42. Lausberg, *Handbuch der literarischen Rhetorik*; ET Lausberg et al., *Handbook of Literary Rhetoric*.

43. An attempt to correct and supplant Lausberg is offered in Martin, *Antike Rhetorik*. Reviews of Lausberg's work, however, have overall been overwhelmingly positive. Rowe ("Style," in Porter, *Handbook of Classical Rhetoric*, 121–58) uses Lausberg's arrangement in his essay overview of style. Apart from Lausberg, other modern works that offer systematic summaries of ancient theories of style include, notably, the older German works of Volkmann, *Die Rhetorik*; and Norden, *Antike Kunstprosa*. See also the dictionary entry on style by de Jonge, and its accompanying bibliography: "Style (lexis), Ancient Theories of."

non-ancient, non-Greco-Roman social and historical contexts. It is, then, not strictly Greco-Roman rhetoric, but something more general—a kind of "universal rhetoric"—that Lausberg describes.

The concept of *universal* rhetoric aligns more closely with the modern, so-called New Rhetoric. Associated especially with the work of Chaïm Perelman and Lucie Olbrechts-Tyteca, this conception of rhetoric deals not only with rhetorical theory as conceived by the Greeks and Romans, but, more broadly, with human persuasion in all its manifestations.[44] Although this conception of rhetoric does not derive from antiquity itself, many scholars regard it as a valid analytical tool for approaching ancient texts;[45] hence, a number of studies conduct rhetorical analyses of Paul's letters through the framework of the New Rhetoric.[46] Of a similar nature are studies that consider stylistic features that, while recognized in ancient rhetorical theory, are regarded for analytic purposes from a grammatical-linguistic perspective rather than the perspective of Greco-Roman theory specifically.[47]

Rhetoric versus the "Art" of Rhetoric

This distinction—between *Greco-Roman* rhetoric and *universal* rhetoric—raises methodological questions about the nature of rhetorical analysis of Paul's letters. Despite the existence of some arguably universal standards, human standards of stylistic virtue are to some extent socially determined and may vary from one context to another. A study of the kind undertaken here therefore must state whether its analysis of Paul's letters presumes, to any degree, his *conscious* application of theoretically derived, *Greco-Roman standards* of eloquence.

---

44. Perelman and Olbrechts-Tyteca, *New Rhetoric*.

45. See Klauck, *Ancient Letters and the New Testament*, 210–11, 225–27; Lampe, "Rhetorical Analysis of Pauline Texts," 5–7.

46. Rhetorical questions: Wuellner, "Paul as Pastor," 49–77.

47. Questions: Estes, *Questions and Rhetoric*; parallelism: Berlin, *Dynamics of Biblical Parallelism*; Johnson, "Romans 1:3–4"; antithesis: Rolland, "L'antithese de Rm 5–8." Several studies examine metaphors in Paul's letters, though not specifically through the framework of ancient rhetorical theory: Williams, *Paul's Metaphors*; others look at specific kinds of metaphors: Burke, *Family Matters*; Finlan, *Background and Content of Paul's Cultic Atonement Metaphors*; Gaventa, *Our Mother Saint Paul*; Hogeterp, *Paul and God's Temple*; Mengestu, *God as Father in Paul*.

Since ancient times Paul's apparent conformity/non-conformity with Greco-Roman standards of eloquence has pressed upon interpreters a sense of obligation to explain what this conformity/non-conformity tells us about his education, or more specifically, whether he had formal training in Greco-Roman rhetoric, and if so how much. In this regard, modern interpreters have widely debated whether Paul completed his education in Tarsus or in Jerusalem, and in the former instance, whether he did so in Hellenistic or in Jewish schools. According to Acts, Paul was "born (γεγεννημένος) in Tarsus" but "brought up (ἀνατεθραμμένος)" and "educated (πεπαιδευμένος)" by Gamaliel in "this city [sc. Jerusalem?]" (22:3); and spent his life "from youth (ἐκ νεότητος) from the beginning (ἀπ' ἀρχῆς)" among his people (26:4). Several aspects of these texts are ambiguous, and many interpreters, speculating that Luke aims to exaggerate Paul's training in Jerusalem, suggest that Paul in fact completed a full rhetorical education in Tarsus, and in Greek rather than Jewish schools. Ryan Schellenberg estimates, as he writes in 2013, that current scholarship shares a "developing consensus" that "Paul's rhetorical ability must have been acquired through formal training" specifically in Greco-Roman theory (an idea to which Schellenberg, however, takes exception).[48] In recent times, even interpreters who see Paul completing his advanced training in Jewish schools have often suggested that he either learned elementary rhetorical exercises in a Hellenistic school in Tarsus[49] or else Greco-Roman rhetorical theory in a Jewish school in Jerusalem.[50]

Complicating the matter of Paul's training are statements made by Paul himself to the effect that—at least as many interpreters understand him (1 Cor 1:17; 2:1–5; 2 Cor 10:10; 11:6; 1 Thess 2:1–10)—he was either not trained in rhetoric or, if he was, chose not to follow its prescriptions, and that he depended instead upon the Spirit for his words and on the Spirit's agency for persuasion (1 Cor 2:1–5).[51] Interpreters have been equally troubled by such passages, since despite Paul's apparent protestations his letters seem to

---

48. Schellenberg, *Rethinking Paul's Rhetorical Education*, 36. Schellenberg's summary of scholarship (36–52) names as taking this view Dale Martin, Jerome Murphy-O'Connor, Ben Witherington, Jerome Neyrey, and Ronald Hock.

49. Stowers, "Apostrophe, προσωποποιία, and Paul's Rhetorical Education," esp. 367–68. Cf. Parsons and Martin, *Ancient Rhetoric and the New Testament*, 2–3.

50. Weiss, "Beiträge zur paulinischen Rhetorik," esp. 184; Witherington, *New Testament Rhetoric*, 99–104.

51. Litfin, *St. Paul's Theology of Proclamation*, 138–39; Levison, "Did the Spirit Inspire Rhetoric?"; Kennedy, *Classical Rhetoric*, 151.

exhibit some substantial rhetorical skill. To this supposed discrepancy interpreters have proposed a variety of solutions: Paul decried only rhetoric used to amuse listeners;[52] he employed "theory" unconsciously or accidentally;[53] he used rhetoric in his letters but not in his preaching;[54] or self-depreciation of his rhetorical ability was itself a rhetorical strategy.[55]

However one understands Paul's claims, it must be said that the appropriateness of stylistic analysis of his letters depends only partly on the question of his formal education. As even Greek and Roman theorists agreed, people could speak eloquently and persuasively without formal training. What was unique about Greco-Roman conceptions of eloquence historically is that the *theoretical* standards were established, first, by comprehensive *description* of the phenomenon of eloquence as people perceived it in those before and contemporary with them, and then the *arrangement* of the constituent features of the descriptive analysis into a system, which one could then use as a *prescriptive* standard for those who aspired to eloquence themselves. In notional distinction from eloquence derived from nature, imitation, or practice, this was rhetoric as an artificial system, or as theorists called it, the "art" (τέχνη, *ars*) of rhetoric.

Theorists differed subtly in their presentation of the relationship between "artificial" and "inartificial" rhetoric. For Aristotle, "rhetoric" (ῥητορική) was a faculty common to all, deployed "either at random (εἰκῇ) or with familiarity arising from habit (διὰ συνήθειαν ἀπὸ ἕξεως)" (*Rhet.* 1.1.1). Since both approaches produce the same result, the two approaches, so to speak, share a common path (ὁδοποιεῖν), and it is possible to reduce the constituent operations into a system (*Rhet.* 1.1.2). This process of examination qualifies as an "art" (τέχνη). And so appears Aristotle's "art" of rhetoric. In sum, *rhetoric* is that which is analyzed, the "*art*" of rhetoric that which analyzes.

In Cicero's dialogue *On the Orator*, the participant Crassus defines rhetoric almost entirely in terms of its non-theoretical qualities. He finds little value in teachers and rhetorical handbooks (*Or.* 3.24.93; 3.30.120—3.31.125). For Crassus rhetoric derives from common practice (*usu*),

---

52. Mihaila, *Paul-Apollos Relationship*, 169, 214. Marshall (*Enmity in Corinth*, 400) suggests that Paul's letters employed an alternative, non-conformist style of rhetoric.

53. Robertson, *Grammar of the Greek New Testament*, 1195-97, 1206; Cranfield, *Epistle to the Romans 1-8*, 1:26.

54. Winter, "Rhetoric," esp. 821.

55. Cf. Judge, "Paul's Boasting."

custom (*more*), and the speech (*sermone*) of mankind (*Or.* 1.3.12), or to put it in the more common terms, from practice (*exercitatus*), imitation (*imitari*), and nature (*natura*) (*Or.* 3.31.125). There is therefore either "no art of speaking at all or a very thin one" (*Or.* 1.23.107). If one is to call rhetoric an "art" it is an art only in the sense that it applies terms to the devices already practiced by those whom we know to be good speakers, and illuminates these practices by classifying and subdividing them (*Or.* 1.23.109). In short, "Eloquence is not the offspring of the art, but the art of eloquence" (*Or.* 1.32.146).

The great Christian teacher of rhetoric St. Augustine expressed much the same view. There was eloquence before the "art" of rhetoric (*Doctr. Chr.* 4.7.21), and many people learn eloquence by imitation (*Doctr. Chr.* 4.3.5). Even those trained in the "rules" of rhetoric do not think about the rules while speaking. Indeed, "it is because they are eloquent that they exemplify these rules; it is not that they use them in order to be eloquent" (*Doctr. Chr.* 4.3.4).[56]

A century after Cicero, Quintilian articulated what sounds again like the view of Cicero's Crassus: the "art" of rhetoric makes only a modest contribution to the human capacity for eloquence. For Quintilian eloquence derives most fundamentally from natural endowment (*natura*), and is then improved upon by study (*studium*), imitation (*imitatio*) and practice (*exercitatio*) (*Inst.* 3.2.1). The natural origin of rhetoric explains why one finds eloquence not only where there are cities and laws and where schools cultivate eloquence for public service, but among peoples who have virtually no social order at all (*Inst.* 3.2.4). Still, the art of rhetoric is not identical to natural rhetoric, but a kind of supplementation or completion of it. As Quintilian says, "Nature (*natura*) . . . gave us the beginnings of speech, observation the beginnings of the art (*initium artis*)" (*Inst.* 3.2.3). Observation at first was a matter of noting what qualities of speech were worthy to be imitated (*imitandum*). The art itself emerged when observation and imitation, supplemented by the original inventions of skilled speakers, were confirmed as useful through experience, and then taught (*docuit*) to others (*Inst.* 3.2.3). In this way, "method and practice" (*ratio et exercitatio*)—or theory and practice—bring natural endowment of speech to completion (*summa sermo*).

---

56. Translation from Shaw in Roberts and Donaldson, *Nicene and Post-Nicene Fathers.*

In all, the sources share a common agreement that the faculty of eloquence is natural in humanity and can exist independently of the art (τέχνη, *ars*), or theory (*ratio, praeceptiones*), since it is endowed by nature and can be enhanced by mere imitation and practice.[57] Sources also agree that the art is descriptive of speech patterns that preexist the art itself. The question whether theory was a *necessary supplement* to other means of acquiring eloquence appears to have been more controversial; but only on the surface. While Crassus is surely correct that the *theory* of eloquence derives from eloquence *itself*, it may be counterposed that theory, by synthesizing and organizing human observations about eloquence, *recommends* the practices that imitate eloquence precisely by highlighting them. It must be recognized, nonetheless, that even students who were trained in the "art" of rhetoric need not have followed the art "by the book,"[58] and that even if their speech improved on account of their training, their basic conformity with the theory in practice need not imply that they followed the rules self-consciously (Augustine, *Doctr. Chr.* 4.3.4). Nor, one might argue, need training imply that students always knew the names of the devices they used. In fact one may seriously doubt that they did.

Paul and Rhetoric

Returning to Paul, an examination of his letters according to the standards of ancient, Greco-Roman rhetoric does not depend for its legitimacy on the question whether he formally studied rhetorical theory, that is, the Greco-Roman *art* of rhetoric. Such examination is also justified by the fact that he lived in the same world that codified this theory, theory based of course on the "best" practices of his time.

In the first place, regardless of the extent of Paul's formative education in Tarsus, he spent time there later as a minister (Acts 9:30; Gal 1:21), and he spent roughly two decades as a missionary across the Hellenistic world

---

57. Similar to the sources cited above, *Rhetorica ad Herennium* describes the "art" (*ars*) as one means through which to acquire the faculty of speech, alongside imitation (*imitatio*) and practice (*exercitatio*) (*Rhet. Her.* 1.2.3).

58. Eloquence itself is achieved in the tension between the rules and poetic license; or put differently, every "virtuous" turn of phrase is achieved by the same license that, when executed less felicitously, instantiates stylistic "vice." See Lausberg, §498; citing among other texts, Quintilian, *Inst.* 1.5.52.

before writing most of his extant letters. One might argue, then, that Paul had an informal, or functional, education in Greco-Roman rhetoric.[59]

Still, it does not go far enough to say that rhetoric was "in the air" (as in fact it was). Rather, Greco-Roman rhetoric took shape within, and as an *expression of*, a more comprehensive socio-linguistic universe. In this respect one needs to see rhetoric, in the theoretical form contrived by Greco-Roman theorists, as a sub-cultural manifestation of standards that were socio-linguistically embedded *in the spoken languages themselves* (i.e., Greek and Latin). The distinction between Hellenistic and so-called "Jewish" rhetoric, then, is finally difficult to uphold not only because Hellenistic rhetoric itself influenced Jewish education,[60] but also because, Jewish or non-Jewish, those who spoke Greek would naturally conform to the "rhetoric" whose very texture was the set of socio-linguistic conventions that constituted the language.[61]

This integral relationship between Greco-Roman rhetoric and the Greek (and Latin) language reflects a more general linguistic principle, namely that rhetorical conventions are "inseparable from the acquisition of language itself." As Schellenberg explains, we "do not learn first to speak and then to speak persuasively. We learn to speak. That is, in short, because there is no speech in the abstract, only speech as social practice."[62] The observation made by ancient theorists, then, to the effect that one may learn rhetoric through imitation, can be qualified in modern, socio-linguistic terms in accordance with the principle that one learns both rhetoric *and* language through imitation, for the former is learned at the *same time* as the latter.

Regardless whether Paul did or did not receive formal training in the Greco-Roman *art* of rhetoric, then, the modern interpreter's use of its specific categories to evaluate his letters remains equally appropriate, for at least three reasons: first, because Greco-Roman theorists themselves acknowledged that the art described rhetorical skills that preceded the art itself (skills acquired by nature, imitation, or practice); second, because

---

59. Kennedy, *New Testament Interpretation through Rhetorical Criticism*, 10; Porter, "Paul of Tarsus and His Letters," 562.

60. Daube, "Rabbinic Methods"; Hidary, *Rabbis and Classical Rhetoric*.

61. While one must make room for varieties of usage according to dialect (e.g., a more "Semitic" dialect), dialects share certain family resemblances that bind them together as belonging to the "same" language.

62. Schellenberg, *Rethinking Paul's Rhetorical Education*, 243; and see his chapter "The Acquisition of Informal Rhetorical Knowledge," on 243–54.

speaking Greek (or Latin) also meant speaking, to varying degrees, in conformity with the theoretical, Greco-Roman, rhetorical principles that were embedded in the socio-linguistic conventions of the language; and third, because those who participated in this socio-linguistic universe would evaluate speakers by the same corresponding standards.

As a qualification to this, it must be acknowledged that ancient audiences would evaluate styles differently depending on their social context. The same conventions could be evaluated as skillful and eloquent, for instance, by an audience of senators, but as pompous and ridiculous by a group of artisans. Variation of standards, however, is not an absolute function of differing social statuses, so much as it is of variation in context more broadly. Even rhetoricians recognized that styles ought to vary with context; this, indeed, is the virtue of "appropriateness," *proprium*. The coining of a "neologism" (§3.1.2), for instance, may be creative, but it will not always be regarded as eloquent (Quintilian, *Inst.* 8.3.30–37). A limitation of the ambitions of this volume is that in the identification of examples it does not take into account variation in context, and hence of the relative standards of the specific audiences Paul addresses in those contexts. Hence, the inventory of ornamental devices collected qualifies examples by their meeting of *formal* criteria that define these devices and leaves description of their function-in-context—and hence evaluation of their respective qualities as "eloquent," or not—to further study.

The Present Volume

Beyond Syntax and Discourse Analysis

While the present book examines style specifically in the rhetorical sense of the term—that is, in the ancient rhetorical sense of *elocutio* or λέξις—linguistic analysis from the perspective of ancient standards of style overlaps with two other analytic approaches to language: specifically, those of *syntactical analysis* and *discourse analysis*.[63]

The overlap of rhetorical analysis with these other types of analysis appears especially in connection with the rhetorical virtues of "correctness" (especially in regard to syntactical analysis) and "clarity" (especially

---

63. This explains why, as Botha observes ("Style in the New Testament," 71), modern interpreters have used the term "style" to describe not only the use of rhetorical figures, but also aspects of grammar and syntax.

in regard to discourse analysis).[64] The overall distinctiveness of rhetorical analysis concerns the combination of qualities that occupy its concerns. For the ancient theorists, "style" referred to the formal character of expression not simply with regard to grammar, but also the other linguistic "virtues." In other words, if grammar was the art of speaking *correctly*, style was the art of speaking beautifully, a quality that depended also on the virtues of *clarity* and *ornament*. Discourse analysis on the other hand (based on modern social-semiotic theory) concerns primarily aspects of thematic prominence and cognitive processing,[65] or in other words, matters of *clarity*. *Ornament* remains a less central concern.

Admittedly, the virtues of style cannot be sharply separated. Hence, neither can rhetorical, syntactical, and discourse analysis. For instance, ornament acquires some of its appeal from the ways in which it serves clarity. This symbiotic relationship is especially evident in the occurrence of figures involving word repetition and schematic arrangements. A repetition of words in the same place in successive clauses (anaphora, epiphora) or schematic arrangements like parallelism (isocolon, homoioteleuton, disiunctio) can elucidate where the speaker's emphasis lies or how emphatically it does so; it can also serve to amplify the thought. This overlap between rhetoric (eloquence) and discourse analysis (clarity) sometimes complicates judgments as to whether a feature can be considered "ornamental" in a truly "rhetorical" sense. In this regard, apparent figures need not always qualify as such.[66] In this study I have often regarded "chiastic" arrangements as more processing-oriented than ornamental (see §3.2.1.1.23). Nonetheless, where formal criteria for stylistic devices are met I have generally considered such instances to be ornamental.

Outline

The present analysis has been arranged according to Quintilian's "virtue"-based structure, with deeper levels of organization following Lausberg's constructive systematization of the broader rhetorical tradition.

---

64. On the ancient virtues of style, see above.

65. For a summary of the linguistic bases for discourse analysis and the discourse grammars that apply them to biblical Greek, see Campbell, *Advances in the Study of Greek*, 148–91.

66. On this issue, see Slings, "Figures of Speech and their Lookalikes."

Consistent with Quintilian, Lausberg arranges his treatment of style under the headings of the primary stylistic virtues (*virtutes*, i.e., correctness, *Latinitas*; clarity, *perspicuitas*; ornament, *ornatus*; and subsumed under ornament, propriety, *proprietas*); he sub-divides each section according to Quintilian's distinction between stylistic qualities embodied *in singulis verbis* and those embodied *in coniunctis verbis*; and he follows further sub-headings where Quintilian provides them. It is Lausberg's contribution (and a true sign of his taxonomic genius and encyclopedic knowledge of ancient rhetoric) that he then devises a system of sub-headings that pushes deeper than Quintilian's visible structure, providing for instance under the heading of ornament *in coniunctis verbis* an additional *nine* levels of organization.

Lausberg's outline provides the general structure for the present analysis, in some places supplying headings up to five levels deep (e.g., under §3.2.1.1.1; etc.; §3.2.1.2.1; etc.; §3.2.2.1.1; etc.). Hence, I have included at most heading levels the corresponding section(s) from Lausberg. I substitute a different method of classification only in §3.1.3, where I organize some tropes (specifically metaphor, allegory, metonymy, and synecdoche), at a fourth heading level, according to Louw and Nida's categories of semantic domain.[67]

Modest criticisms of Lausberg's work notwithstanding, our adoption of his system has substantial benefits and ample justification. In the first place, Lausberg provides a ready-made outline for organization of stylistic features, and one that, despite any limitations it might have, I am happy to admit I could not improve upon myself. Second, although Lausberg's system draws disproportionately from the theory of Quintilian, one might argue that there is no method more appropriate. Quintilian's work reflects the culmination of several preceding centuries of theorization, and a comprehensive systematization of it at that. Moreover, Quintilian is as near a contemporary of Paul as any other theorist (ca. 35–100 CE), and as such preserves rhetorical tradition as it was at almost precisely the time of Paul's activity. Finally, while Quintilian provides Lausberg with his basic outline, Lausberg's handbook also draws from ancient theorists more comprehensively. A synthetic approach of this type allows Lausberg not only to achieve, but in some sense to *reveal*, a uniformity in the tradition that is concealed somewhat by the inconsistency of terminology used in the sources. Apart from the application of both Greek and Latin rhetorical

---

67. Louw and Nida, *Greek-English Lexicon*.

terms among ancient theorists, even theorists who wrote in the same language assign various names to what are functionally the same, or very nearly the same, rhetorical devices. In such cases, Lausberg's descriptive taxonomy of rhetorical phenomena allows common headings to associate functionally similar devices.

Format

Arrangement of examples. At the most subordinate levels of the book's outline, I have used various criteria for arranging material. Within subsections under §1. *Correctness* and §2. *Clarity*, I have generally grouped examples conceptually or thematically, supplying paragraph headings in italics where possible. I have followed the same procedure in §3.2.2. *Composition*. In the remaining sections under §3. *Ornament*—covering archaisms (§3.1.1), neologisms (§3.1.2), figures of speech (§3.2.1.1), and figures of thought (§3.2.1.2)—I have generally presented examples in a formatted list and in canonical order.

Citation of the original text. When discussing examples in paragraph form, I sometimes cite the original text and sometimes provide only the citations. In sections consisting only in the citation of the original text, i.e., where individual examples are separated by paragraph breaks (generally, under figures of speech, §3.2.1.1; figures of thought, §3.2.1.2), I provide the original text sometimes in Greek and sometimes in English. Greek prevails in the section on *figures of speech* (§3.2.1.1), where figures are sometimes manifest only in the original language. Since *figures of thought* (§3.2.1.2) depend more on the conceptual content than on the shape of the wording, English has sufficed. Translations are original unless otherwise indicated.

Text formatting. When displaying devices that require the original Greek for identification, I have generally used formatting on the most relevant portion of the text, simultaneously using bold type and italics for visibility.

Letters Analyzed

I treat as the subject of analysis the seven undisputed Pauline letters, plus Ephesians, Colossians, and 2 Thessalonians. The decision about scope was not an easy one, for the rationale must take into account several ponderable considerations: first, differences in epistolary type, and specifically the intrinsic rhetorical differences manifested between more "personal" letters (like 1–2 Thessalonians) and more "diplomatic" letters (like Romans and 1 Corinthians);[68] second, expected differences in style between letters ostensibly addressed to individuals (Philemon, 1–2 Timothy, Titus) and those addressed to churches (the remaining letters); third, the question of which letters to consider authentic; and fourth, the decision whether to include letters even if they are indeed inauthentic. My final decision was to treat all the letters internally addressed to churches, but to add Philemon, because of its universally agreed status as an authentic letter of Paul, because of the noticeable rhetorical finesse involved in its composition, and because, despite the initial address to "Philemon," it is in fact addressed to an entire church (Phlm 2). I have taken no consideration for the impact that co-authorship or use of an amanuensis might have on stylistic differences—naturally, since as far as the Pauline letters are concerned, the extent of the impact is impossible to determine.

Inclusiveness of Examples

A few remarks need to be made about the selection and the distribution of examples.

First, in evaluating each letter I have attempted to be exhaustive in the identification of ornamental features (i.e., figures of speech, figures of thought, and tropes); though, undoubtedly, I have missed examples, particularly as I was not always tuned in to the same kinds of features across the span of time during which I collected examples.[69]

Second, I have excluded rhetorical features manifested in citations of the OT, except where it is apparent that Paul has made original adaptations (1 Cor 15:54). I have also included instances where many interpreters suspect the incorporation of pre-Pauline traditions (Rom 12:9–21; 1 Thess 4:14; 5:16–22), since the pre-Pauline nature of this material is not altogether certain.

Third, I have identified rhetorical devices against the definitions provided in the relevant sections of Lausberg; though I have also compared the terminology and definitions given in Anderson, Lanham, MacDonald,

---

68. On the distinction between personal and diplomatic letters, see Klauck, *Ancient Letter Writing and the New Testament*, 68–69.

69. A vast majority of examples derive from my own analysis, though some derive from other sources, most notably Bullinger, *Figures of Speech Used in the Bible*.

Rowe, and Smith where I felt further clarity was needed.[70] Accordingly, the definitions I have provided are essentially adaptations from Lausberg. For the names of figures, I generally cite both the Greek and Latin terms; though where one term or the other has become standard in modern discourse, I use the corresponding term. Where terms have developed unique English spellings, I employ the modern spellings.

Fourth, in deciding about qualifying examples, some subjectivity in evaluating the difference between "virtuous" and "vicious" configurations of speech was unavoidable. Hence, in some instances I have included the same material under both "solecisms" (§1.2) and "ornament" (§3.2), especially instances of "ellipsis" (§3.2.1.1.19) and "zeugma" (§3.2.1.1.20). This subjectivity is not merely a function of the interpreter's distance from the ancient writer, but as noted above, is a function of the varying standards of Paul's audiences (and even of sub-sections within them) and of contingencies in the rhetorical situations that Paul's addressed. In this respect, examples are included, and categorized, on the basis of their *formal* qualities, not necessarily their relative rhetorical *value* in context.

Fifth, I have said the most by far about the virtue of "ornament," in keeping with the weight attributed to this virtue by ancient theorists. For as Crassus remarks in Cicero's *On the Orator*, "ornament" is "the highest distinction of eloquence" (*Or.* 3.104); "correctness," by contrast, does not elicit praise, but only serves to preclude criticism; for, "nobody ever admired an orator for correct grammar, they only laugh at him if his grammar is bad" (*Or.* 3.52).

Sixth, I have taken a maximalist approach in the identification of tropes. Despite the development of "conceptual metaphor theory" over the last decades and its valid cognitive-linguistic underpinnings,[71] the "conceptual" nature of metaphors need not diminish the conceptualizer's *awareness* of the expression's metaphorical (or "tropical," *tropicus*) nature, or its intended use as such. This point has relevance, for instance, in the question whether to consider Paul's language of "pouring," "filling," etc. in connection with the Spirit as metaphorical or physical: the former does not require the latter. I have also included in the spectrum of tropes what may be called "weak," or "lexicalized tropes" (see §3.1.3).

---

70. Anderson, *Glossary of Greek Rhetorical Terms*; Lanham, *Handlist of Rhetorical Terms*; MacDonald, *Glossary of Greek and Latin Rhetorical Terms*; Rowe, "Style"; Smith, *Glossary of Terms*.

71. Lakoff and Johnson, *Metaphors We Live By*.

INTRODUCTION

Finally, it has been my primary purpose to collect examples, not to analyze their interpretive significance. While the full value of rhetorical analysis lies in the latter, as I suggest below the present collection should be a valuable resource that future studies can use toward that end.

Approaches to the Book

This book is intended as a reference tool, offering for rhetorical analysis what traditional tools like Smyth, Robertson, and BDF offer for syntactical analysis.[72] As such, I suggest several ways in which the reader might approach the book's contents.

(1) *Verse-by-verse rhetorical analysis.* Readers translating sequentially through a letter or letters of Paul may wish to follow the scripture index of this book as they translate. In this way the reader is shown any stylistic devices deployed, verse-by-verse, as they appear in each letter.

(2) *Original application.* One might follow the reverse approach, reading the book section-by-section and then conducting one's own analysis of the Pauline text, identifying any places where they find the relevant devices.

(3) *Device focus.* Those interested in a particular rhetorical device might consult the relevant section of the book using the table of contents, thereby accessing any examples of the device that occur in Paul's letters.

(4) *Stylistic comparison.* One might use the book for stylistic comparison between letters by following the scripture index and noting which letters, or which sections, have the densest concentration of stylistic devices or which devices are most common across particular letters.

(5) *Translation help.* The reader might also access the book for interpretation assistance, consulting it alongside syntax tools where a letter's meaning is obscure or further clarity is sought.

Purpose

This book is a reference tool. Its main purpose is to collect, in one place and as comprehensively as possible, the data illustrating Paul's "style" as evaluated by the standards of Greco-Roman rhetorical theory. While I provide little commentary on the exegetical payoff of this material, I shall note here

---

72. Smyth, *Greek Grammar*; Robertson, *Grammar of the Greek New Testament in the Light of Historical Research*; Blass et al., *Greek Grammar of the New Testament and Other Early Christian Literature*.

a few areas in which I believe this data makes such a contribution and could be fruitfully utilized in future research.

(1) *Paul's education.* This collection provides a more extensive database of stylistic aspects of Paul's letters to be considered in evaluating the question of Paul's education.

(2) *Stylistic tendencies.* The organization and exhaustiveness of this database (however imperfect) reveals more clearly patterns and stylistic tendencies in Paul's letters. Striking tendencies include, for instance, the prevalence in Paul's use of complicated zeugma (see §1.2.2. on ellipsis by subtraction, as well as §3.2.1.1.20 on zeugma), anaphora (§3.2.1.1.5), various kinds of wordplay (§3.2.1.1.9–14), and especially various types of isocolon (§3.2.1.1.22–31).

(3) *Theological motifs.* This material reveals, through the organization of tropes by semantic domain, those domains that are most salient and most prevalent in Paul's letters theologically. One notices from the section on tropes (§3.1.3) the predominance of tropes that draw from the *source domains* of Constructions (#7), the Body, Body Parts, and Body Products (#8), Kinship (#10), Physiological Processes (#23), Control, Rule (#37), Religious Activities (#53), Military Activities (#55), Possess, Transfer, Exchange (#57), Quantity (#59), Spatial Positions (#83), and Spatial Extensions (#84).[73] Key *target domains* include Understand (#32), Control, Rule (#37), Behavior and Related States (#41), Status (#87), and Moral and Ethical Qualities (#88).

(4) *Epistolary types.* This collection provides, as it were, a synopsis of the stylistic variety (a) contained within letters and (b) exhibited between letters. (a) Some letter sections contain a noticeably dense concentration of stylistic devices (e.g., Rom 1:18—3:8; 9:1–9; 1 Cor 3:5–23; 11:2–16; 15:39–56; 2 Cor 10–13; esp. 11:19–29). (b) The well accepted characterization of Romans as more formal and diplomatic on the one hand, and the Thessalonian letters as informal and personal on the other hand, is confirmed, as the present scripture index reveals, by the astonishing abundance of stylistic ornament in Romans and the comparative absence of ornamental features in the Thessalonian letters.

(5) *Letter distinctives.* Similarly, this collection provides a synopsis that reveals what rhetorical features are most distinctive of *particular* letters. An

---

73. And to a lesser degree: Physical Events (#14), Linear Movement (#15), Stances (#17), Violence, Harm, Destroy, Kill (#20), Sensory Events (#24), Hostility, Strife (#39), Perform, do (#42), Building, Constructing (#45), Clothing, Adorning (#49), Contests and Play (#50), Courts and Legal Procedures (#56), and Weight (#86).

awareness of the *comparative* prevalence and distribution of specific tropes and figures in Paul's letters, one suspects, could be enlightening. One notes for instance the distinctive abundance of antithetical isocolon and subiectio in Romans; of climax, paronomasia, and erōtēsis in Romans and 1 Corinthians; of anaphora, antistrophe, isocolon, tricolon, and sententiae in 1 Corinthians; of correctio in 2 Corinthians; and of oxymoron in 1–2 Corinthians. An awareness of the patterns of variation between letters could offer further clues not only about Paul's contingent rhetorical purposes, but also about the social profiles of his respective audiences.

(6) *Form criticism.* The emergence of stylistic tendencies allows the interpreter to assess the possible correlation between certain rhetorical "styles" and certain literary "forms" as understood in the vein of form criticism prior to the age of rhetorical criticism. For instance, the "loose" style (§916–20) commonly characterizes "parenetic" sections (Rom 12:9–17; 14:13–23; 1 Cor 7:18–23; 15:33–34; 16:13–14; 2 Cor 13:11; Col 4:2; 1 Thess 5:12–22).

(7) *Pauline authorship.* The question of the authorship of the disputed letters is complex and can in no way be resolved by a comparison of rhetorical styles. However, the present resource offers a convenient synopsis of the distribution of stylistic devices across letters, and therefore a useful tool for comparing devices in the disputed and undisputed letters.

(8) *Interpretive clarity.* Perhaps the most serious relevance of this data for exegetes consists in its usefulness for elucidating what Paul is saying. One's failure to understand the rhetorical dimensions of Paul's form of speech can result in misapprehension of his meaning, just as recognition of the devices he uses can offer clarity. I offer just a few examples where exegetical payoff is evident.

(a) Recognition of Paul's use of isocolon (§3.2.1.1.22) in Rom 11:25 clarifies that he refers not to a "partial hardening" of Israel,[74] but rather to the hardening of "part of Israel," for ἀπὸ μέρους corresponds structurally with τὸ πλήρωμα:

πώρωσις [A] ἀπὸ μέρους [B] τῷ Ἰσραὴλ [C] γέγονεν

ἄχρις οὗ [A] τὸ πλήρωμα [B] τῶν ἐθνῶν [C] εἰσέλθῃ

(b) On the other hand, parallel structures can be misleading, since the correspondence of elements is not always exact. For instance, despite the use of isocolon in Rom 5:18 the interpreter need not conclude, *ipso*

---

74. As in the ESV; NASB; Fitzmyer, *Romans*, 621.

facto, that there is *semantic* equivalency of πάντας in the corresponding elements εἰς πάντας ἀνθρώπους and εἰς πάντας ἀνθρώπους.[75] One would first need to determine tendencies as seen in the more exhaustive collection of examples of isocolon and related devices (especially interpretatio, §3.2.1.1.31). In this regard, one may note that διά appears to have two different meanings in the parallel phrases of Rom 4:25 ("delivered *because of* our trespasses," "raised *because of* our justification"). Both Rom 5:18 and 4:25 suggest that Paul's penchant for parallel *structure* sometimes overcomes the appropriateness of the parallel in *sense*.

(c) Familiarity with common rhetorical devices that entail verbal or conceptual repetition can help prevent over-interpretation when encountering semantic variation. Indeed, Paul frequently resorts to semantic redundancy to amplify a thought. It is tenuous, for instance, to look for significant semantic distinctions in the coordination of terms like "fleshly (σαρκίνοις)" and "immature (νηπίοις)" (1 Cor 3:1), for coordinated synonymy occurs so frequently in Paul's letters as to rightly be considered a stylistic tendency (see §3.2.1.1.11. *Synonymy*).[76]

(d) Interpreters sometimes make strong assertions as to the pre-Pauline or pseudonymous origins of material based on the putative standard of Paul's "normal" style. Charles Wannamaker asserts, for instance, that the "repeated use of synonymous parallelism in [2 Thess 1:7b–10] is not typical of Paul's normal epistolary style."[77] This is a most surprising assertion, given the abundance of such structures noted in this collection (twenty-two examples of synonymous parallelism cited under §3.2.1.1.31. *Interpretatio*).

(e) Paul's adaptations of OT citations may not always be motivated by theological considerations. In at least one instance, Paul adapts a citation apparently for the purpose of producing anaphora (1 Cor 15:54 substitutes θάνατε for the ᾅδη of LXX Hos 13:14).

(f) A great deal is learned from this collection about Paul's tendency toward ellipsis and economy of expression. (i) One notices that ellipses

---

75. Boring ("Language of Universal Salvation in Paul") claims that "all" in the second instance indicates universalism. For the use of parallel phrasing without parallel meaning, note also the different senses of διά in the parallel phrases of Rom 4:25.

76. For a similar example, note "times and seasons" (1 Thess 5:1). The use of coordinated synonymity occurs in the Thessalonian letters alone quite a few times: "in a holy and righteous and blameless manner," 1 Thess 2:10; "distress and tribulation," 1 Thess 3:7; "abound and increase," 1 Thess 3:12; "signs and wonders," 2 Thess 2:9; "labor and toil," 1 Thess 2:9; 2 Thess 3:8.

77. Wanamaker, *Epistles to the Thessalonians*, 232.

need not imply repetition of the same grammatical forms, for "complicated zeugma" (see §1.2.2. on ellipsis by subtraction, as well as §3.2.1.1.20 on zeugma)—where the omitted element requires a different form than the one used in the parallel part—is widely prevalent in Paul's letters. (ii) Paul's tendency toward parsimony in the interest of brevity should discourage wooden interpretation of his grammar. Often this point has theological importance. For instance, the pregnant expression ἠγέρθη διὰ τὴν δικαίωσιν ἡμῶν in Rom 4:25 does not mean that Jesus was "raised because of our justification," i.e., "because we had been justified" (as some interpreters have taken him to mean),[78] but that he was raised in order to *effect* our justification. (iii) A similar rigidity occurs where the interpreter misses the "tropical" nature of Paul's language. Metonymies (§3.1.3.3) involving Christ are frequent and often theologically significant. That God "made [Christ] to be sin" is evidently a metonymy for "made Christ to be a sin-offering [or perhaps sinner]" (2 Cor 5:21); in the same way, Christ's having "become our curse" is metonymy for "became the victim of our curse" (Gal 3:13); "become righteousness" is a metonymy that substitutes cause for effect (2 Cor 5:21), as also in the expression "became wisdom . . . righteousness . . . sanctification . . . redemption" (1 Cor 1:30); "whom God set forth as a propitiation" is metonymy for "whom God set forth as the means to propitiation" (Rom 3:25).[79] Theologically significant examples could be multiplied; e.g., the Law as "sin" = product for producer (Rom 7:7). It is not special (theological) pleading that motivates the interpretation of these examples as metonymies; rather the sheer prevalence of metonymies in Paul's letters (see hundreds of examples in §3.1.3.3) exposes the *non*-metonymic interpretations likely as overly wooden. (iv) Paul's verbal omissions are sometimes rhetorically motivated, as where they serve to obviate shock (omission of the direct object in 1 Cor 10:9) or to hint at something too bold to speak (aposiopesis in Rom 9:22; perhaps also in Rom 7:12). (v) Due recognition of aposiopesis together with its rhetorical function in the context helps one to avoid recourse, in some instances, to the label of anacoluthon (Rom 9:22; 2 Thess 2:4).

One cannot anticipate the full range of potential this material has to aid interpretation of Paul's letters. The above examples, however, offer indications of its value and point toward hopeful avenues for further research.

---

78. Schreiner (*Romans*, 244) takes this view on the basis of parallelism with the prior διά phrase. Fitzmyer (*Romans*, 389) cites Schlatter as taking this view.

79. Compare also "so also is the Christ" (1 Cor 15:12), which is either a pregnant expression for "so also is [the body of] Christ" or a metonymy in which Christ substitutes for the church; though most commentators interpret it according to the latter.

STYLE IN PAUL'S LETTERS

1. Correctness (Lausberg, §463–527)

"Correctness," "Greekness" (ἑλληνισμός), or "Latinity" (*Latinitas*) refers to the idiomatically correct manner of expression (Lausberg, §463). Correctness counts as stylistic virtue. Lack of correctness counts as stylistic vice.

Correctness is assessed both at the level of single words and at the level of combinations of words. Therefore, two types of stylistic vice are possible under the heading of correctness. Barbarisms (§1.1) are unintentional alterations of single words. Solecisms (§1.2) are grammatical errors committed through the faulty combination of words. When committed intentionally and under certain conditions, barbarisms and solecisms count as stylistic virtues.

Little need be said about correctness. Learning correctness was the first matter of primary education (Quintilian, *Inst.* 1.4–9), and students who continued beyond elementary education can be expected to have mastered it. Thus, in Cicero's *De Oratore*, Crassus expresses his desire to quickly "pass over" the rules of correctness, which he says "are imparted by education in boyhood and fostered by a more intensive and systematic study of literature, or else by the habit of daily conversation in the family circle, and confirmed by books and by reading the old orators and poets" (*Or.* 3.49 [LCL, Rackham]). Accordingly, "nobody ever admired an orator for correct grammar, they only laugh at him if his grammar is bad, and not only think him no orator but not even a human being; no one ever sang the praises of a speaker whose style succeeded in marking his meaning intelligible to his audience, but only despised one deficient in capacity to do so" (*Or.* 3.52 [LCL, Rackham]). For this reason attention is given below only to incorrectness, or barbarisms and solecisms.

1.1. Barbarisms (Lausberg, §479-95)

Barbarisms are unintentional alterations of single words, and are committed through addition, omission, transposition, or substitution of sounds, syllables, or letters. Virtuous alteration of a single word is known as μεταπλασμός (Lausberg, §479; cf. Quintilian, *Inst.* 1.5.5).

Examples of barbarism in Paul's letters are almost impossible to locate with certainty. Errors of pronunciation are of course impossible to detect in literature, and the origins of spelling errors could not be traced with certainty through the history of transmission back to the original text. Some grammatical "errors" could qualify as barbarism. For instance, in 1 Cor 3:5 ἑκάστῳ functions as a nominative (appositive to διάκονοι) but proleptically takes on the dative case by attraction to the case of the implied indirect object of ἔδωκεν.

See also vices considered under "Composition" (§3.2.2).

1.2. Solecisms (Lausberg, §496-527)

Solecisms are grammatical errors committed through the faulty combination of words, and are created through addition, omission, transposition, or substitution of words (Lausberg, §501).

Virtuous alterations of combinations of words are called σχήματα / *figurae*, or "figures" (Lausberg, §498). There is a corresponding figure for almost every kind of vice (Quintilian, *Inst.* 1.5.52; 9.3.11, 18; cf. Seneca, *Contr.* 7.pr.5; *Suas.* 2.13ff; *Contr.* 2.3.21). On "figures," see §3.2.1 below.

1.2.1. *By addition (Lausberg, §502-3)*

1.2.1.1. PLEONASM

Solecisms committed by the addition of one or two words are called *pleonasms* (Quintilian, *Inst.* 1.5.40; 8.3.53; Lausberg §502).

Note "yield in subjection" (Gal 2:5); "shameful talk out of your mouth" (Col 3:8); and (unless these genitives are "epexegetical") several examples involving construct forms, including "likeness of an image" (Rom 1:23); "house of dwelling" (2 Cor 5:1); and "attitude of your mind," (Eph 4:23).

ἐκτὸς εἰ μή, a pleonasm for "unless," occurs in the Greek bible only in the Pauline corpus (1 Cor 14:5; 15:2; cf. 1 Tim 5:19).

Some superfluous additions owe to Semitic influence, e.g., the redundant personal pronoun after relative pronoun: "to remember the poor, which thing (ὅ) I also hastened to do this very thing (αὐτὸ τοῦτο)" (Gal 2:10). Semitic tendencies in Paul's letters are usually common to other NT writings as well (see BDF, "Semitisms").

The cognate accusative (αὐξ- in Col 2:19) and other instances of semantic repetition (χαρ- in 2 Cor 7:13) could be considered conventional (see BDF, §153). σήμερον ἡμέρα = "today" (2 Cor 3:14, 15), a more intensive expression for σήμερον ("this very day"), is in fact commonplace in both Classical and Koine Greek.

1.2.1.2. Anacoluthon

ὅτι resumes ὅτι in Eph 2:11, 12, though the intervening addition does not make the sentence ungrammatical. Note also ἵνα . . . ἵνα in 1 Thess 4:1.

Anacoluthon also occurs as a result of ungrammatical substitutions (see below under §1.2.4.4).

1.2.2. By subtraction (Lausberg, §504)

The omission of a necessary part of a sentence is known as *ellipsis* (Lausberg, §504; Quintilian, *Inst.* 5.4.40; 8.3.50; BDF §479–82). Ellipsis counts as a vice only when it offends clarity. Ellipsis committed in the interest of brevity (Lausberg, §297) may count as a virtue; such ellipses can often be regarded, like zeugma, as figures (Lausberg, §690–708; cf. BDF §479.2); see below under "Ellipsis" (§3.2.1.1.19) and "Zeugma" (§3.2.1.1.20).

Lightfoot noted that Paul's use of ellipsis caused scribes much difficulty.[1] Ellipsis in his letters is especially common in parallel, antithetical, and parallel constructions, where the element needing to be supplied is generally self-evident. Yet, in many cases the omitted element needs to be supplied in a different form than is stated in the parallel part. In these cases, the line between vicious ellipsis and "complicated zeugma" (see §3.2.1.1.20 below) is not easy to draw.

---

1. Lightfoot, *Notes*, 168.

1.2.2.1. Ellipsis of a Nominal

1.2.2.1.1. Subject not explicit

The switch from a singular verb to a plural in 1 Cor 7:36 does not come with a marked change in subject: "If someone thinks . . . he does not sin; let *them* marry." A new subject is needed with the infinitives in 1 Thess 4:9 (γράφειν); 5:1 (γράφεσθαι).

1.2.2.1.2. Direct object omitted in ellipsis

Normally a direct object is omitted if it was made explicit in a prior parallel part. Yet, in 1 Cor 11:2 τὰς παραδόσεις is omitted in the first instance, and stated in the second (this perhaps suggests an editorial error in placing the punctuation). In Phil 3:12–14, several clauses build up before the object is finally revealed: "Not that I have *already* attained—or have been *already* perfected—but I press on if indeed I *might* obtain, (that) in which I also have *been* laid hold of by Christ Jesus—no, rather, forgetting what is behind and pressing on to what is ahead, I *press on* according to the goal to the *prize* . . . " The suspense perhaps makes the initial omission of the object stylistically virtuous.

At times, what is to be supplied is not sufficiently clear (1 Cor 11:4; 14:38; Phil 4:10). 1 Thess 5:24 requires some indefinite object ("who also will do [obj.]"). ἀγνοεῖ may need an object in 1 Cor 14:38. The omitted object is clarified by the embedded ending of the verb in 1 Cor 11:17 (ὑμᾶς known from συνέρχεσθε).

Some omissions have theological significance. The omission of the direct object after ἔχων in 1 Cor 11:4 has created a major interpretive crux: is it "having [something/a veil] coming down from the head" or "having [hair] coming down from the head"? In 1 Cor 10:9, the identity of the object has christological significance: did those in the wilderness "test [the Christ]"?

1.2.2.1.3. Case changes in ellipsis

Direct objects are sometimes omitted in the second of two parallel lines where a change of verb would have required a change in the case of the object, e.g., διότι **γνόντες τὸν θεὸν** οὐχ ὡς θεὸν ἐδόξασαν ἢ **ηὐχαρίστησαν** [τῷ θεῷ] (Rom 1:21). In Phlm 8, ἐπιτάσσειν takes the dative σοι as its complement; the complement is omitted in v. 9 after παρακαλῶ, though a switch to the accusative, σε, would be required.

1.2.2.2. Ellipsis of a Verbal

1.2.2.2.1. Number changes in ellipsis

In 1 Cor 14:27, a singular verb switches to plural in the ellipsis: εἴτε γλώσσῃ τις **λαλεῖ**, κατὰ δύο ἢ τὸ πλεῖστον τρεῖς καὶ ἀνὰ μέρος [**λαλείτωσαν**]. In Rom 2:6, 8 both the voice (active, passive) and number of the verb changes (singular, plural): "who *will give* (ἀποδώσει) ... eternal life ... wrath and anger [*will be given*, ἀποδοθήσονται]." Note 2 Cor 11:6, where the subject switches from singular to plural, though no verb appears at all.

1.2.2.2.2. Person changes in ellipsis

Changes in person almost always involve parallel—for instance, antithetical (Rom 7:17, 20; 1 Cor 7:10, 12; 9:25; 15:10), restrictive (Phil 4:15); complementary (1 Cor 9:12; Gal 6:14), comparative (1 Cor 9:5; 10:7; 2 Cor 3:1; 11:12; 1 Thess 2:14; 4:13), conditional (1 Cor 9:12; 2 Cor 2:10), or reciprocal (1 Thess 1:12)—constructions.

In 1 Cor 7:10 there is double ellipsis of the verb, where in the first instance it needs to be supplied in the first person, and in the second instance the third person: τοῖς δὲ γεγαμηκόσιν παραγγέλλω, οὐκ [**παραγγέλλω**] ἐγὼ ἀλλ' ὁ κύριος [**παραγγέλλει**]; cf. 1 Cor 9:25. See also 7:12; 9:12, 25; Gal 6:1, 14. There is a change perhaps of both number and tense in the omissions in 1 Cor 15:48 (οἷος ὁ χοϊκός, τοιοῦτοι καὶ οἱ χοϊκοί, etc.).

1 Thessalonians 5:4 probably requires an object other than ὑμᾶς in the elliptical ὡς clause.

1.2.2.2.3. Tense changes in ellipsis

Occasionally, the verb needs to be supplied in a different tense: **βλέπομεν** γὰρ ἄρτι δι' ἐσόπτρου ἐν αἰνίγματι, τότε δὲ [**βλέψομεν**] πρόσωπον πρὸς πρόσωπον (1 Cor 13:12; see also 15:21). Also: "I suffer birth pangs over you [and will continue to] until Christ is formed in you" (Gal 4:19); "It is bearing fruit and increasing among you, [and has been] from which day you heard it..." (Col 1:6); "from which day we heard, [we prayed and we] do not cease praying..." (Col 1:9). For durative constructions that extend from past to present but describe the action using only the present tense, see below on pregnant expressions (§1.2.2.6).

A double ellipsis of the verb in 1 Cor 15:21 involves an implied present indicative in the first instance and an implied future indicative in the second. Similarly, a double ellipsis in 2 Cor 11:22, 26–27 involves an implied present indicative in the first instance and an implied perfect participle in the other: "Are they ... I [*am*] more so, [*having been*] in labors more abundantly, etc." Determination of the main verb in 1 Cor 15:24 depends upon the anchoring temporal moment (thus a future indicative or a futuristic present). A choice between the present and future is difficult in 1 Cor 15:32 ("what [...] the benefit to me?").

1.2.2.2.4. Voice changes in ellipsis

In Rom 2:6, 8 both the voice (active, passive) and number of the verb changes (singular, plural): "who *will give* (ἀποδώσει) ... eternal life ... wrath and anger [*will be given*, ἀποδοθήσονται]."

1.2.2.2.5. Mood changes in ellipsis

In ellipses requiring a change of mood, usually the change occurs in the second of two complementary clauses; e.g., in the apodosis of conditions (indicative to imperative, 1 Cor 14:27); in the tenor of comparisons (indicative to imperative, Eph 5:24; imperative to either a modal construction or an indicative, Eph 6:5; tenor in subjunctive, indicative probably required in vehicle, 1 Thess 5:4; Rom 1:13).

In other cases a finite verb becomes an infinitive or a participle (or vice versa) in the ellipsis. A participial form (ἐπιποθοῦντες) becomes an indicative in the ellipsis (ἐπιποθῶ) in 1 Thess 3:6. An indicative becomes a participle in the ellipsis of 1 Cor 8:12. Ellipsis of the verb in 1 Thess 3:12 picks up from the verbal idea in the noun ἀγάπη.

In 1 Cor 3:1 displacement of the negative creates an ellipsis that requires a change of verb form or construction: "I was not able to speak to you (οὐκ ἠδυνήθην λαλῆσαι) as to spiritual people but [had to speak to you] as to fleshly people."

1.2.2.2.6. Mood and person changes in the ellipsis

In Col 3:13 ἐχαρίσατο becomes either an imperative χαρίζετε (imperative, second person sg) or a modal construction (ὀφείλετε χαρίζειν). In 1 Thess 3:12, the third-person optatives (πλεονάσαι καὶ περισσεύσαι) apparently change to the first-person indicative (sc. πλεονάζομεν καὶ περισσεύομεν) in the ellipsis.

1.2.2.2.7. The antithesis in ellipsis

Where antitheses are involved, the omitted element is sometimes the negative of the remaining, parallel element: "circumcision is *nothing* and uncircumcision is *nothing*, but keeping the commandments of God [is *something/everything*]" (1 Cor 7:19); "neither circumcision nor uncircumcision is of any value, but faith worked out in love [is of value]" (Gal 5:6; similarly, 6:15). See also 2 Cor 5:15; 13:8; Eph 4:29; 5:3.

1.2.2.2.8. Lexical unit changes in ellipsis

In Phil 2:17, θυσία works after σπένδομαι, but λειτουργία requires a different verb. ἐπότισα does not suit the parallel part in 1 Cor 3:2a–b.

1.2.2.2.9. Semantics change in ellipsis

In Rom 13:8, the original verb needs to be supplied, but with a different meaning: "owe (ὀφείλετε) no one anything except that [you ought] to love one another." See also below under traductio/antanaklasis (§3.2.1.1.12).

1.2.2.2.10. Complement missing

A complement is needed after ἠκαιρεῖσθε in Phil 4:10.

1.2.2.2.11. Required verb or form not definitely known

μή πως ἐπείρασεν ὑμᾶς ὁ πειράζων (1 Thess 3:5) appears to be set off by an implied verb of fear: "To ascertain the state of your faith, [fearing] lest...." Note the omission of an introductory verb prior to ἵνα clauses of command (1 Cor 7:29; 2 Cor 8:7; Gal 2:10; Eph 5:33); the omission of a verb after ἵνα (1 Cor 1:31; Gal 2:9). Verbs are sometimes missing before citations of scripture (1 Cor 1:31; 2:9). εἰ γὰρ πιστεύομεν ὅτι Ἰησοῦς ἀπέθανεν καὶ ἀνέστη, οὕτως καὶ ὁ θεὸς τοὺς κοιμηθέντας διὰ τοῦ Ἰησοῦ ἄξει σὺν αὐτῷ (1 Thess 4:14) appears to mean "If we believe ... so also [we ought to believe that] God ... " 1 Cor 5:10 requires something like "not at all [meaning] the sexually immoral ... (οὐ πάντως τοῖς πόρνοις)." Some or other verb of speaking is needed in the ὡς clauses in 2 Cor 2:17. The general sense of 1 Cor 3:2c is clear enough without a complement (οὔπω γὰρ ἐδύνασθε [...]). The sense is also clear in 1 Cor 7:8 (ὡς κἀγώ [...]); Gal 2:9 (ἡμεῖς μὲν εἰς τὰ ἔθνη [...], αὐτοὶ δὲ εἰς τὴν περιτομήν [...]). In Rom 13:11, Καὶ τοῦτο εἰδότες τὸν καιρόν lacks a verb.

Fairly frequently the omitted verb is complemented with a prepositional phrase in the predicate: 1 Cor 2:4a ([...] ἐν πειθοῖς ἀνθρωπίνης σοφίας λόγοις ἀλλ᾽ ἐν ἀποδείξει); 4:19 ([...] ἐν λόγῳ ... ἐν δυνάμει).

Even in parallel constructions, the element required in the ellipsis is sometimes unclear. In 1 Thess 3:12, the verb required in "as also we [...] towards you" perhaps derives from the dative noun ἀγάπῃ in the preceding clause ("as also [we have love] toward you"). Note ellipsis in the comparative construction in 1 Cor 11:1: μιμηταί μου γίνεσθε καθὼς κἀγὼ Χριστοῦ [...]; and in 5:1, καὶ τοιαύτη πορνεία [...].

1.2.2.3. OMISSION OF QUALIFIER OR QUALIFYING PHRASE

"The *power* [of those puffed up]" (1 Cor 4:19) does not have the same validity as the fuller, parallel part, "the *word* of those puffed up," since the relevant subjects are presumed to have "words" but *not* to have power.

1.2.2.4. MISSING PARTICLE

μέν is wanted after ἦτε to complement ὑπηκούσατε δὲ in Rom 6:17.

1.2.2.5. ABBREVIATED EXPRESSIONS

Abbreviation of syntax results in ungrammatical constructions in 1 Cor 1:25: "the foolishness of God is wiser than humans, and the weakness of God is stronger than humans" (unless "God's foolishness" / "the weakness of God" is in fact synonymous with "Christ-crucified," with which "humans" are then compared). In 2 Thess 3:7 πῶς δεῖ μιμεῖσθαι ἡμᾶς = "how you should [walk] so as to imitate us."

1.2.2.6. Time-Lapse and Event-Lapse Ellipsis

1.2.2.6.1. *Time lapses involving durative actions*

In not a few instances, a time-lapse occurs between the beginning and endpoint of an action that is apparently continuous in nature: "complete it [such that it lasts] until the day of Christ" (Phil 1:6); "was added because of transgressions, [and it continued] until the seed to whom it was promised came" (Gal 3:19); "I suffer birth pangs over you [and will continue to] until Christ is formed in you" (Gal 4:19); "it is bearing fruit and increasing among you, [and it has been doing so] from which day you heard it . . . " (Col 1:6); "from which day we heard, [we have prayed and we now] do not cease praying . . . " (Col 1:9); "may your spirit and body . . . be blamelessly preserved [so that they will blameless] on the day of our Lord Jesus Christ" (1 Thess 5:23); "in whom you were sealed [and will remain sealed] until the day of redemption" (Eph 4:30).

1.2.2.6.2. *Lapse between cause and effect*

In cases a time lapse occurs between a cause, indicated by the verb, and its result, indicated by its accusative complement: "who will strengthen you [so that you are] blameless on the day of our Lord Jesus" (1 Cor 1:8); "who will transform our body of humiliation, [so that it becomes] conformed to the body of his glory" (Phil 3:21); "to strengthen your hearts [so that they are] blameless in sanctification before our God and Father at the Parousia" (1 Thess 3:13); "whoever eats and drinks eats and drinks [in such a way as to result in] judgment" (1 Cor 11:29); similarly, "the one who prophesies speaks to people [in such a way as to result in] edification, etc." (1 Cor 14:3).

1.2.2.6.3. *Reduced chain of events*

In 2 Thess 3:12, ἵνα μετὰ ἡσυχίας ἐργαζόμενοι τὸν ἑαυτῶν ἄρτον ἐσθίωσιν means, "that by working quietly they might eat their own bread [thereby earned]."

1.2.2.7. Pregnant Expressions

Prepositional phrases are very often pregnant. ἐν δὲ εἰρήνῃ κέκληκεν ὑμᾶς ὁ θεός means "but God has called you [so that you might live] in a state of peace" (1 Cor 7:15); οὐ γὰρ ἐλάβετε πνεῦμα δουλείας πάλιν εἰς φόβον = "you did not receive a spirit of slavery [such that you should fall back] into fear" (Rom 8:15); τὸ ἑαυτοῦ σκεῦος κτᾶσθαι ἐν ἁγιασμῷ καὶ τιμῇ = "to get control of his vessel [and thus to live] in sanctification and honor" (1 Thess 4:4); οὐ γὰρ ἐκάλεσεν ἡμᾶς ὁ θεὸς ἐπὶ ἀκαθαρσίᾳ ἀλλ᾽ ἐν ἁγιασμω = "God did not call you [to live] in impurity but in sanctification" (1 Thess 4:7; here with some equivalency between ἐπί and ἐν).

"These I will send *through letters* [δι᾽ ἐπιστολῶν]" (1 Cor 16:3) means, "These I will send with letters of authorization"; "a pedagogue unto Christ" = "a pedagogue [that leads us] to Christ" (Gal 3:24); ἐνώπιον τοῦ θεοῦ = "as if standing before God I tell you" (Gal 1:20). The Pauline idiom ἐν Χριστῷ (cf. ἐν αὐτῷ, ἐν ᾧ, ἐν Κυρίω) is in many cases pregnant: "have become evident in Christ" = "have become evident [as being] in/for Christ" (Phil 1:13); some apparently adjectival usages appear to function adverbially when filled out, and vice versa: "pleasing in the Lord" (adverbial) = "pleasing [with respect to those who are] in the Lord" (adjectival). Note ἐν κυρίω also in 1 Cor 7:22; εἰς χριστόν in Rom 16:5. In Gal 1:20, ἐνώπιον τοῦ θεοῦ = "as if standing before God I tell you." In Rom 4:25, it is not that Jesus was handed over "because of our sins" and raised "because of our justification"; rather each prepositional phrase reduces a whole series of events into one related act or thing: he was delivered up in order to *forgive* us of the sins (or because we had committed sins that needed forgiveness; cf. Rom 8:23); he was raised in order to *effect* our justification (or "because justification [was necessary]"). In Rom 10:4, εἰς δικαιοσύνην παντὶ τῷ πιστεύοντι means "[and Christ's being the end of the law acts] unto righteousness to every person who believes." In Rom 13:5, διὸ ἀνάγκη ὑποτάσσεσθαι, οὐ μόνον διὰ τὴν ὀργὴν ἀλλὰ καὶ διὰ τὴν συνείδησιν, the preposition διά is causal in both instances, but each phrase requires supplementary material: "because of [the threat of] wrath ... because of conscience [that is, our knowing that God has ordained the governing authorities]." εἰ γὰρ Ἀβραὰμ ἐξ ἔργων ἐδικαιώθη, ἔχει καύχημα· ἀλλ᾽ οὐ πρὸς θεόν apparently means, "For if Abraham was justified by works, he has a right to boast, but in the eyes of God he does not [have a right to boast, i.e., did not do such works as to give him this right]" (Rom 4:2). In 2 Thess 1:9, ἀπὸ προσώπου τοῦ κυρίου καὶ ἀπὸ τῆς δόξης τῆς ἰσχύος αὐτοῦ means, "[separated] from ... "

1.2.2.8. Unknown Element

The location of the ellipsis in Rom 6:22 is difficult to determine: is the thought (1) "and [you have] the end, eternal life," (2) "unto sanctification and [unto] the end," or (3) "unto sanctification, and the end [is] eternal life"? If a contrast between "now" (νυνί) and "the end" (τέλος) is present, then (1) is probably the sense: "*now* you have your fruit unto sanctification; and as the *end*, you have eternal life."

In 2 Thess 2:7, μόνον ὁ κατέχων ἄρτι ἕως ἐκ μέσου γένηται could mean, (1) "only, the one who restrains [restrains] until he is out of the way," or (2) "only, [the mystery of lawlessness must work in secret and remain unrevealed] until the one who restrains is out of the way."

Something is missing also in 2 Cor 12:6.

1.2.3. By transposition (Lausberg, §505)

1.2.3.1. Displaced Modifiers

The infelicitous position of certain words or phrases can lead the listener to take those words with the wrong part of the sentence. In Phil 2:23 ἐξαυτῆς belongs with πέμψαι, which occurs seven words earlier. Note the displacement of ἐν ὑμῖν in 1 Cor 3:18 and 11:18; and of κατὰ ἄνθρωπον in 1 Cor 15:32. Irenaeus (*Haer.* 3.7.1), however, is incorrect that τοῦ αἰῶνος τούτου in 2 Cor 4:4 belongs with τῶν ἀπίστων (several words later) rather than ὁ θεός (with which it is juxtaposed).

The demonstrative τούτου at first appears to have been inappropriately transferred from τοῦ σώματος to τοῦ θανάτου in Rom 7:24 (ἐκ τοῦ σώματος τοῦ θανάτου τούτου), but sense shows (and grammar allows) that it in fact does modify the former.

If ἐν τῇ ἡμέρᾳ ἐκείνῃ modifies ἔλθῃ 2 Thess 1:10, it has probably been delayed until the end for emphasis.

1.2.3.2. Postpositives

Placement of postpositives like δέ and γάρ in third, fourth, or even fifth position in their respective clauses is conventional in classical (BDF §475.2), and not uncommon in Paul's letters. In Paul's letters the delayed position often serves to avoid disruption in the grouping of grammatical components (δέ third in 1 Cor 1:30; 3:8; 4:18; 9:15; 10:4, 20; 11:7; 12:21; γάρ third in 1 Cor 1:18; 10:1, 26); though in other instances it comes second even though grammatical units are thereby disrupted (e.g., δέ in 1 Cor 2:14, 15; 7:1; 12:4; 14:3, 4; etc.; γάρ in 1 Cor 3:13, 17, 19; 9:9; etc.).

1.2.3.3. Negatives

In 1 Cor 2:2, οὐ γὰρ ἔκρινά τι εἰδέναι ἐν ὑμῖν εἰ μὴ Ἰησοῦν Χριστὸν καὶ τοῦτον ἐσταυρωμένον, the negative belongs not with ἔκρινά but with εἰδέναι (compare English: "I don't think that I want to," where the negative properly goes with "want" rather than "think"). The negative is misplaced in 1 Thess 1:8. οὐκ goes with ἐκ τοῦ σώματος in 1 Cor 12:15.

The negative is often transposed where "universal" subjects are involved, as where "all . . . not" means "not all . . . ": ὅπως μὴ καυχήσηται πᾶσα σὰρξ ἐνώπιον τοῦ θεοῦ (1 Cor 1:29) = not, "in order that *not all flesh* might boast before God" (as if *some* flesh could), but rather "in order that all flesh might *not* boast," or, "that *no* flesh might boast before God" (1 Cor 1:29). See also Rom 3:20; 1 Cor 1:15; 15:51; Gal 2:16; Eph 4:29; cf. Luke 1:37; *Poly. Mart.* 3:1; *Did.* 2:7; Rev 7:1; 9:4; and note a similar construction with indefinite pronouns (John 10:28; Ignatius, *Phil.* 6:3; *Poly. Mart.* 2:2; 8:3; *Did.* 6:1). οὐ πάντως ("not in every way") appears to be equally unidiomatic, for the sense rather is "not in any way" (Rom 3:9; cf. πάντως οὐ in 1 Cor 5:9; 16:12; 15:51).

Displacement of the negative sometimes explains the rise of textual variants: in 1 Cor 15:51 it is evident that "all will not sleep" (1 Cor 15:51) is not the sense, but rather "not all will sleep."

οὐ(κ) is often thrown to the beginning of its clause for emphasis. In 1 Cor 12:15, οὐ belongs with ἐκ τοῦ σώματος . . . . and should not be taken introducing a leading question. In Rom 9:8 οὐ belongs with ταῦτα. Paul's placement of οὐ μόνον with ἐν τῇ Μακεδονίᾳ, etc. ruins its correlation with ἀλλ' ἐν παντὶ τόπῳ, etc. (1 Thess. 1:8). Note that οὐ πάντες belongs before οὗτοι Ἰσραήλ in Rom 9:6, 8. In 1 Cor 3:1 displacement of the negative creates an ellipsis that requires a new verb form: "I was not able to speak to you (οὐκ ἠδυνήθην λαλῆσαι) as to spiritual people but [had to speak to you] as to fleshly people"; here the negative belongs more properly before the substantives: "was able to speak to you *not* as to spiritual people but as to fleshly people."

1.2.3.4. Ambiguous Juxtaposition

In 2 Thess 2:8–9, Paul mentions τῆς παρουσίας αὐτοῦ, and continues immediately thereafter with οὗ ... ἡ παρουσία. The two pronouns, however, have different referents (Jesus, then the "man of lawlessness"), and thus the two "parousias" belong to different entities, as only the context makes clear (as noted by Irenaeus, *Haer.* 3.7.2).

1.2.3.5. Left-Dislocations

Some apparently ungrammatical constructions are better understood as involving left-dislocation, which serve the purpose of emphasis. Such is common among the best orators (Cicero, *Fin.* 3.21: *cum positum sit in eo quod ... cum igitur in eo sit*; Cicero, *Nat. d.* 2.95: *cum ... vidissent ... cum viderent ...* ; also *Tusc.* 1.28.68–70). In this regard, 1 Cor 5:3–5 is quite grammatical, though the direct object (v. 3, τὸν ... κατεργασάμενον) is separated by a great distance from the verb (v. 5, παραδοῦναι) and has to be resumed by τὸν τοιοῦτον (v. 5).

Left-dislocation of ὁ κατέχων in 2 Thess 2:7 makes the ellipsis more obscure, though the meaning is probably, "until the one who restrains is out of the way." In 1 Cor 11:18, the genitive absolute belongs within the content of the indirect discourse set off by ἀκούω. In 1 Cor 14:9, the prepositional phrase (διὰ τῆς γλώσσης) belongs within the protasis. τίνα is fronted for emphasis in 2 Cor 12:17.

On Eph 2:1–5, see above under "By Addition."

1.2.3.6. Separation of Complement

The complementary infinitive is separated by a great distance from its governing verb in Phil 2:25: ἡγησάμην ... πέμψαι (cf. παραγγέλλω ... τηρῆσαί in 1 Tim 6:13, 14). In 1 Cor 5:3–5, the main verb (v. 3, κέκρικα) must wait quite some time for its infinitive complement (v. 5, παραδοῦναι).

1.2.3.7. Syntactical Sequence

Irenaeus (*Haer.* 3.7.2) is probably correct that the final clause in Gal 3:19 belongs prior to the preceding clause; thus, not τῶν παραβάσεων χάριν προσετέθη, ἄχρις οὗ ἔλθῃ τὸ σπέρμα ᾧ ἐπήγγελται, διαταγεὶς δι' ἀγγέλων ἐν χειρὶ μεσίτου, but τῶν παραβάσεων χάριν προσετέθη, διαταγεὶς δι' ἀγγέλων ἐν χειρὶ μεσίτου ἄχρις οὗ ἔλθῃ τὸ σπέρμα ᾧ ἐπήγγελται.

In 1 Thess 4:14, omission of the verb "believe" in the apodosis throws off the sequence of thought. εἰ γὰρ πιστεύομεν ὅτι Ἰησοῦς ἀπέθανεν καὶ ἀνέστη, οὕτως καὶ ὁ θεὸς τοὺς κοιμηθέντας διὰ τοῦ Ἰησοῦ ἄξει σὺν αὐτῷ appears to mean that only "if we believe" (εἰ γὰρ πιστεύομεν) that Jesus died and rose will God raise us with him. But the meaning could also be, "If, *as* we believe, Jesus died and rose again, God will also raise those who sleep as well" (where καὶ is understood with τους κοιμηθεντας rather than the verb). Romans 6:8 is similar in both syntax and content, and likewise involves an issue with the placement of πιστεύομεν: now εἰ δὲ ἀπεθάνομεν σὺν Χριστῷ, πιστεύομεν ὅτι καὶ συζήσομεν αὐτῷ, appears really to mean, "We believe (πιστεύομεν) that if we died with Christ, we shall also live with him."

1.2.4. *By substitution (Lausberg, §506–27)*

1.2.4.1. Substitution of Part of Speech (Lausberg, §512–14)

The noun ζηλώτης has adjectival force in Gal 1:14.

Substitutions between participle and finite verb are common in parallel constructions (in point/counterpoint in Rom 12:19; 1 Cor 7:37; 2 Cor 5:12; 7:5; cf. μὴ ἔχουσαν σπίλον ... ἀλλ' ἵνα ᾖ ἁγία ... in Eph 5:27); this exchange has good rhetorical effect in 2 Cor 6:9: ὡς ἀποθνῄσκοντες καὶ ἰδοὺ ζῶμεν. But sometimes what appears to be anacoluthon could actually be ellipsis; e.g., the change from indicative to participle in 2 Thess 3:8: "We did not eat (ἐφάγομεν) anyone's bread free of charge, but rather, working night and day (ἐργαζόμενοι) [we ate our own bread]"; or perhaps the parallel components express manner: "we ate not freely (δωρεὰν) but working night and day (νυκτὸς καὶ ἡμέρας ἐργαζόμενοι)."

1.2.4.2. Substitution of Number (Lausberg §518–19)

Philippians 2:1 has τις in place of τινά (σπλάγχνα) and τινές (οἰκτιρμοί), though Paul probably treats each as a collective singular.

Use of the second person plural in the genitive with a singular head-noun need not indicate collectivity: ἐν καρδίᾳ ὑμῶν (Eph 3:7); τῆς καρδίας ὑμῶν (Eph 6:5); αὐτῶν τὴν συνείδησιν (1 Cor 8:12; see BDF §140); πίστιν ὑμῶν (1 Thess 3:5); ὑμῶν τὸ πρόσωπον (1 Thess 3:10); τοῦ πνεύματος ὑμῶν (Gal 6:18); πᾶσαν χρείαν ὑμῶν (Phil 4:19); τοῦ σώματος ἡμῶν (Rom 8:23); τῇ ἑαυτῶν κοιλίᾳ (Rom 16:18), as the pronoun could in each case be distributive ("each of you"); for instance, slaves of different masters do not share a singular heart (Eph 6:5); the weak do not share one conscience (1 Cor 8:12); and the wicked do not share just one belly (Rom 16:18). Both the genitive and head-noun are plural in ὑμῶν τὰς καρδίας (2 Thess 3:5); τὰς καρδίας τῶν ἀκάκων (Rom 16:18).

1.2.4.3. Substitution of Case (Lausberg, §520–21)

The nominative participle is unexpected in Col 1:20 (εἰρηνοποιήσας; the agent evidently being υἱός, 1:13). In Phil 1:29–30 the nominative participle ἔχοντες (v. 30) refers to the dative referent of ὑμῖν (v. 29).

The reason for the accusative τὸ . . . ἀδύνατον in Rom 8:3 is not apparent.

Sometimes a left-dislocation gets the case that would be required of the resumed referent (ἑκάστῳ should be nominative in 1 Cor 3:5; so also in Rom 12:3, unless εκαστω agrees with παντί earlier in the verse). A switch from the accusative to nominative in Rom 11:22 could be ungrammatical, unless ἀποτομία . . . χρηστότης are subjects of a copulative. Rom 2:8 has the nominative (ὀργὴ καὶ θυμός) where one expects the accusative, due to the accusative in the parallel construction of the previous verse (ζωὴν αἰώνιον). See a similar switch between nominative and accusative in Rom 12:6, 7.

Construction *ad sensum* can scarcely be considered a vice; e.g., the neuter pronoun for the masculine (τί in 1 Cor 3:5; ὅ in Eph 5:5; Col 3:14) or a singular for a collective (οὗ in reference to οὐρανοῖς in Phil 3:20).

1.2.4.4. Substitution through "What Is not Fitting" (Lausberg, §527)

Included here are anacoluthon and parenthesis (Quintilian, *Inst.* 1.5.51).

One finds many instances of anacoluthon involving isolated participles (Rom 12:6–17; 2 Cor 5:6, 12; 7:5; 8:20; 9:11, 13). The participles in Eph 5:19–21 relate to the main verb only loosely (see also Col 3:16). Sometimes Paul begins with a participle but never gets to a finite verb (Rom 7:13; 13:11, but this could just involve ellipsis of the verb). He can switch from the indicative to a participle in point/counterpoint constructions (2 Cor 5:12), or from participle to indicative in εἴτε-εἴτε constructions (Phil

1:27). One finds parallel clauses where a participle changes to a finite verb (Rom 12:19; 1 Cor 7:37; 2 Cor 6:9; 12:1) or an adjective changes to a finite verb (2 Cor 10:1).

Longer sentences tend to meander into anacoluthon (Rom 5:12–18; 12:6–8; 15:23–28; 2 Cor 8:18–21; Col 1:9–23). νυν(ὶ) δὲ changes the arrangement of the sentence in Col 1:22; 1:26. In some instances a construction is never resolved with a predicate (Rom 5:12; 2 Cor 5:6). At other times Paul comes back and resolves the thread after much intervening material: the thought in Rom 5:12 is resolved perhaps at 5:15 or 5:18 (cf. Kirby 1987 on the structure of Rom 5:12); the parenthesis that begins in Eph 3:1 (εἴ γε ἠκούσατε) is finally resolved in v. 14 (τούτου χάριν ἐγὼ Παῦλος . . . τούτου χάριν κάμπτω). Eph 2:1–5 and Col 1:21–23 begin with accusatives that one expects to be left-dislocations, but the syntax is ultimately never resolved (cf. in Col 2:13 an accusative in left-dislocation that does not result in anacoluthon); note also ἕνα ἕκαστον ὑμῶν . . . ὑμᾶς in 1 Thess 2:11–12. The doxology in Rom 16:25–27 involves a left-dislocation in the dative, but when the dative is resumed after much intervening material, it is resumed by the relative pronoun ᾧ rather than the required αὐτῷ.

In some places we find a pendent accusative with a subsequent shift in thought (Rom 8:3; Eph 2:1–5; Col 1:21–23). The change from accusative to nominative in Rom 11:22; 12:7 could be seen as ungrammatical.

The clause introduced by γάρ in Gal 2:6 actually grounds the preceding parenthesis, which intervenes before the main clause (Ἀπὸ δὲ τῶν δοκούντων εἶναί τι) is resolved.

Some apparent examples of anacoluthon are on further consideration grammatical. The obscure citation in 1 Cor 2:9 (with affinities to LXX Isa 64:3; 65:16e) is syntactically difficult (ἃ ὀφθαλμὸς οὐκ εἶδεν καὶ οὖς οὐκ ἤκουσεν καὶ ἐπὶ καρδίαν ἀνθρώπου οὐκ ἀνέβη, ἃ ἡτοίμασεν ὁ θεὸς τοῖς ἀγαπῶσιν αὐτόν), but the difficulties are alleviated if the second relative resumes the first (ἃ . . . ἃ = "*those things* that eye has not seen . . . *these very things* God has prepared for those who . . . "). In some longer sentences Paul comes back and resolves the thread after much intervening material (Rom 5:12, being resolved perhaps at 5:15 or 5:18; cf. Kirby 1987 on the structure of Rom 5:12); the parenthesis that begins in Eph 3:1 (εἴ γε ἠκούσατε) is finally resolved in v. 14 (τούτου χάριν ἐγὼ Παῦλος . . . τούτου χάριν κάμπτω). The main clause is omitted in Rom 15:23–24 (νυνὶ δὲ μηκέτι τόπον ἔχων ἐν τοῖς κλίμασιν τούτοις, . . . ὡς ἂν πορεύωμαι εἰς τὴν Σπανίαν), though "I will come to you" is readily understood from the context. The sentence fragment in Rom 7:13 (ἡ ἁμαρτία... κατεργαζομένη θάνατον) should be understood elliptically as the answer to a question and is not really anacoluthon ("Has the good [i.e., the Law] become death to me? No, rather *Sin-producing-death* has become death to me"). εἰ + ἀλλά (1 Cor 9:2; Col 2:5; Mark 14:29; Ignatius, *Phil.* 7:1), εἴπερ + ἀλλά (1 Cor 8:5–6) strikes the modern reader as ungrammatical ("if... but") though it actually reflects normal Classical style (LSJ I.2). Note also the concessive participle + δέ (Col 1:21–22).

Both anacoluthon and parenthesis can also function as figures (Lausberg, §924; 860). For this, see below on "aposiopesis" (§3.2.1.2.25).

1.2.4.5. Substitution of a Word

While Phil 3:11 would appear to require ὥστε or ἵνα in place of εἰ, the given construction could be understood as an indirect question (BDF § 368; 375), i.e., "[to see] if I might attain."

The correlation of τοιαύτη and ὥστε in 1 Cor 5:1 seems inappropriate, for Paul does not mean that such a kind (τοιαύτη) of sexual immorality has occurred *that* (ὥστε) a certain man's having his father's wife has *resulted*; rather, the relative points ahead to the *content* of the sexual immorality ("*such* a kind... namely, *that*...; cf. τοῦτο... ἵνα, 1 Cor 7:29).

2. Clarity (Lausberg, §528–37)

Clarity, or *perspicuitas*, refers to the quality of using language that is immediately apprehensible to the audience. It is achieved both by employing the proper words (*verba propria*) and by correctly joining these words. Conversely, one fails to achieve clarity (commits the vice of *obscuritas*) when one uses words, or joins them, incorrectly; though, the use of improper words (*verba impropria*) can in some cases be considered virtuous (e.g., certain neologisms or archaisms).

In Cicero's *de Oratore*, Crassus offers the following definition of *perspicuitas*: "obviously this [speaking clearly] will be by talking correct Latin, and employing words in customary use that indicate literally the meaning that we desire to be conveyed and made clear, without ambiguity of language or style, avoiding excessively long periodic structure, not spinning out metaphors drawn from other things, not breaking the structure of the sentences, not using the wrong tenses, not mixing up the persons, not perverting the order" (*Or.* 3.39).

Crassus, however, proceeds to say that he can pass over this topic quickly, since like the matter of correctness, clarity of speech is an ordinary expectation (*Or.* 3.49, 52). Accordingly, the clarity of style in Paul's letters can, from a rhetorical perspective, be assumed as a general feature, and analysis of his letters from this perspective is best approached through the exceptions, insofar as these can be discerned by modern speakers. Moreover, it is evident from Crassus's definition, that the virtues of style (correctness, clarity, and ornament) overlap and serve one another: one cannot be lucid, let alone eloquent, without also speaking correctly. Thus, many of the features noted above under "Solecisms" and "Barbarisms" as to correctness can be considered pertinent also in the area of lucidity, and will not be repeated here.

We discuss here only the matter of the coordination of clauses and of logical argumentation.

Paul frequently leaves an ellipsis of the thought. ἤ sometimes poses a disjunction between an idea that is expressed and an idea that is left unexpressed. "Or (ἤ) do you not know . . . " (1 Cor 6:2) leaves implicit the premise that they "do know" (cf. 8:1), i.e., "As you know—or do you *not* know . . . ?" Misunderstanding of the ellipsis of thought here leads Caragounis (208–11) to prefer the variant reading ἦ ("truly"). The conjunction functions similarly in 1 Thess 2:19: "or (ἤ) is it not you?" = "you think you are not special to me—or *are you not* you special to me . . . ?" Note "or (ἤ) do you *not* know . . . " also in 1 Cor 6:9, 19. In 1 Cor 10:22, ἤ introduces a disjunction between "provoking the Lord to jealousy" and, implicitly, not doing so, with the implicit idea being an extrapolation from the idea of avoiding idolatry (cf. vv. 14–22). In 1 Cor 14:36, the same conjunction introduces a contrast between, on the one hand, the way things ought to be, as dictated by the customs of all the churches (14:33), and on the other hand, the way the Corinthians have acted (with vv. 34–35 being an interpolation); effectively the question asks how the Corinthians could act as though this incongruity were acceptable: "*Or* (ἤ) perhaps it is because you think *you* were the very source of the gospel that you act in this way?" The prior alternative must be supplied also in 1 Cor 11:22.

The pronominal component contained in inferential connectives (διὰ τοῦτο, διά + ὅ) sometimes refers to the *opposite* of what has been asserted; e.g., διὰ τοῦτο in 1 Cor 11:30 means, "Since many have *not* observed the principles just stated."

The contrast introduced by δέ in 1 Cor 11:28 is not directly expressed and requires the listener to supply, "instead of eating unworthily." Similarly, δέ in 1 Cor 14:2 requires one to substitute "they do not speak an intelligible human language" for "no one understands." In 1 Cor 10:20, ἀλλ' introduces a correction to the implied negative answer to the preceding question: "(I do not mean that) *but* that . . . " Similarly, in 1 Cor 15:46 ἀλλ' indicates a contrast, not with the quotation immediately preceding, but with the erroneous presupposition against which vv. 45 and 46 bear witness, namely that the spiritual precedes the physical. Note the inexplicitedness of the contrast (ἀλλά) also in 1 Cor 6:6.

The logical connection shown by γάρ in Gal 1:10 is loose; "for am I trying to persuade men or God" follows not from what has been said explicitly, but from something like, "you can trust what I say above all others" (paraphrasing 1:6–9); one must then further supply the premise, "those who are trying to please God are trustworthy."

Misunderstanding of logical ellipses can lead interpreters to conjecture anomalous new means of conjunctions. Modern translations offer new renderings in many places, though perhaps only for purposes of simplification. For instance, translations often render ἀλλά as "indeed." The ESV renders γάλα ὑμᾶς ἐπότισα, οὐ βρῶμα, οὔπω γὰρ ἐδύνασθε. <u>ἀλλ'</u> οὐδὲ ἔτι νῦν δύνασθε (1 Cor 3:2) as, "I gave you milk to drink, not solid food; for you were not yet able to receive it. *Indeed* (ἀλλ'), even now you are not yet able . . . " (ESV). However, the deep meaning is, "You were not able to eat solid food. *Nay, (so far from being able to eat solid food)*, you are not able even now." At 1 Cor 4:3, the NIV renders ἐμοὶ δὲ εἰς ἐλάχιστόν ἐστιν ἵνα ὑφ' ὑμῶν ἀνακριθῶ ἢ ὑπὸ ἀνθρωπίνης ἡμέρας. <u>ἀλλ'</u> οὐδὲ ἐμαυτὸν ἀνακρίνω as, "I care very little if I am judged by you or by any human court; *indeed* (ἀλλ'), I do not even judge myself." The sense, however, is, "But to me it is of little consequence that I should be judged by you, or by any human court. *Yet, (while you might then expect me to judge myself)*, I do not even do *that*." Likewise, the NAB renders ἀλλά in 1 Cor 12:22 as "indeed," though the sense is, "*but* (rather than asserting its autonomy) each part of the body should recognize how necessary all of the parts are." In 2 Cor 1:8–9, the sense is not "*[i]ndeed* (ἀλλά), in our hearts we felt the sentence of death," but "it is true, we despaired of life, *[b]ut* but the reason we experienced this sentence of death was to learn not to rely on ourselves."

Again, in Phil 1:18 it is not "I rejoice. Indeed (ἀλλά) I will rejoice," but "I rejoice now. But I also *will* rejoice when through your prayers and the Spirit I am delivered" (1:18–19). One must fill in a logical gap between οὖν and what precedes in 1 Cor 3:4–5. The NAB, NIV, and NLT render the conjunction "after all," as if it expressed grounds. The meaning, however, is, "(If by making such claims about Paul and Apollos you show yourselves to be merely 'human,' i.e., mistaken), Paul and Apollos must, therefore (οὖν), be of different character than you suppose." In 1 Cor 9:10, γάρ itself does not mean "yes" (NIV, NASB, CSB) or "indeed" (NRSV) but rather provides the grounds for what is to be be supplied by the listener: "does it not say this entirely for our sake? (Yes), *for* (γάρ) . . . " In 1 Cor 14:2d, δέ does not mean "for" (NRSV) or "since" (CSB), provided one understands "no one hears" to mean "they do not speak an intelligible human language."

New meanings have also been proposed in instances where interpreters link the wrong clauses together. For instance, οὖν is not "adversative" in 1 Cor 11:20 but has its ordinary inferential meaning,[2] connecting back, not with v. 19, but with v. 18a. 1 Cor 11:10 (διὰ τοῦτο) states a conclusion not to v. 9 but to v. 7b ("but the woman is man's glory"), provided the listener supplies two additional premises: "an uncovered head entices angels" and "intercourse with angels compromises the glory of the woman's head, man." One must conjecture "since (*car*)" (Senft 1990: 94) as the meaning of δέ in 1 Cor 7:15d only if one sees this verse grounding v. 15ab; but in fact, it grounds v. 15c and thus means "but." The NRSV renders γάρ as "but" in 2 Cor 12:6, though this is evidently because the translators see it connecting with v. 5b rather than, as it does, with v. 5a. Not infrequently, then, conjunctions link clauses between which other material intervenes. γάρ links Rom 7:8b with 7:7; it links 1 Cor 3:9b with 3:8; it links 1 Cor 7:22 with 7:21ab; and it links 1 Cor 8:11 with 8:9 (probably why manuscript A has emended to οὖν). ἀλλά jumps back from Rom 10:19 to 10:17; and from Rom 12:20 to 12:19a. ὥστε in 1 Cor 1:7 links back with 1:5.

3. Ornament (Lausberg, §538–1054)

Ornament, or *ornatus*, refers to the quality of elegance or adornment of speech. Among the virtues, ornament and propriety are the "big matters," for "nobody ever admired an orator for correct grammar, they only laugh at him if his grammar is bad" (*Or.* 3.52; cf. *Off.* 1.2, which omits reference

---

2. Porter, *Idioms*, 215.

to correctness); and "all success in winning credit for talent and applause for eloquence" depends upon ornament and correctness (*Or.* 3.52). Moreover, ornament itself is "the highest distinction of eloquence" (*Or.* 3.104). It serves the rhetorical purpose of "delighting" the audience (Quintilian, *Inst.* 8.3.5), a purpose fulfilled through the varying effect of ornament and the consequent avoidance of tedium (Cicero, *Or.* 3.100; cf. Lausberg, §257.2b; 538). Thus all ornament in a sense amounts to "stylistic variation."

Ornament is realized either in single words (Lausberg §541–98) or in the conjunction of words (Lausberg §599–1054).

3.1. In Single Words

Ornament realized through single words includes the use of archaisms (Lausberg §546), neologisms (Lausberg §547–51), and tropes (Lausberg §552–98). While these devices violate strict propriety of usage, they are virtuous insofar as they open up new semantic possibilities (explored usually because of a "poverty" of preexisting options) without sacrificing the speaker's semantic intention.

3.1.1. *Archaisms (Lausberg §546)*

Archaism consists in the use of antiquated words or phrases for purposes of an "increased *dignitas* (in keeping with *ornatus*; cf. §539) conditioned by age." Since old words have aged out of usage, "they give *elocutio* that touch which one admires on old paintings" (Lausberg, §246).

3.1.2. *Neologisms (Lausberg §547–51)*

A neologism is a new word created on the basis of onomatopoeia, derivation, or compounding of derivatives (Quintilian, *Inst.* 8.3.30–37). It is impossible to determine definitively whether one is encountering an original coinage. However, several words that appear in Paul's letters appear nowhere else in antecedent literature. Several examples appear to be compounds of lexical units that appear in proximity in passages from the LXX.

ἀρσενοκοίτης (1 Cor 6:9; cf. 1 Tim 1:10). A compound of ἄρσην ("male") and κοιμᾶν ("to lie down") formed on the basis of Lev 18:22; 20:13.

εἰδωλολατρία (1 Cor 10:14; Gal 5:20; Col 3:5). A compound of εἴδωλον ("idol") and λατρεύειν ("to worship") formed on the basis of 2 Kgs 17:12. Usage of this word in 1 Pet 4:3 postdates Paul's usages.

θεοδίδακτος (1 Thess 4:9). A compound of θεός ("god) and δίδακτος ("taught") formed on the basis of Isa 54:13.³

3.1.3. *Tropes (Lausberg §552–98)*

A "trope" (τρόπος, "turn [of phrase]"; *modus elocutionis*, "manner of speaking") consists in the substitution, in place of the "proper" word, of a word not semantically related, where the substituted word is intended to have the same meaning as the word it replaces, the meaning of which becomes comprehensible in light of the context. Every trope is technically an impropriety, but when the impropriety keeps within certain limits, it serves to break up the tedium of the discourse and can serve the ideal of eloquence.

Two considerations problematize attempts to identify legitimate tropes. First, some tropes are customary; some are partial inventions of the speaker; and some are total inventions. Tropes that become current in colloquial language can descend to the level of "proper use," and will no longer be perceived as tropes but as common idiom (e.g., σπλάγχνα, "bowels" for "affection"). Consequently, many apparent examples of tropes may not qualify as such from a *pure* rhetorical standpoint. On the other hand, even unconscious examples can be counted as metaphor in a sense (Quintilian says that metaphor is "a gift which Nature herself confers on us, and which is therefore used even by uneducated persons and unconsciously"; *Inst.* 8.6.4). Second, expressions that may seem to be metaphorical from a "modern" standpoint, ancient speakers may have understood in quite a literal sense. Though, here also one should be aware of the middle ground of the "lexicalized trope," or "catachresis" (Lausberg §562), i.e., a trope that is invented due to a poverty of expressive options and subsequently lexicalized out of necessity. The lexicalized trope is especially common in discourse about transcendent realities.

In ancient times debate raged among grammarians and philosophers "as to the genera, species, number and classification of Tropes" (Quintilian, *Inst.* 8.6.1, referring to an "endless battle" over this question). Included in §3.1.3 here are the tropes of metaphor, allegory, metonymy,

---

3. Witmer, "θεοδίδακτος 1 Thessalonians 4.9."

synecdoche, hyperbole, antonomasia, irony, periphrasis, catachresis, litotes, and hyperbaton.

3.1.3.1. Metaphor (Lausberg, §558–64)

Metaphor (μεταφορά, *translatio*) consists in the substitution of one thing (an improper thing) for another (the proper thing). Substitutions may be of either nouns or verbs (Quintilian, *Inst.* 8.6.5). Far-fetched, or "daring" metaphors, are often introduced by speakers with formulas of caution, like "so to speak," "if it is permitted to say," etc. (Lausberg, §558); cf. "I speak in human terms" (Rom 6:18–19; 1 Cor 15:32; Gal 3:15). Here we have been quite inclusive, qualifying as metaphors many examples that surely qualify merely as "lexicalized tropes" (see §3.1.3 above). We also treat as metaphorical all language that refers to the transcendent realm or abstract reality, or at least, that reality that people, even ancient ones, typically do not conceptualize as material in the *same* sense as tangible reality.

See also "Simile/Similitudo" (§3.2.1.2.19) and "Allegory" (§3.1.3.2).

The following catalog groups metaphors according to the semantic domain of the source term. Categories and enumeration (e.g., Geographical objects and features [#1]) are from Louw and Nida.[4]

3.1.3.1.1. Plants (#3)

Non-fruit part of plants. The church as "rooted" (Eph 3:17; Col 2:7).

Fruit part of plants. A "fruitless" mind (1 Cor 14:14); make spiritual "fruit (καρπός)" (Rom 1:13; 6:21, 22; 15:28); "bear fruit (καρποφορεῖν)" (Rom 7:4; Col 1:6, 9); the "fruit" of righteousness (Phil 1:11); the "fruit" of work (Phil 1:22); the "fruit" of the Spirit (Gal 5:22).

3.1.3.1.2. Animals (#4)

Animals. Paul's opponents as "dogs" (Phil 3:2).

---

4. Louw and Nida, *Greek-English Lexicon*.

3.1.3.1.3. FOOD AND CONDIMENTS (#5)

Food. Church as a "loaf" of bread (1 Cor 10:17); Christ's body as a "loaf" of bread (1 Cor 11:24; citing Jesus); the "old leaven," the "leaven of malice and wickedness" (1 Cor 5:8).

3.1.3.1.4. ARTIFACTS (#6)

Traps, snares. "Stumbling-block (πρόσκομμα)" to the weak (1 Cor 8:9); "stumbling-block (σκάνδαλον)" of the cross (Gal 5:11); "cause [one] to stumble" (1 Cor 8:13); "hindrance (προσκοπή)" (2 Cor 6:3).

Weapons and armor. Presenting one's members as "weapons" (Rom 6:13); "weapons" of righteousness (2 Cor 6:7).

Instruments in marking and writing. See "Allegory" on the extended metaphor of the "letter" and "tablet" (2 Cor 3:3).

Musical instruments. Paul as "clanging cymbal" (1 Cor 13:1).

Adornments. The church as Paul's "crown" (Phil 4:1; 1 Thess 2:19; for both examples see also under "Metonymy"). On the "crown" of eternal life (1 Cor 9:25), the "prize" of the upward call (Phil 3:13–14), see under "Allegory."

Containers. The male body as a "vessel" (1 Thess 4:4).

Anything pointed. Messenger of Satan as a "thorn" in Paul's flesh (2 Cor 12:7).

3.1.3.1.5. CONSTRUCTIONS (#7)

Buildings. The (human?) body as a "temple" of God (1 Cor 6:19); the human body as a "house" (2 Cor 5:2, 8). On the church as a "building" (1 Cor 3:9), "temple" (1 Cor 3:17; 2 Cor 6:16), see under "Allegory."

Parts and areas of buildings. Christ as "cornerstone" (Eph 2:20).

3.1.3.1.6. BODY, BODY PARTS, AND BODY PRODUCTS (#8)

Body. The human (or else the church's) body as "temple" of the Holy Spirit (1 Cor 6:19); the church as "body" (Rom 12:4–5; 1 Cor 10:16–17;

12:12–27; Eph 2:16; 3:6; 4:4, 12; Col 1:24; 3:15; with Christ as the "head" in Eph 1:22–23; 4:15; 5:23; Col 1:18; 2:19). On the church as a "body," see also under "Allegory."

Parts of the body. The bodies of believers as "members" of Christ versus "members" of a prostitute (1 Cor 6:15–17); believers as "members" of the body (1 Cor 12:14, 18, 19, 20, 22, 25, 26, 27; Eph 4:25); the "foot," "hand," "ear," "eye" as members of the church (1 Cor 12:15–17). Christ as "head" of the church body (Eph 1:22; 4:15; 5:23; Col 1:18; 2:19), as "head" of every man (1 Cor 11:3), as "head" of every other power (Col 2:10); man as "head" of woman (1 Cor 11:3).

Physiological products. The world's status markers as "excrement (σκύβαλον)" (Phil 3:8).

3.1.3.1.7. People (#9)

Males. Thinking like a "man (ἀνήρ)" (1 Cor 13:11).

Children. "Children (νήπιοι)" as to spiritual maturity (1 Cor 3:1; cf. Rom 2:20). Thinking like a "child (νήπιος)" (1 Cor 13:11), or "think like children (νηπιάζετε)," "be infants (νηπιάζετε)" toward evil (1 Cor 14:20). Paul's converts as his spiritual "children (τέκνα)" (Gal 4:19). "We became little children (νήπιοι) in your midst" (1 Thess 2:7).

3.1.3.1.8. Kinship Terms (#10)

Groups and members of groups of persons regarded as related by blood but without special reference to successive generations. "Those of the household of faith" (Gal 6:10).

Successive generations. Christ as "firstborn (πρωτότοκος)" among many brothers (Rom 8:29), as "firstborn (πρωτότοκος)" of all creation (Col 1:15), as "firstborn" from among the dead (Col 1:18).

Father. Paul as spiritual "father (πατήρ)" of Timothy (Phil 2:22). God as "Father (πατήρ)" (Rom 1:7; passim). Abraham as spiritual "father (πατήρ)" of believers (Rom 4:11; 9:7–13; Gal 3:7); Israelites as spiritual "fathers (πατέρες)" of believers (1 Cor 10:1); Abraham as "father (πατήρ)" of all ethnic Israel (Rom 4:1); the patriarchs as "fathers (πατέρες)" of all ethnic Israel (Rom 9:5; 11:28); Isaac as "father (πατήρ)" of all ethnic Israel (Rom 9:10).

Mother. Jerusalem-above as "mother (μήτηρ)" of believers (Gal 4:26); Rufus's mother as Paul's spiritual or foster "mother (μήτηρ)" (Rom 16:13).

Son. Believers as "sons (υἱοί)" of God (Rom 8:14), "sons and daughters (υἱοὺς καὶ θυγατέρας)" of God (2 Cor 6:18; citing Isa 43:6). Believers receive "adoption" as God's children (Rom 8:15; Gal 4:5; cf. Rom 8:29); the sons of God await their "adoption" (8:21–23); Israel enjoyed God's "adoption" as sons (Rom 9:4). The Man of Lawlessness as "the son of destruction" (2 Thess 2:3).

Child. Paul's converts as his spiritual "children (τέκνα)" (2 Cor 6:13; Gal 4:19); Timothy as Paul's spiritual "child (τέκνον)" (Phil 2:22); Onesimus as Paul's "child (τέκνον)" (Phlm 10). Believers as "children (τέκνα)" of God (Rom 8:16, 21; Eph 5:1), as "children (τέκνα) of the promise" (Gal 4:28). Believers as "children (τέκνα) of the freewoman" (Gal 4:31).

Brother. Believers as "brothers (ἀδελφοί)" of one another (passim, with uses most concentrated in 1 Corinthians and 1 Thessalonians). False-teachers as "false-brothers (ψευδαδελφοί)" (Gal 2:4).

Sister. Fellow-believer as "sister (ἀδελφή)" (Rom 16:1; 1 Cor 7:15; Phlm 2).

3.1.3.1.9. GROUPS AND CLASSES OF PERSONS AND MEMBERS OF SUCH GROUPS AND CLASSES (#11)

Socio-religious. Unbelievers as "the sons of disobedience" (Eph 2:2; 5:6; Col 3:6); believers as "children of light" (Eph 5:8).

Socio-political. The term "assembly (ἐκκλησία)" as a reference to the corporate body of believers (1 Cor 1:2; passim) is metaphorical, not only in that it characterizes the church in terms of a *political* body, but also to the extent that it refers to an "ideal" entity whose nature transcends the physical gathering or even physical location (ἐκκλησία is probably translocal in 1 Cor 10:32; 11:22; 15:9). Jews and gentiles as "fellow-citizens (συμπολῖται)" (Eph 2:19); believers have a "citizenship (πολίτευμα)" in heaven (Phil 3:20);

"live as citizens (πολιτεύεσθε)" in a manner worthy of Christ (Phil 1:27). Paul and Apollos as "assistants (ὑπηρέται)" of Christ (1 Cor 4:1).

3.1.3.1.10. *Physical Events and States (#14)*

Light, darkness. "Darkened" in their understanding (Eph 4:18); the saints "in the light" (Col 1:12); the power of "darkness" (Col 1:13); a "shadow" of what is to come (Col 2:17); unrighteous people as "darkness," righteous people as "light" (Eph 5:8).

Burning. To "burn" with desire (Rom 1:27) or anger (2 Cor 11:29); to "flame" with passion (1 Cor 7:9); not to "quench" the Spirit (1 Thess 5:19).

3.1.3.1.11. *Linear Movement (#15)*

Travel, journey. A "more excellent path (ὁδόν)" (1 Cor 12:31).

Leave, depart, flee, escape, send. "Escape" the judgment of God (Rom 2:3); "flee" from idolatry (1 Cor 10:14).

Come, come to, arrive. Have "access" to grace (Rom 5:2).

Fall. "Falling" as dying (1 Cor 10:8), as lapsing spiritually (Rom 11:11; 1 Cor 10:12); "have fallen away" from grace (Gal 5:4).

Run. "Running" as making an effort or striving (Rom 9:16; Gal 2:2; Phil 2:16), as making spiritual progress (Gal 5:7; cf. Phil 3:13–14), or as advancing toward the goal in one's spiritual journey (1 Cor 9:24–25); the word of the gospel as "running" to meet new audiences (2 Thess 3:1).

Walk, step. "Walk in step" (στοιχῶμεν) with the Spirit" (Gal 5:25); "walk (στοιχήσουσιν) according to this standard" (Gal 6:16); "walk (στοχεῖν)" in the way one has been walking (Phil 3:16); "walking" (περιπατεῖν) for living or conducting oneself in a righteous way (Rom 8:4; 13:13; 1 Cor 7:17; 2 Cor 5:7; 12:18; Gal 5:16; Eph 2:2, 10; 4:1, 17; 5:2, 8, 15; Phil 3:17; Col 1:10; 2:6; 4:5; 1 Thess 2:12; 4:1, 12), in an unrighteous way (1 Cor 3:3; 2 Cor 4:2; 10:2; Phil 3:18; Col 3:7; 2 Thess 3:6, 11); "not walking rightly (ὀρθοποδοῦσιν)" (Gal 2:14).

3.1.3.1.12. Non-linear Movement (#16)

Be "shaken" out of one's mind (2 Thess 2:2).

3.1.3.1.13. Stances and Events Related to Stances (#17)

Stand. "Stand" in grace (Rom 5:2); "stand" in the gospel (1 Cor 15:1).

3.1.3.1.14. Attachment (#18)

Fasten, stick. "Clinging" to good (Rom 12:9).

3.1.3.1.15. Physical Impact (#19)

Press. "Pressure (ἐπίστασις)" upon Paul (2 Cor 11:28); be "pressed between (συνέχομαι)" two things (Phil 1:23).

3.1.3.1.16. Violence, Harm, Destroy, Kill (#20)

Destroy. "Tearing down (καθαίρεσις)" (2 Cor 10:8; 13:10); not to "destroy (κατάλυε)" the work of God (Rom 14:20); "destroyed (κατέλυσα)" (Gal 2:18); pure thoughts being "destroyed (φθαρῇ)" (2 Cor 11:3); not to be "destroyed (ἀναλωθῆτε)" by each other (Gal 5:15).

Kill. The old self being "crucified with him" (Rom 6:6); sin "killing" through the Law (Rom 7:11); "crucified with Christ" (Gal 2:19); the world "has been crucified to me, and I [crucified] to the world" (Gal 6:14).

3.1.3.1.17. Danger, Risk, Safe, Save (#21)

Become safe, free from danger. An "exit" from temptation (1 Cor 10:13).

Cause to be safe, free from danger. "Salvation" (σωτήρια), "save" (σῳζω) might qualify as a lexicalized trope (see §3.1.3 above), where save from danger = save in a religious sense.

3.1.3.1.18. TROUBLE, HARDSHIP, RELIEF, FAVORABLE CIRCUMSTANCES (#22)

Relief from trouble. No "rest" for the spirit (2 Cor 2:13); one's spirit "refreshed" (2 Cor 7:13).

3.1.3.1.19. PHYSIOLOGICAL PROCESSES AND STATES (#23)

Eat, drink. "Bite" and "devour" each other (Gal 5:15). "Drink" of the Spirit (1 Cor 12:13); be "sober" (1 Cor 15:34; 1 Thess 5:8).

Processes involving the mouth, other than eating and drinking. Not to be "swallowed up" by sorrow (2 Cor 2:7); that the mortal body might be "swallowed up" by life (2 Cor 5:4).

Birth, procreation. Onesimus as Paul's child, whom he has "begotten" (Phlm 10). Paul as an "untimely birth (ἔκτρωμα)," i.e., an aborted fetus (1 Cor 15:8).

Tire, rest. "Rest on" the Law (Rom 2:17).

Sleep, waking. "Stay awake (γρηγορεῖτε)" (1 Cor 16:13); "staying awake (ἀγρυπνοῦντες)" (Eph 6:18); "staying awake (γρηγοροῦντες)" in prayer (Col 4:2); to "wake from sleep" (Rom 13:11).

Live, die. "Raised" from spiritual death to walk (now) in a new way (Rom 6:4; Col 3:1).

Sickness, disease, weakness. "Weak" in faith (Rom 14:1, 2); "weak" in conscience (1 Cor 8:7, 9, 10, 11); possibly, "make stiff (καταναρκᾶν)" (2 Cor 11:9; 12:13, 14).

Rot, decay. Creation enslaved in bondage of "decay (φθορᾶς)" (Rom 8:21).

3.1.3.1.20. SENSORY EVENTS (#24)

See. Hope that is "seen" is not hope (Rom 8:24). Mystery "hidden," "now revealed" (Col 1:26).

But see especially under "Allegory" (§3.1.3.2).

STYLE IN PAUL'S LETTERS

3.1.3.1.21. LEARN *(#27)*

Try to learn. God "searches" hearts (Rom 8:27).

3.1.3.1.22. KNOW *(#28)*

Well known, clearly shown, revealed. Mystery "hidden," "now revealed" (Col 1:26).

3.1.3.1.23. COMMUNICATION *(#33)*

Written language. "Book of life" (Phil 4:3).

Assert, declare. Word "has rung out" (1 Thess 1:8).

Non-verbal communication. The Corinthians as "seal" of Paul's apostleship (1 Cor 9:2); God "sealed" us by giving the Spirit (2 Cor 1:22); sign of circumcision as a "seal" of righteousness (Rom 4:11); "put a seal" on a financial contribution (Rom 15:28); church "sealed" for the day of redemption (Eph 4:30).

3.1.3.1.24. HELP, CARE FOR *(#35)*

Serve. "Eye-service" (Col 3:22).

3.1.3.1.25. CONTROL, RULE *(#37)*

Control, restrain. Be "bound" to a spouse (Rom 7:2); "enslaved" to a spouse (1 Cor 7:15); "slaves" to people (1 Cor 7:23); "enslaved" (2 Cor 11:20); "slave" of Jesus Christ (Rom 1:1; 1 Cor 7:22; Col 4:12), "slaves" of Christ Jesus (Phil 1:1); "fellow-slave" (Col 1:7; 4:7).

Rule, govern. Death "ruled" (Rom 5:14, 17); believers "rule" (Rom 5:17); sin "ruled" (Rom 5:21); grace "ruled" (Rom 5:21); the Corinthians "reign as kings" (1 Cor 4:8); to let the peace of God "control (βραβευέτω)" (Col 3:15). "Under" the Law (Rom 6:14, 15; 1 Cor 9:20; Gal 3:23; 4:4, 5, 21; 5:18); "under" grace (Rom 6:14, 15); "under" sin (Rom 3:9; 7:14; Gal 3:22); God treads Satan "under" his feet (Rom 16:20). "Subject" all things to himself

(Phil 3:21), "subjected" all things under his feet (1 Cor 15:27 = LXX Psa 8:6; Eph 1:22); all things "subjected" (1 Cor 15:28).

Assign to a role or function. God having "anointed" believers (2 Cor 1:21); Paul as "separated" for the gospel (Rom 1:1).

Imprison. God "shut in" (συνέκλεισεν) all people in disobedience (Rom 11:32); "make captive" (Col 2:8); "prisoner" of Christ Jesus (Phlm 9); the "bonds" of the gospel (Phlm 13).

Guard, watch over. The peace of God will "guard" their hearts (Phil 4:7).

Release, set free. "Redemption (ἀπολύτρωσις)" (Rom 3:24; 8:23; 1 Cor 1:30; Eph 1:14; 4:30; Col 1:14); Christ "redeemed (ἐξηγόρασεν)" believers (Gal 3:13).

3.1.3.1.26. PUNISH, REWARD (#38)

Reward, recompense. God "giving back" what is due for one's works (Rom 2:6; 12:19//Deut 32:35). See also domain #57 (§3.1.3.1.40).

3.1.3.1.27. HOSTILITY, STRIFE (#39)

Opposition, hostility. The carnal mind as "enemy" against God (Rom 8:7); flesh and Spirit "opposed" to each other (Gal 5:17); "enemies" in understanding (Col 1:21).

Conquer. "Lead in triumphal procession" (2 Cor 2:14).

Strife, struggle. Perseverance through suffering as a "contest" (Phil 1:30); a "contest" on behalf of others (Col 2:1); "contending" in prayer (Col 4:12).

3.1.3.1.28. RECONCILIATION AND FORGIVENESS (#40)

Reconciliation. Pre-converted people as "estranged (ἀπηλλοτριωμένοι)" from God (Col 1:21); "reconciliation" (Rom 5:11; 11:15; 2 Cor 5:18, 19), "reconcile" (Rom 5:10; 2 Cor 5:18, 19, 20; Col 1:20).

3.1.3.1.29. BEHAVIOR AND RELATED STATES (#41)

Uncivilized. Tongues-speaker as "barbarian" (1 Cor 14:11).

3.1.3.1.30. PERFORM, DO (#42)

Make, create. The "work (ἔργον)" of God (Rom 14:20); the Corinthians as Paul's "work (ἔργον)" (1 Cor 9:1); "building up" of the church (Eph 4:16, 29); believers as God's "creation (ποίημα)" (Eph 2:10); the person in Christ as "new creation" (2 Cor 5:17).

3.1.3.1.31. AGRICULTURE (#43)

A body "sown" and raised (1 Cor 15:42, 43, 44); "first-fruit" (Rom 8:23; 11:16; 16:5; 1 Cor 15:20, 23; 16:15; 2 Thess 2:13).

3.1.3.1.32. ANIMAL HUSBANDRY (#44)

Not to be "unequally yoked" (2 Cor 6:14).

3.1.3.1.33. BUILDING, CONSTRUCTING (#45)

Paul as "wise master-builder" (1 Cor 3:10). "Building up (οἰκοδομή)" of people (Rom 14:19; 15:2; 1 Cor 14:3, 5, 12; 2 Cor 10:8; 12:19; 13:10); "build up (οἰκοδομέω)" someone (1 Cor 8:1, 10; 10:23; 14:4 [x2], 17; Gal 2:18; 1 Thess 5:11); "build up" the old order of reality (Gal 2:18). Believers as "built upon" the foundation of the apostles and prophets (Eph 2:19); as "founded upon him" (Eph 3:17), as "well-founded and firm and not moved" (Col 1:23), as "built upon him and established in the faith" (Col 2:7).

3.1.3.1.34. HOUSEHOLD ACTIVITIES (#46)

Steward. Paul and Apollos as God's "stewards" (1 Cor 4:1, 2); Paul entrusted with a "stewardship" (1 Cor 9:17; Eph 3:2; Col 1:25).

3.1.3.1.35. Activities Involving Liquids or Masses (#47)

Movement of liquids or masses. God's love "poured out" (Rom 5:5).

Application and removal of liquids or masses. God having "anointed" believers (2 Cor 1:21); "having wiped out" the handwriting (Col 2:14).

3.1.3.1.36. Activities Involving Adorning (#49)

Clothe, unclothe. "Put on" the armor of light (Rom 13:12); "put on" the Lord Jesus Christ (Rom 13:14); "put on" incorruptibility, immortality (1 Cor 15:53, 54); "wear" the image (1 Cor 15:49); the "stripping off" of the body of the flesh (Col 2:11); "having stripped" the powers and authorities (Col 2:15); "put on" feelings of compassion, etc. (Col 3:12).

3.1.3.1.37. Funerals and Burial (#52)

"Buried" with Christ (Rom 6:4; Col 2:12).

3.1.3.1.38. Religious Activities (#53)

Religious practice / roles and functions. λειτουργ- derives from the domain of public service or cultic activity: Paul as "minister (λειτουργός)" of Christ Jesus to the gentiles (Rom 15:16); Epaphroditus as "minister (λειτουργός)" of Paul's needs (Phil 2:25); the Philippians' "service (λειτουργία)" to Paul (Phil 2:30); to "serve (λειτουργεῖν)" God (Rom 1:9; 12:1); to "minister to (λειτουργεῖν)" the Jews (Rom 15:27). So also διακον-: Epaphras as "servant (διάκονος)" (Col 1:7); Paul and Apollos as "servants (διάκονοι)" (1 Cor 3:5); Paul as "servant (διάκονοι)" (2 Cor 3:6; 6:4; 11:23), "servant (διάκονος)" (Col 1:23, 25); Christ as "servant (διάκονος)" (Rom 15:8); devoted themselves to "ministry (διακονία) for the saints (1 Cor 16:15). The collection effort for Jerusalem as "ministry of this service (διακονία τῆς λειτουργίας)" (2 Cor 9:12). Also cultic is ὑπηρέτης (1 Cor 4:1).

Offering and sacrifice. "First-fruit" as a religious offering (Rom 8:23; 11:16; 16:5; 1 Cor 15:20, 23; 16:15; 2 Thess 2:13); "for us" as vicarious sacrifice (2 Cor 5:8, 21; Gal 3:13); likewise, "for our sins" (1 Cor 15:3), "for the ungodly" (Rom 5:6), handed over "for our transgressions" (Rom 4:25).

Purify, cleanse. "Pure" (Phil 2:15); "sanctification" (ἁγιωσύνη: 2 Cor 7:1; 1 Thess 3:13; ἁγιασμος: Rom 6:19, 22; 1 Cor 1:30; 1 Thess 4:3, 4, 7; 2 Thess 2:13, 15).

Defiled, unclean, common. Conscience is "defiled" (1 Cor 8:7); minds "corrupted" (2 Cor 11:3); "impurity" (Rom 6:19; Gal 5:19); "uncircumcision" (Rom 2:25).

Dedicate, consecrate. "Circumcision" as being of the heart (Rom 2:29).

3.1.3.1.39. MILITARY ACTIVITIES (#55)

Arm, fight. "Stand firm" (Rom 14:4; 1 Cor 16:13; Gal 5:1; Phil 1:27; 4:1; 1 Thess 3:8; 2 Thess 2:15); present members as "weapons" (Rom 6:13), "weapons" of righteousness (2 Cor 6:7).

Soldiers, officers. "Fellow-soldier" (Phil 2:25; Phlm 2).

3.1.3.1.40. COURTS AND LEGAL PROCEDURES (#56)

Judicial hearing, inquiry. God "searches" the hearts (Rom 8:27).

Judge, condemn, acquit. God as "witness" (Rom 1:9; 2 Cor 1:23; Phil 1:8; 1 Thess 2:5, 10); the Thessalonians as "witnesses" (1 Thess 2:10). A legal (moral) "defeat" (1 Cor 6:7). "Justification" (Rom 4:3, 5, 6; etc.), "justify" (Rom 2:13; 3:20, 24; etc.).

3.1.3.1.41. POSSESS, TRANSFER, EXCHANGE (#57)

Have, possess, property, owner. "Have" the Spirit (Rom 8:9); "have in full" (Phil 4:18).

Be rich, wealthy. God's "riches" (Rom 2:4; Eph 1:7, 18; 2:7; 3:8, 16), God as "rich" (Rom 10:12; Eph 2:4; Phil 4:19); Christ as "rich" (2 Cor 8:9); the "riches" of the wisdom and knowledge of God (Rom 11:33); the "riches" of the glory of this mystery (Col 1:27); the "riches" of the fullness of understanding (Col 2:2); believers as "rich" (2 Cor 6:10; 8:9), "enriched" (1 Cor 1:5; 2 Cor 9:11), as having "riches" (Rom 11:12); Paul calls the Corinthians "rich" in an ironic sense (1 Cor 4:8). "Treasures" of wisdom and knowledge

(Col 2:3); a "wealth" of generosity (2 Cor 8:2). "Filled up" what was lacking in meeting Paul's needs (2 Cor 11:9).

Take, obtain. Count things as "gain," "loss" (Phil 3:7).

Receive. Receive an "inheritance" (κληρονομία: Gal 3:18; Eph 5:5; Col 3:24; κλῆρος: Col 1:12); "receive" the Spirit (Gal 3:2); receive "adoption" (Gal 4:5); believers as "heirs" (Gal 3:29; 4:1–7); "inherit" the kingdom (1 Cor 6:9, 10; Gal 5:21); receive a "reward" (Col 3:24); receive "recompense" (Rom 1:27); "receive as reward" (Col 3:24). Press on for the "prize" of the upward call (Phil 3:13)

Spend, waste. "I will spend and will be spent" for your souls (2 Cor 12:15).

Pay, price, cost. The Holy Spirit as a "pledge" (2 Cor 1:22; 5:5); death as the "wages" received from sin (Rom 6:23); ministers will receive "wages" at the judgment (1 Cor 3:8).

Sell, buy, price. "Sold" under sin (Rom 7:14).

Earn, gain, do business. "Peddling" the word of God (2 Cor 2:17).

Owe, debt, cancel. Paul as "debtor" to Greeks and barbarians (Rom 1:14); believers as "debtors" not to the flesh (Rom 8:12); the gentiles as "debtors" to the Jews (Rom 15:27).

3.1.3.1.42. QUANTITY (#59)

Full, empty. That God would "fill" the church with joy and peace (Rom 15:13); the church as "full (μεστοί)" of goodness and "filled" with knowledge (Rom 15:14); be "filled" with the Spirit (Eph 5:18); be "filled" with the fruit of righteousness (Phil 1:11); be "filled" with the knowledge of his will (Col 1:9); "fill up" what is lacking in afflictions (Col 1:24); "fill up" their sins (1 Thess 2:16); "filled" with comfort (2 Cor 7:4). That Paul's boast would not be "made empty" (2 Cor 9:3); "be (ful)filled" by someone's company (Rom 15:24); the "fulfillment" of the Law (Rom 13:10); "fulfill" the gospel of Christ (Rom 15:19). "Emptied" himself (Phil 2:7).

Be in abundance. "Superabound" in joy (2 Cor 7:4); the "surpassing" grace of God (2 Cor 9:14); "increasing grace," that thanksgiving "might abound" (2 Cor 4:15); that grace might "increase" (Rom 6:1); that God might "increase" grace, that they might "increase" in every good work (2 Cor 9:8); God's truth "abounds" (Rom 3:7); "abound" in hope (Rom 15:13); "abound" in faith and speech and knowledge, etc. (2 Cor 8:7).

3.1.3.1.43. WHOLE, UNITE, PART, DIVIDE (#63)

Whole. "Joined together" in love (Col 2:2).

Separate. "Separate" us from the love of Christ (Rom 8:35); "separate" us from the love of God that is in Christ Jesus (Rom 8:39)

3.1.3.1.44. VALUE (#65)

Valuable, lacking in value. "Storing up" (in an ironic sense) wrath (Rom 6:5); hope "stored up" in heaven (Col 1:5).

3.1.3.1.45. GENUINE, PHONY (#73)

If alluding to testing the genuineness of artefacts (i.e., coinage, documents, etc.): "test" and "approve" oneself (2 Cor 13:5); "approved," "disapproved" (2 Cor 13:6–7).

3.1.3.1.46. FEATURES OF OBJECTS (#79)

Fragrance, odor. "Scent" of knowledge" (2 Cor 2:14), "fragrance" of Christ (2 Cor 2:15); "scent" (2 Cor 2:16).

Solid, liquid. God "hardens" someone or someone is "hardened" (Rom 9:18; 11:7; 11:25; 2 Cor 3:14); "hardness" of heart (Rom 2:5; Eph 4:18).

Clean, dirty. The apostles as "refuse," "off-scouring" (1 Cor 4:13). Conscience as "defiled" (1 Cor 8:7).

Blemished, unblemished. "Unblemished" (Eph 1:4; 5:27; Phil 2:15; Col 1:22).

Strong, weak. "Steadfastness" of faith in Christ (Col 2:5); man who "stands firm" in his heart (1 Cor 7:37).

Straight, crooked. "Crooked," "perverted" (Phil 2:15).

Open, closed. An "open" mouth, "open" heart (2 Cor 6:11).

Covered over. The gospel as "veiled" among those who are perishing (2 Cor 4:3).

Large, small. Knowledge "puffs up" (1 Cor 8:1); a person is "puffed up" (1 Cor 4:6, 18, 19; 5:2; 8:1; Col 2:18); love not "puffed up" (1 Cor 13:4).

3.1.3.1.47. SPATIAL POSITIONS (#83)

Above, below. To put *below* as "subjecting" all things to himself (Phil 3:21), "subjected all things under his feet" (1 Cor 15:27 = LXX Psa 8:6; Eph 1:22); all things "subjected" (1 Cor 15:28). "Under" the Law (Rom 6:14, 15; 1 Cor 9:20; Gal 3:23; 4:4, 5, 21; 5:18); "under" grace (Rom 6:14, 15); "under" sin (Rom 3:9; 7:14; Gal 3:22); God treads Satan "under" his feet (Rom 16:20). Not "lifted up" with pride (2 Cor 12:7).

Among, between, in, inside. The Spirit "in" the heart (2 Cor 1:22); Christ "in" people (Rom 8:10; 2 Cor 13:5; Col 1:27), "in" one's heart (Eph 3:17); believers "in" Christ (Rom 3:24; 6:11; 8:1; 12:5; 1 Cor 15:28; 2 Cor 5:17; Gal 3:26; passim); have a person "in" one's heart (2 Cor 7:3; Phil 1:7); be convinced "in" one's own mind (Rom 14:5); have earnestness "in" one's heart (2 Cor 8:16); sin being "in" a person (Rom 7:17, 18, 20); a person being "in" sin (Rom 6:2), "in" one's sins (1 Cor 15:17). The "inner" person (Rom 7:22; 2 Cor 4:16; Eph 3:16); "insider" (1 Cor 15:12); "outsider" (1 Cor 5:12, 13); "fightings *without*, fears *within*" (2 Cor 7:5). God "among" people (1 Cor 14:25).

At, beside, near, far. To be "near" to death (Phil 2:27), "came near" to death (Phil 2:30). "Salvation is nearer," "the night is far advanced, the day is near" (Rom 13:12).

In front of, face to face, in back of, behind. Standing "before" God (κατέναντι: 2 Cor 2:17; 12:19; ἔμπροσθεν: 1 Thess 1:3; 3:9, 13; παρά: Rom 2:11, 13; 9:14; 1 Cor 7:24; Gal 3:11); "forgetting the things *behind*," "straining toward the things *ahead*" (Phil 3:13–14).

On, upon, on the surface of. God's grace "upon" people (2 Cor 9:14); peace and mercy "upon" the Israel of God (Gal 6:16); "grief upon grief" (Phil 2:27); the power of Christ "upon" (2 Cor 12:9).

3.1.3.1.48. Spatial Extensions (#84)

Extension from a source. All things "from" God, "to" God (1 Cor 8:6); woman "from" man, man "through" (source) woman, all things "from" God (1 Cor 11:12); "through" him, "to" him (Col 1:16); "through" him, reconcile all things "to" himself (Col 1:20).

Extension to a goal. All things "from" God, "to" God (1 Cor 8:6); "through" him, "to" him (Col 1:16); "through" him, reconcile all things "to" himself (Col 1:20); baptized "into" Christ (Rom 6:3; Gal 3:27), "into" one body (1 Cor 12:13); "to whom" the ages have reached, the old and the new meeting at this point (1 Cor 10:11). Straining "toward" the things ahead, press on "toward" the goal (Phil 3:13, 14), "to which we have attained" (Phil 3:16); the "upward" call (Phil 3:14). The love of God poured "into" the heart (Rom 5:5); the Spirit sent "into" one's heart (Gal 4:6).

3.1.3.1.49. Existence in Space (#85)

This category is complex, involving both events/states and spatial positions.

Put, place. "Bestow upon" (1 Cor 12:23); "put aside" vices (Col 3:8).

Dwell, reside. "In whatever [circumstances] I am in" (Phil 4:11). The Spirit "dwells in" people (Rom 8:9, 11); the power of Christ "dwells in" Paul (2 Cor 12:9); the fullness of God "dwells" in Christ (Col 1:19; 2:9); that the word of God would "dwell in" them (Col 3:16); A person as being "in the tent" of the body (2 Cor 5:4), "at home in" the body (2 Cor 5:6, 8, 9).

3.1.3.1.50. Weight (#86)

Heavy, light. Be "burdened" (2 Cor 1:8), "burdened" by the body (2 Cor 5:4); "burden" someone (2 Cor 2:5; 12:16); not to "burden" someone (1 Thess 2:9; 2 Thess 3:8); carry someone's "burdens" (Gal 6:2); carry one's own "load" (Gal 6:5); be "burdensome" (1 Thess 2:7); "for-*bear*-ance" (Rom 3:25); grief piled "upon" grief (Phil 2:27); "heavy" epistles (2 Cor 10:10, as sermocinatio).

3.1.3.1.51. RELATIONS (#89)

Dissociation. Dwelling "away from" the Lord (2 Cor 5:6, 8, 9); "separated from the Lord" (2 Thess 1:9).

3.1.3.2. ALLEGORY (LAUSBERG §895–901)

"Allegory," ἀλληγορία, *permutatio* (Ps.-Cicero, *Rhet. Her.* 4.46), *inversio* (Quintilian, *Inst.* 8.6.44), or *immutatio* (Cicero, *Or.* 2.261) is like metaphor, only the substitution is of an idea rather than a single word. Allegory may can consist of a succession of metaphors and can occupy the length of a whole sentence, and beyond. Thus, Lausberg places this under Figures of Thought (§895).

Extended allegories are relatively scarce in Paul's letters (e.g., Rom 11:16–24; 1 Cor 3:6–9, 9–15; 6:15–17; 12:12–27; 15:35–38, 39–42; 2 Cor 3:2–3; 4:3–6; Gal 4:21—5:1; Eph 6:11–18). In some cases allegories consist only of two or three words; though short, such instances do not qualify as "metaphors" by ancient rhetorical criteria, since metaphors technically consist only of a single word.

The following catalog groups allegories according to the semantic domain of the source terms. Categories and enumeration (e.g., Geographical objects and features [#1]) are from Louw and Nida.[5]

3.1.3.2.1. GEOGRAPHICAL OBJECTS AND FEATURES (#1)

Pastures and cultivated lands. The church as a field, planted and watered by ministers, grown by God (1 Cor 3:6–9).

3.1.3.2.2. PLANTS (#3)

Non-fruit parts of plants. The church as an olive tree, with "root" and "branches," some grafted in and others broken off (Rom 11:16–24).

---

5. Louw and Nida, *Greek-English Lexicon*.

3.1.3.2.3. FOOD AND CONDIMENTS (#5)

Food. "Milk" for elementary teaching, solid food for advanced teaching (1 Cor 3:2); "a little yeast leavens the whole batch" (1 Cor 5:6; Gal 5:9).

Condiments. "Seasoned with salt" (Col 4:6).

3.1.3.2.4. ARTIFACTS (#6)

Instruments used in marking and writing. The church as a "letter of Christ, prepared by us, written not with ink but with the Spirit of the living God, not on tablets of stone but on tablets of human hearts" (2 Cor 3:3).

Containers. The potter making various objects from same lump of clay (Rom 9:21); "treasure in earthen vessels" (2 Cor 4:7).

3.1.3.2.5. CONSTRUCTIONS (#7)

Buildings. The church as a "building," foundation laid by Paul, built upon with various materials by other builders (1 Cor 3:9–15); the church as God's "temple," destroying God's temple, which is "holy" (1 Cor 3:16–17); the church "built upon the foundation of the apostles and prophets," Christ Jesus as "cornerstone," the structure joined together and built into a holy Temple, where God dwells (Eph 2:20–22).

3.1.3.2.6. BODY, BODY PARTS, AND BODY PRODUCTS (#8)

Body. The church as a "body" with "many parts," each with its own function (Rom 12:4–5; 1 Cor 12:12–27); church as "body," with Christ as its "head" (Eph 1:22–23; 4:15; 5:23; Col 1:18; 2:19; cf. Col 1:24); the "body" versus its "shadow" (Col 2:17).

Parts of the body. Church members as "parts" of Christ's body (1 Cor 6:15–17). Death as a creature that uses a "sting(er)" to kill (1 Cor 15:54–56).

3.1.3.2.7. KINSHIP TERMS (#10)

Child. Onesimus as Paul's "child," whom he has "begotten" (Phlm 10). Believers as God's "children" through adoption (Rom 8:15–17; Gal 4:1–7). Isaac, the son of the free woman receives the inheritance, believers as "children" of Isaac (Gal 4:21—5:1).

Son. Christ as "son" and "firstborn among many brothers" (Rom 8:29). Gal 4:1–7 involves a slight shift within the kinship domain, resulting in some inconsistency: Paul says that as "minors," "heirs" remain "under guardians and trustees until the date set by the father" (NRSV), but then refers to their "adoption" as children, as if they had not already been considered children who were, as he had said, minors and future heirs.

3.1.3.2.8. PHYSICAL EVENTS AND STATES (#14)

Wind, events involving liquids and dry masses. "Billowed and carried about by every wind of doctrine" (Eph 4:14).

Light, darkness. A "light to those who are in darkness" (Rom 2:19); "the night is far gone, the day is near. Let us then lay aside the works of darkness and put on the armor of light; let us live honorably as in the day" (Rom 13:12–13); "who will bring to light the things now hidden in darkness" (1 Cor 4:5); "once you were darkness, but now in the Lord you are light. Live as children of light" (Eph 5:8); "you, beloved, are not in darkness, . . . for you are all children of light and children of the day; we are not of the night or of darkness" (1 Thess 5:4–5); "those who sleep sleep at night, and those who are drunk get drunk at night. But since we belong to the day . . . " (1 Thess 5:7–8).

3.1.3.2.9. LINEAR MOVEMENT (#15)

Fall. "It is before their own lord that they stand or fall. And they will be upheld, for the Lord is able to make them stand" (Rom 14:4).

Walk, step. "Move in line with the footsteps" (Rom 4:12); "walk in the same spirit," "in the same steps" (2 Cor 12:18).

3.1.3.2.10. STANCES AND EVENTS RELATED TO STANCES (#17)

Stand. "It is before their own lord that they stand or fall. And they will be upheld, for the Lord is able to make them stand" (Rom 14:4); "standing" against evil powers in a spiritual "battle" (Eph 6:11–14).

3.1.3.2.11. PHYSICAL IMPACT (#19)

Press. "The God of peace will shortly crush (συντρίψει) Satan under your feet" (Rom 16:20).

Hit, strike. "For they stumbled over the stone of stumbling (προσέκοψαν γὰρ τῷ λίθῳ τοῦ προσκόμματος)" (Rom 9:32).

3.1.3.2.12. VIOLENCE, HARM, DESTROY, KILL (#20)

Kill. As a battle metaphor: "taking an opportunity," "it killed" (Rom 7:11; cf. 7:8). "Crucified the flesh with its passions and desires" (Gal 5:24); "nailed it to the cross" (Col 2:14); "put to death the members that are on the earth" (Col 3:5).

3.1.3.2.13. DANGER, RISK, SAFE, SAVE (#21)

Cause to be safe, free from danger. God has "rescued us from the power of darkness and transferred us into the kingdom of his beloved Son" (Col 1:13). The language of physical health and safety, i.e., "salvation (σωτηρία)," is extended into the realm of spiritual salvation (Rom 1:16; 10:1, 10; 11:11; 13:11; 2 Cor 1:6; 6:2 [x2]; 7:10; Eph 1:13; Phil 1:10, 28; 2:12; 1 Thess 5:8, 9; 2 Thess 2:13); likewise, Christ as "Savior (σωτήρ)" (Eph 5:23; Phil 3:20).

3.1.3.2.14. PHYSIOLOGICAL PROCESSES AND STATES (#23)

Birth, procreation. Creation "groans and labors in child birth (συστενάζει καὶ συνωδίνει)" (Rom 8:22); the "fullness of time" may allude to the full-term of a pregnancy, particularly in light of the context (Gal 4:4); "for whom I am again in the pain of childbirth until Christ is formed in you" (Gal 4:19). See also the simile in 1 Thess 5:3.

Live, die. Being "dead" to sin, baptized into Jesus's "death," being "buried with him," then being raised in "newness of life," "live with him" "death no longer reigns," etc. (Rom 6:2–11); being "dead" to the Law, sin as "dead" apart from the Law, "sin revived and I died," etc. (Rom 7:4–13); "when you were dead in trespasses and the uncircumcision of your flesh, God made you alive together with him" (Col 2:13); "[i]f with Christ you died to the elemental spirits of the universe, why do you live as if you still belonged to the world?" (Col 2:20); "you have died, and your life is hidden with Christ in God. When Christ who is your life is revealed . . . " (Col 3:3–4).

Sleep, waking. "Time to awake from sleep" (Rom 13:11); "let us not sleep like the rest, but let us stay awake" (1 Thess 5:6).

3.1.3.2.15. SENSORY EVENTS AND STATES (#24)

See. A "light to those who are in darkness" (Rom 2:19); "let their eyes be darkened so they cannot see" (Rom 11:10 = LXX Ps 68:23); "revelation (ἀποκάλυψιν) . . . now having been made visible (φανερωθέντος)" (Rom 16:26); "see through a glass in a riddle . . . [see] face to face" (1 Cor 13:12); gospel "veiled" to people, "blinded" in their thoughts, not "seeing the light" of Christ, who is the "image" of God, "light shine out of darkness" (2 Cor 4:3–6).

3.1.3.2.16. COMMUNICATION (#33)

Written language. A "law," "written" on the heart (Rom 2:14–15); an "epistle," "written on our hearts," "known and read by all," "letter of Christ," "written not with ink but with the living spirit," "not on stone tablets but on flesh-heart tablets" (2 Cor 3:2–3).

3.1.3.2.17. ASSOCIATION (#34)

Belong to, be included in membership of, be excluded from. "Estranged and enemies" in understanding (Col 1:21).

Marriage, divorce. "I promised you in marriage to one husband, to present you as a chaste virgin to Christ" (2 Cor 11:2 NRSV). The marriage of Christ and the church is developed more extensively in Eph 5:22–32.

3.1.3.2.18. HELP, CARE FOR (#35)

Rear, bring up. The Corinthians have "many pedagogues" in Christ (1 Cor 4:15). Paul comes with a "rod" of discipline (1 Cor 4:21). "As a nurse cares for her own children, so also we, longing for you, were pleased to share with you not only the gospel of God but also our very lives, for you became dear to us" (1 Thess 2:7–8).

3.1.3.2.19. CONTROL, RULE (#37)

Control, restrain. "Having been set free from sin you became slaves of righteousness" (Rom 6:18); "slaves to sin . . . free with regard to righteousness" (Rom 6:20); "set you free from the law of sin and death" (Rom 8:2); marriage to the Law as slavery, end of this marriage as freedom (Rom 7:1–6); "sold" to live "under" the rule of sin (Rom 7:14); "slave of Christ," "do not become slaves of humans" (1 Cor 7:22, 23); "throw a noose" around someone (1 Cor 7:35); "although being free from all, I have enslaved myself to all" (1 Cor 9:19); "spy out our freedom," "in order to enslave us" (Gal 2:4); people are "slaves" until they are liberated by God's son (Gal 4:1–7; see also above under "Kinship"); "enslaved to beings that by nature are not gods," "serve" the "elemental spirits" (Gal 4:8–9 NRSV); the "slave" and "free" woman, "slavery" to the Law and "freedom" from it (Gal 4:22—5:1).

Rule, govern. Death "rules," a person "obeys" and is "slave" to it (Rom 6:12–23); "might rule over the dead and the living" (Rom 14:9); Paul comes with a "rod" (1 Cor 4:21).

Guard, watch over. Gal 4:1–7 blends the metaphors of sonship and slavery, subsuming both under an allegory in which sons and slaves (both being pre-converted believers) are said to be subordinate to a guardian (Gal 4:1–7).

Imprison. "Confined" (συνέκλεισεν), "shut up" (συγκλειόμενοι), "guarded" (ἐφρουρούμεθα) (Gal 3:22–23).

Release, set free. "Having been set free from sin you became slaves of righteousness" (Rom 6:18); "slaves to sin . . . free with regard to righteousness" (Rom 6:20); creation "subjected" but will be "set free from its bondage to decay and will obtain the freedom . . . " (Rom 8:20–21); "bought with a price" (1 Cor 6:20); "freed-person of Christ," "bought with a price; do not become slaves of humans" (1 Cor 7:22, 23); "spy out our freedom," "in order to enslave us" (Gal 2:4); the "slave" and "free" woman, "slavery" to the Law and "freedom" from it (Gal 4:22—5:1); "redemption through his blood" (Eph 1:7).

3.1.3.2.20. HOSTILITY, STRIFE (#39)

Opposition, hostility. "Fought wild beasts in Ephesus" (1 Cor 15:32); an open "door" for Paul and many "oppose" him (1 Cor 16:9).

Strife, struggle. "Stand firm against," "struggle," "resist," etc. (Eph 6:11–18); "acted boldly, in much struggle" (1 Thess 2:2).

Conquer. Against every form of opposition believers are "super-conquerors through him who loved us" (Rom 8:35–37); death "swallowed up in victory," death loses its "sting," believers have "victory" over death through Jesus (1 Cor 15:54–57); "having stripped the rulers and authorities, he made a public spectacle of them, triumphing over them in it" (Col 2:15).

3.1.3.2.21. PERFORM, DO (#42)

Make, create. "Potter" making a "vessel" out of "clay" (Rom 9:21–22).

3.1.3.2.22. AGRICULTURE (#43)

"Root" and "branches," "olive tree," "branches are broken off," "grafted in" (Rom 11:16–24).

Just as a person "plows," "threshes," "shares" in the crop, so Paul has "sown" spiritual things and is entitled to "reap" the benefits (1 Cor 9:10); one "reaps" what one "sows" (2 Cor 9:6; Gal 6:7–9); "he who supplies seed to the sower and bread for food will supply and multiply your seed for sowing and increase the harvest of your righteousness" (2 Cor 9:10); "seek the fruit that increases to your account" (Phil 4:17); the body as a seed that is sown, dies, and comes to life (1 Cor 15:35–38, 42–44). The church as a field, planted and watered by ministers, grown by God (1 Cor 3:6–9).

3.1.3.2.23. ANIMAL HUSBANDRY (#44)

"You shall not muzzle the ox while it is treading," citing Deut 25:4 but interpreting the content as a figure for work and wages (1 Cor 9:9).

3.1.3.2.24. BUILDING, CONSTRUCTING (#45)

"Not to build upon another person's foundation" (Rom 15:20). Paul as "wise master-builder" who "laid the foundation" of the church, another person "builds upon it" using a variety of materials, some of which are consumed by flames (1 Cor 3:10–15).

3.1.3.2.25. ACTIVITIES INVOLVING ADORNING (#49)

Clothe, unclothe. Clothed with new body, stripped of the old (2 Cor 5:2–4); "having stripped off the old self with its actions and having put on the new" (Col 3:9–10).

3.1.3.2.26. CONTESTS AND PLAY (#50)

To "run" in a race in order to "attain the prize," an "incorruptible crown" (1 Cor 9:24–25); "take hold of" the prize, "forgetting what lies behind and straining forward to what lies ahead, I press on toward the goal for the prize of the heavenly call of God in Christ Jesus" (Phil 3:12, 13–14 NRSV). "I run in such a way, as not without aim; I box in such a way, as not beating the air; but I buffet my body and make it my slave" (1 Cor 9:26–27 NASB).

"For this I toil, struggling (ἀγωνιζόμενος) with all the energy that he powerfully inspires within me" (Col 1:29).

The apostles as a "spectacle" in which they are condemned to death, with spectators witnessing (1 Cor 4:9; with "scum of the world" in v. 13 perhaps alluding to the status of condemned criminals); "fought wild beasts in Ephesus" (1 Cor 15:32).

3.1.3.2.27. RELIGIOUS ACTIVITIES (#53)

Roles and functions / offering, sacrifice. Paul as "minister," "serving as priest" and making an "offering" of the gentiles that is "acceptable" and "consecrated" (Rom 15:16).

Offering, sacrifice. A gift received from the Philippians, a "scent of good fragrance, an acceptable sacrifice, pleasing to God" (Phil 4:18). Paul "poured out as a drink offering and religious service (λειτουργία)" (Phil 2:17). "Refuse," "off-scouring," i.e., sacrificial waste (1 Cor 4:13). "Our Passover lamb has been sacrificed" (1 Cor 5:7). Christ's "offering and sacrifice" as a "scent of good fragrance" (Eph 5:2). "Present your bodies as a living sacrifice, holy, acceptable to God, which is your reasonable service (λατρεία)" (Rom 12:1). Christ "died on behalf of all" (2 Cor 5:14, 15), "died for us" (Rom 5:8); God presented Christ as a "propitiation ... by his blood" (Rom 3:25).

Purify, cleanse. Christ "consecrated" the church, having "cleansed it with the washing of water," so that it would be "without spot or wrinkle but holy and without blemish" (Eph 5:26–27); "he has now reconciled in his fleshly body through death, so as to present you holy and blameless and irreproachable before him" (Col 1:22 NRSV).

Defiled, unclean, common. "Let us cleanse ourselves from every defilement of body and of spirit, making holiness perfect in the fear of God" (2 Cor 7:1 NRSV).

Dedicate, consecrate. "You were circumcised with a spiritual circumcision, by putting off the body of the flesh in the circumcision of Christ" (Col 2:11 NRSV).

3.1.3.2.28. FESTIVALS (#51)

Passover illusions, including "unleavened" bread, the "paschal lamb was sacrificed," "celebrate the feast" (1 Cor 5:6–8).

STYLE IN PAUL'S LETTERS

3.1.3.2.29. FUNERALS AND BURIAL (#52)

"Buried" with Christ and "raised" in newness of life (Rom 6:4); seed goes into the ground and "dies," before growing into "body to be" (1 Cor 15:36–37).

3.1.3.2.30. MILITARY ACTIVITIES (#55)

To arm. "Let us thrust off the works of darkness and put on the weapons of light" (Rom 13:12).

Arm, fight. "Waging war," "bringing me into captivity" (Rom 7:23); "keep alert, stand firm in your faith, be courageous, be strong" (1 Cor 16:13); "that you stand firm . . . striving together" (Phil 1:27); "having put on the breastplate of faith and love and the helmet, the hope of salvation" (1 Thess 5:8); "wage war," "weapons of warfare," "destruction of fortresses," "destroying," "raised up against the knowledge of God," "take captive," "avenge" (2 Cor 10:3–6). The allegory of fighting is most extensive in Eph 6:10–17: "be strengthened," "strength of his might," "the armor of God," "stand against," "battle," "against," "take up the armor of God," "stand," "girded," "having put on the breastplate," "having shod the feet," "shield," "withstand the missiles," "the helmet" (Eph 6:10–17).

3.1.3.2.31. COURTS AND LEGAL PROCEDURES (#56)

Judge, condemn, acquit. "We will all stand before the judgment seat of God" (Rom 14:10); "we must all appear before the judgment seat of Christ, so that each may receive recompense for what one has done" (2 Cor 5:10).

3.1.3.2.32. POSSESS, TRANSFER, EXCHANGE (#57)

Take, obtain, gain, lose. "Attain" the "prize," an incorruptible "crown" (1 Cor 9:24–25); "take hold of" the "prize" (Phil 3:12).

Receive. "Received the Spirit of adoption," are "heirs," "co-heirs" (Rom 8:15–17; cf. 8:29); "adoption" as "sons" who receive the "inheritance" (Gal 4:1–7); the son of the free woman receives the "inheritance" (Gal 4:21—5:1); receive the "riches of the glory of his inheritance" (Eph 1:18).

Keep records. "Fruit increasing to your account" (Phil 4:17).

3.1.3.2.33. QUANTITY (#59)

Be in abundance. "Abundance," "wealth," overflowed" (2 Cor 8:2); "treasures," "hidden" (Col 2:3).

3.1.3.2.34. ARRANGE, ORGANIZE (#62)

Organize (of events and states). "Order" as a military metaphor: those resurrected (1 Cor 15:23); "good order" and "steadfastness" (Col 2:5).

3.1.3.2.35. VALUE (#65)

Valuable, lacking in value. "Treasure in earthen vessels" (2 Cor 4:7).

3.1.3.2.36. TIME (#67)

Duration of time without reference to points or units of time. "Old" versus "new" (in a spiritual sense) person (Eph 4:22, 24; Col 3:9, 10).

3.1.3.2.37. MODE (#71)

Possible, impossible. An open "door" for Paul, while many "oppose" him (1 Cor 16:9); "door" of opportunity was "opened" (2 Cor 2:12); that God might "open the door" to speak the word (Col 4:3).

3.1.3.2.38. GENUINE, PHONY (#73)

"Testing the genuineness" of love (2 Cor 8:8).

3.1.3.2.39. SPATIAL POSITIONS (#83)

Above, below. Man "from earth," man "from heaven" (1 Cor 15:47; or possibly #84, Spatial Extensions); the "present Jerusalem," the "Jerusalem above" (Gal 4:25, 26).

3.1.3.2.40. Spatial Extensions (#84)

Extension from a source. Man "from earth," man "from heaven" (1 Cor 15:47; or possibly #83, Spatial Positions).

3.1.3.3. Metonymy (Lausberg, §565–71)

The replacement of a proper word by another, qualitatively different, word whose actual meanings stands in a real relationship (rather than a comparative relationship, as in simile) to the intended meaning. Common types of metonymy include: the substitution of cause for effect, person for object, author for work, divinities for area of function, possessor for possessed, invented for inventor, greater for lesser, instrument for possessor, and content for container; and vice versa. As with metaphor (§3.1.3.1) and synecdoche (§3.1.3.4), a high degree of habitualization in the use of a particular metonymy results in lexicalization of the given term, so that its figurative quality becomes diminished.

The following catalog groups examples according to the semantic domain of the source term. Categories and enumeration (e.g., Geographical objects and features [#1]) are from Louw and Nida.[6]

3.1.3.3.1. Geographical Objects and Features (#1)

The earth's surface. "Earthly things" for sin (Phil 3:19); "world" for the unrighteous people that inhabit it (Rom 3:6; 1 Cor 1:21; 6:2; 11:32; 2 Cor 5:19), for gentiles (Rom 11:15), for an evil cosmic order (1 Cor 2:12; 7:31; Eph 2:2; Col 2:8, 20), for the people of the world (Col 1:6).

3.1.3.3.2. Food and Condiments (#5)

Food. "Food" for the eating of food (1 Cor 8:13), for eating habits (Rom 14:17; Col 2:16); "bread" for the eating of food (Rom 14:15; 1 Cor 10:16).

---

6. Louw and Nida, *Greek-English Lexicon.*

3.1.3.3.3. ARTIFACTS (#6)

Instruments used in binding and fastening. "Chains" for imprisonment (Phil 1:14, 17; Col 4:18; Phlm 10; 13).

Instruments used in punishment and execution. "Cross" for Jesus's death for the unworthy (Gal 6:12, 14), "cross" for Jesus's death (Col 1:20).

Weapons and armor. "Sword" for what it causes (Rom 8:35).

Adornments. "Crown" for the means by which the crown was received (Phil 4:1; 1 Thess 2:19).

Musical instruments. "Bronze" for an instrument made of bronze (1 Cor 13:1).

Containers. "Cup" for its contents (1 Cor 10:21; 11:25); "cup" for the drinking of its contents (1 Cor 10:16).

Furniture. "Table" for meal (1 Cor 10:21).

3.1.3.3.4. CONSTRUCTIONS (#7)

Buildings. "Courthouses" for the cases tried therein (1 Cor 6:2); "house (οἶκος)" for household (οἰκία) (1 Cor 1:16).

Open constructions. A "place of viewing (θέατρον)" for what is viewed there (1 Cor 4:9); a "race track" for a "race" (1 Cor 9:24).

3.1.3.3.5. BODY, BODY PARTS, AND BODY PRODUCTS (#8)

Parts of the body. The "belly" (κοιλία) for the sensation of pleasure (Phil 3:19) or desire for pleasure (Rom 16:18); "face" (πρόσωπον) for the outward appearance of something (2 Cor 10:7). "Blood" (αἷμα) for death (Rom 3:25; 5:9; 1 Cor 10:16; Eph 1:7; 2:13; Col 1:20). "Bowels" (σπλάγχνα) for feelings (2 Cor 6:12; 7:15; Phil 1:8; 2:1; Phlm 7; 20 [with double meaning]), for the person or thing about which one has feelings (Phlm 12; 20 [with double meaning]); the "soul" for its intentions (2 Cor 1:23), "soul" for life (Rom 16:4; Phil 2:30), for person (Rom 13:1; 2 Cor 12:15; perhaps in Rom 2:9); the "spirit" for the whole person (2 Cor 2:13; Phil 4:23; Phlm

25); the "heart" for a person's feelings (Rom 9:2; 10:1), morale (Eph 6:22; Col 2:2; 4:8; 2 Thess 2:17), will (2 Cor 9:7), good-will (Col 3:16; 1 Thess 2:17), intentions (Col 3:22; 1 Thess 2:4), desires (bad desires, Rom 1:24; good desires, 1 Thess 3:13), or convictions (Rom 10:9, 10). "Foreskin" for uncircumcision (Rom 2:25, 26; 4:10, 11, 12; 1 Cor 7:18, 19; Gal 5:6; 6:15; Col 2:13; 3:11); "hand" for handwriting (Col 4:18; 1 Cor 16:21); "hand" for mediation or instrumentality (Gal 3:19); "tongue" (1 Cor 14:2), "tongues" (1 Cor 13:1, "tongues of angels"; 14:18) for a (spiritual) language; "tongue" for a (spiritual) message (1 Cor 14:26).

Body. "Flesh" (σάρξ) for ordinary human existence (1 Cor 7:28), for existence in the present body (Phil 1:22, 24), for life within the present social order (Col 3:22; Phlm 16), for one's ethnicity (Rom 4:1), for the members of a certain ethnicity (Rom 11:14), for ordinary human standards (2 Cor 1:17; 11:18), for human credentials (Phil 3:3–4), for the power or agency of sin (Rom 8:4, 5, 6, 8, 9, 12, 13; Gal 3:3; 5:13, 16, 17, 19; Col 2:18), for humanity in its sinful aspect (Rom 8:7; 1 Cor 5:5), for a human being (Rom 3:20; Gal 2:16), for human ancestry (Rom 1:3; 9:3, 5), for natural human limitations (Rom 6:19), for natural desires (Col 2:23), for life under the Law (Gal 3:3; 4:23, 29), for the real as opposed to the imagined person (Col 2:1); "fleshly" for earthly (2 Cor 1:12); "bodies" for whole selves (Eph 5:28), "body" for the person conceived as a sinful creature (Rom 8:13).

3.1.3.3.6. SUPERNATURAL BEINGS AND POWERS (#12)

Supernatural beings. "Spirits" for the manifestations of spirits (1 Cor 14:12, 32).

Supernatural powers. "Powers" for the effects they produce (1 Cor 12:6); spiritual gifts for the people that possess them (1 Cor 12:28, 29).

3.1.3.3.7. NON-LINEAR MOVEMENT (#16)

"Trembling" for an attitude that results in trembling (Phil 2:12).

3.1.3.3.8. PHYSICAL IMPACT (#19)

Pierce, cut. "Mutilation" for people who are circumcised (Phil 3:2).

3.1.3.3.9. Danger, Risk, Safe, Save (#21)

Cause to be safe, free from danger. "Save" for being the instrument through which another saves (1 Cor 7:16); "salvation" (an event) as a location (Rom 13:11).

3.1.3.3.10. Physiological Processes and States (#23)

Live, die. Fleshly thinking as "death" (Rom 8:6); the Spirit as "life and peace" puts effect for cause (Rom 8:6); likewise, the Spirit as "life" (Rom 8:10).

Rot, decay. "The corruption" for the body, i.e., quality for possessor (1 Cor 15:50).

3.1.3.3.11. Attitudes and Emotions (#25)

Love, affection, compassion. "Love" for the one who possesses it (Rom 13:10).

Hope, look forward to. "In this hope we were saved" puts an action (hope) in place of its object (that in which the hope is placed) (Rom 8:24); the Thessalonians as Paul's "hope and joy" = effect (Paul's emotional state) for cause (the Thessalonians' faith) (1 Thess 2:19; "joy" again in 2:20), likewise the Philippians as Paul's "joy" (Phil 4:1).

3.1.3.3.12. Think (#30)

To choose, select, to prefer. "Election" for those who are elected (Rom 11:7).

3.1.3.3.13. Hold a View, Believe, Trust (#31)

Trust, rely. "Faith" as effect for cause (Gal 3:23).

3.1.3.3.14. Understand (#32)

Understand. Jesus as "wisdom" = the cause of understanding for the effect (1 Cor 1:30).

3.1.3.3.15. Communication (#33)

Written language. "Scripture" for its divine or human author (Gal 3:8). The "letter," or what is visible on the textual surface as opposed to its deep meaning or embodiment in action (Rom 2:27; "letter" commonly opposed with the "intention," i.e, *scriptum* vs. *voluntas* in Cicero, *Top.* 96; Quintilian, *Inst.* 3.6.66; *scriptum* vs. *sententia* in *Rhet. Her.* 1.19).

Boast. "Boasting" for mouth, i.e., it is the boasting *mouth* that is "shut" (2 Cor 11:10).

Law, regulation, ordinance. The gentiles as "a law" = word for deeds (Rom 2:14).

Name. "Name" for the very person (Rom 1:5; 1 Cor 1:2, 10; 2 Thess 1:12).

Bless, curse. Christ as a "curse" = Christ as object of a curse (Gal 3:13; cf. Rom 3:25; 1 Cor 1:30).

Boast. Person as a "boast" = effect in place of cause (2 Cor 1:14).

3.1.3.3.16. Control, Rule (#37)

Rule, govern. "Throne" for power to rule (Col 1:16); "power, etc." for the people that possess it (Rom 13:1, 2, 3; Eph 1:21).

Release, set free. Jesus as "redemption" = Jesus as cause of redemption (1 Cor 1:30; cf. Rom 3:25; Gal 3:13).

3.1.3.3.17. Punish, Reward (#38)

Punish. A "rebuke" (cause) for its effect (shame and grief) (2 Cor 2:6).

3.1.3.3.18. Reconciliation, Forgiveness (#40)

Forgiveness. Christ as "propitiation" = effect for cause (Rom 3:25; cf. 1 Cor 1:30; Gal 3:13).

3.1.3.3.19. Perform, Do (#42)

Do, perform. "Work" for the people that do the work (Rom 13:3).

Make, create. "Creation" for creature (2 Cor 5:17; Col 1:23)

3.1.3.3.20. Agriculture (#43)

"Seed" for descendents (Rom 4:13, 16; 9:7; Gal 3:29) or descendent (2 Cor 11:22; Gal 3:16).

3.1.3.3.21. Contests and Play (#50)

"Crown" for the means by which the crown is attained (Phil 4:1; Col 2:19).

3.1.3.3.22. Festivals (#51)

"Feast or new-moon or Sabbath" = the observing of such days (Col 2:16); "Passover" for lamb sacrificed at Passover (1 Cor 5:7).

3.1.3.3.23. Religious Activities (#53)

Offering, sacrifice. "Blood" (αἷμα) for death/sacrifice (Rom 3:25; 5:9; 1 Cor 10:16; Eph 1:7; 2:13; Col 1:20). Christ as "propitiation" = effect for cause (Rom 3:25);

Dedicate, consecrate. "Circumcision" for those who are circumcised (Rom 4:9; Gal 2:7; Phil 3:3); Jesus as "sanctification" = effect for cause (1 Cor 1:30).

Purify, cleanse, defiled. "Impurity" as effect for cause (Rom 6:19).

3.1.3.3.24. Courts and Legal Procedures (#56)

Judge, condemn, acquit. "Sentence of death" for the feelings produced by such a sentence (2 Cor 1:9).

3.1.3.3.25. POSSESS, TRANSFER, EXCHANGE (#57)

Receive. The Thessalonians as Paul's "crown" = effect (Paul's reward) for cause (the Thessalonians) (1 Thess 2:19); likewise the Philippians as Paul's "crown" (Phil 4:1).

3.1.3.3.26. TIME (#67)

Beginning. Christ, rather than the Christ-event, described as the "beginning" (Col 1:18).

Indefinite units of time. "Age" for the deeds committed within it (Rom 12:2; Gal 1:4; Eph 2:2).

Definite units of time. "The time," "hour" for a period of time or an age (Rom 13:11); "the time of an hour" for a short period of time (1 Thess 2:17); "the (evil) day" for a time of evil (Eph 6:13); "days and months and seasons and years" for the calendrical laws (Gal 4:10); "day" for an event that happens on it, i.e, the Parousia (1 Cor 5:5; Phil 2:16).

3.1.3.3.27. MODE (#71)

Possible, impossible. "Door" for an opportunity (1 Cor 16:9).

3.1.3.3.28. POWER, FORCE (#76)

In πνεύματος καὶ δυνάμεως (1 Cor 2:4), the latter term may be metonymy for "Spirit," making the coordinated terms roughly synonymous.

3.1.3.3.29. SPATIAL ORIENTATIONS (#82)

Left, right, straight ahead, opposite. "Right-handed" for closely-cooperating (Gal 2:9).

3.1.3.3.30. SPATIAL POSITIONS (#83)

Above, below. "Things above" for the things pertaining to life in Christ (Col 3:1, 2), "earthly things" for things pertaining to the sinful activities of the world (Col 3:2; cf. 3:5), "earthly things" for the sinful activities of the world (Phil 3:19); "the heavens" for the realm of Christ's influence or activity (Phil 3:20).

3.1.3.3.31. STATUS (#87)

Honor or respect in relation to status. The Thessalonians as Paul's "glory" = effect (Paul's reward) for cause (the Thessalonians' faith) for (1 Thess 2:20).

3.1.3.3.32. MORAL AND ETHICAL QUALITIES AND RELATED BEHAVIOR (#88)

Self-control, lack of self-control. "Weakness" for sexual sin (1 Cor 7:5).

Just, righteous. "Righteousness" for the person who possesses righteousness (2 Cor 5:21); Jesus as "righteousness" = effect for cause (1 Cor 1:30; cf. Rom 3:25; Gal 3:13; 2 Cor 5:21).

Sin, wrongdoing, guilt. Christ as "sin" = sin for sin offering (2 Cor 5:21; cf. Rom 3:25; 1 Cor 1:30; Gal 3:13); "sins" for sinners (1 Cor 15:3); the Law as "sin" = product for producer (Rom 7:7).

Anger, be indignant with. "Wrath" for its effects (Rom 13:5).

3.1.3.3.33. NAMES OF PERSONS AND PLACES (#93)

"Christ" for the church (1 Cor 1:13; 6:15; 8:12; 12:12); "Christ" for the serving of Christ (Phil 1:21); "Jesus" for the message about Jesus (2 Cor 11:4); "Moses" for what Moses wrote, i.e., the Law (2 Cor 3:15); "the Lord" for time of the coming of the Lord (Phil 4:5); "Jacob," "Esau" for the peoples descended therefrom (Rom 9:13 = Mal 1:2–3); "Adam," "Moses" for the time during which Adam, Moses lived (Rom 5:14); "Apollos and myself" for the (cooperative) activities of Apollos and Paul (1 Cor 4:6).

3.1.3.4. SYNECDOCHE (LAUSBERG, §572–77)

A substitution of part for whole, species for genus, singular for plural, and vice versa. Thus, synecdoche functions as a subcategory of metonymy in which the relationship between the word used and the meaning intended is quantitative (rather than qualitative) in nature. As with metaphor and metonymy, a high degree of habitualization in the use of particular synecdoches results in lexicalization of the given term. Synecdoche is sometimes also catachrestic (§3.1.3.10).

The following catalog groups examples according to the semantic domain of the source term. Categories and enumeration (e.g., Food and Condiments [#5]) are from Louw and Nida.[7]

3.1.3.4.1. FOOD AND CONDIMENTS (#5)

Food. "Bread" for any food (2 Thess 3:8, 12); "milk," "meat" for any food (Rom 8:29); "meat" for any food (Rom 14:21).

3.1.3.4.2. ARTIFACTS (#6)

Instruments used in punishment and execution. "Cross" for the whole gospel message, including both Jesus's death and resurrection (1 Cor 1:17, 18; Gal 6:12, 14; Phil 3:18; though in Gal 6:12, 14, and perhaps other instances, the "cross" may put special emphasis on the shameful aspects of the message).

Containers. If "vessel" refers specifically to the male sexual member, it could still refer, by synecdoche, to one's whole self (1 Thess 4:4).

3.1.3.4.3. BODY, BODY PARTS, AND BODY PRODUCTS (#8)

Body. "Bodies" for whole selves (Rom 12:1). "Foreskin" for people who are uncircumcised (Rom 2:26, 27; 3:30; 4:9; Gal 2:7, 8, 9; Eph 2:11; Col 3:11).

Body parts. "Eye" or "ear" for a person (1 Cor 2:9; cf. LXX Isa 64:3). The Lord's "face" for his manifestation (2 Thess 1:9), or for the person of Christ (2 Cor 2:10); "face" for a person (Col 2:1; 1 Thess 2:17; 3:10), for a particular identity (Gal 2:6), for the whole person as oriented toward (i.e., "facing") another (Gal 2:11), (possibly) for external or surface appearances (2 Cor 10:7); "face to face" for "person to person" (1 Cor 13:12); "face well (εὐπροσωπῆσαι)" for looking good by external social criteria (Gal 6:12). "Flesh and blood" for human beings (Gal 1:16; Eph 6:12), for an earthly

---

7. Louw and Nida, *Greek-English Lexicon.*

(ψύχικος) type of body (1 Cor 15:50); "flesh" for the kind of body that consists of flesh (Col 1:22), for the physical body (2 Cor 7:5; Gal 4:13, 14; Col 1:24; 2:1, 5), for a part of the body (Gal 6:13, though a double meaning here), for a human being (1 Cor 1:29; Gal 2:16), for the sinful part of a person (Rom 7:18); "fleshly" for immature or sinful behavior (1 Cor 3:1). "Shames his head" = "shames himself [and God]" (1 Cor 11:4); "disgraces her head" = "disgraces herself [and her husband]" (1 Cor 11:5). "Knee" for the person (Phil 2:10); "tongue" for the person (Phil 2:11); "neck" for life (Rom 16:4). Working with the "hands" for the exertion of the body, though with special emphasis on the hands (1 Thess 4:11).

3.1.3.4.4. KINSHIP TERMS (#10)

Kinship terms based on marriage. "Wife" for all wives, "husband" for every husband (1 Cor 7:16).

3.1.3.4.5. PHYSIOLOGICAL PROCESSES AND STATES (#23)

Eat, drink. "Eat with" as species for the genus "associate with" (1 Cor 5:11).

3.1.3.4.6. COMMUNICATION (#33)

Law, regulation, ordinance. "Days and months and seasons and years" for the calendrical regulations of the Law (Gal 4:10).

Written language. "Letter" for a complete text, i.e., the Law (2 Cor 3:6–7).

3.1.3.4.7. COURTS AND LEGAL PROCEDURES (#56)

Judge, condemn, acquit. "Judgments" (final verdict) for the whole process of prosecution (1 Cor 6:7).

3.1.3.4.8. QUANTITY (#59)

All, any, each, every. "All" for "every kind of" (1 Cor 9:22).

3.1.3.4.9. TIME (#67)

Duration of time with reference to some point of time. "Night and day" for portions of the night and day (1 Thess 2:9; 3:10; 2 Thess 3:8); "Sabbath" for week (1 Cor 16:2);

3.1.3.5. HYPERBOLE (LAUSBERG, §579)

An extreme, literally implausible onomastic surpassing of the "right" word.

Wish oneself "accursed" (Rom 9:3[8]); Abraham's body as "dead," the "deadness" of Sarah's womb (Rom 4:19); faith to move "mountains" (1 Cor 13:2); "naked" (1 Cor 4:11); "ten thousand" pedagogues (1 Cor 4:15); "enslaving" the body (1 Cor 9:27); short hair as equivalent to a "shaved" head (1 Cor 11:5, 6); one person hungry, another "drunk" (1 Cor 11:21); speak "ten thousand" words in a tongue (1 Cor 14:19); writing "through many tears" (2 Cor 2:4); always carrying around the "dying" of Jesus (2 Cor 4:10); "terrify" them (with some irony), i.e., because his letters are "weighty and strong" (2 Cor 10:9, 10); "deaths" as near death encounters (2 Cor 11:23); even if "an angel from heaven" preaches a different gospel (Gal 1:8); "digging out" their eyes and giving them to Paul (Gal 4:15); "castrate" themselves (Gal 5:12); that the Jews oppose "all" people (1 Thess 2:15).

Hyperbole is sometimes catachrestic (see §3.1.3.10). Hyperbolic catachresis consists in a kind of "biased use of synonyms" (Lausberg, §562; cf. "incrementum," §402; Quintilian, *Inst.* 8.4.1–4; 8.6.36): e.g., "robbed" other churches by receiving wages from them (2 Cor 11:8); "mutilation" in reference to people who are circumcised (Phil 3:2).

Hyperbole also occurs at the level of the thought, e.g., "such as occurs not even among the Gentiles" (1 Cor 5:1); "will surely not eat meat for all eternity" (1 Cor 8:13); "so that we have no need to say anything" (1 Thess 1:8).

3.1.3.6. ANTONOMASIA (LAUSBERG, §§580–81)

The substitution of an appellative or periphrasis for a proper name. The substitution is often made in service of praise or censure, or to highlight physical attributes, qualities of character, or external circumstances.

---

8. Bullinger, *Figures of Speech Used in the Bible*, 428.

"Those who are despised" (1 Cor 6:4); "the slave woman," "the free woman" (Gal 4:22, 23, 31); "those who do not know God" (1 Thess 4:5); "those who are outside" (1 Cor 5:12; Col 4:5; 1 Thess 4:12); "those who are inside" (1 Cor 5:12); "the rest, who do not have hope" (1 Thess 4:13). Frequently of opponents or offenders within the church: "the man who acted thusly" (1 Cor 5:3); "those who seem to be somebodies" (Gal 2:6 [x2]), "those who seem to be pillars" (Gal 2:7); "certain men from James" (Gal 2:12); "those of the circumcision" (Gal 2:12). For Christ: "the one who was to come" (Rom 5:14); "the Lord of glory" (1 Cor 2:8); "the beloved" (Eph 1:6). For God: "the one who is calling you" (1 Thess 5:24). "The man of lawlessness," "the son of destruction" (2 Thess 2:3), "the one who opposes and elevates himself above everthing considered a god or object of worship (2 Thess 2:4); "the lawless one" (2 Thess 2:8). Use of the definite article in names like "the Adversary" (Rom 16:20; 1 Cor 5:5; 7:5; 2 Cor 2:11; 11:14; 1 Thess 2:19; 2 Thess 2:9) and "the Slanderer" (Eph 4:27; 6:11) suggests that these designations function as epithets and highlight the qualities of the referent, though common usage probably pushes them near to proper names.

3.1.3.7. Irony (Lausberg, §582–85)

Irony, like reflexio (§3.2.1.1.14), consists in the repetition of a word or phrase in which the language of one speaker is received by a second speaker in a changed sense that emphasizes the new speaker's point of view. Whereas reflexio, however, plays on meanings that both parties agree to be usual, irony represents the view of the opposing party as being false or nonsensical. Since repetition of the word is not explicit, irony counts as a trope (change *in verbis singulis*) and not as a figure (change *in verbis coniunctis*). See also the figure of thought called "irony" (§3.2.1.2.27).

In Rom 2:5, the sense seems to be: you are indeed "storing up" (θησαυρίζειν) something for yourself, but it is not any kind of treasure (as in θησαυρός) but rather wrath (Rom 2:5). Irony is especially common in the Corinthian letters: the "foolishness" of the message (1 Cor 1:21); God's "foolishness," human "wisdom" (1 Cor 1:25); the "wisdom" of the world (1 Cor 3:19); "be rich," "reign as kings" (1 Cor 4:8); "those who are despised," i.e., from a worldly perspective (1 Cor 6:4); a "wise person" (1 Cor 6:5); "prudent," "strong," "distinguished" (1 Cor 4:10); "prudent" (1 Cor 10:15); imitators of Christ as "off-scourings" (1 Cor 4:13); be "built up" to eat idol-meat, i.e., you are not enlightening them with your "knowledge" but destroying them (1 Cor 8:10); "stronger" (those who deem themselves stronger) than God (1 Cor 10:22); "approved," though not in the way that the Corinthians measure approval (1 Cor 11:19); ψύχικος, πνευμάτικος from Paul's perspective versus the perspective of the Corinthians (1 Cor 2:14, 15; 15:44, 46); "that freedom of yours" (1 Cor 8:9), where "freedom" is a freedom to do what one wants rather than a freedom to choose what is beneficial (1 Cor 9:1–27); "terrify" them (as a kind of ironic catachresis), i.e., because his letters are "weighty and strong" (2 Cor 10:9, 10); not "dare" to compare, i.e., since the "super-apostles" are so superior (2 Cor 10:12); "super-apostles" (2 Cor 11:5; 12:11); "fools," "wise" (2 Cor 11:19); "fool" (2 Cor 11:21); those who are "outstandingly" apostolic (2 Cor 12:11); "worse off," "injustice" (2 Cor 12:13); "crafty," "deceit" (2 Cor 12:16); "those seeming to be pillars," i.e, those whose word should mean something! (Gal 2:9); an "enemy" as opposed to a friend (Gal 4:16).[9]

3.1.3.8. Periphrasis (Lausberg, §589–98)

The paraphrasing of one word by several words. See also "antonomasia" (§3.1.3.7), as well as "periphrasis" the thought-figure (§3.2.1.2.28).

"The earthly house of the tent" = body (2 Cor 5:1); "speaks edification and exhortation and comfort" = edifies, exhorts, comforts (1 Cor 14:3).

3.1.3.9. Catachresis (Lausberg, §562, 577)

An intentional "misuse" (κατά + χρῆσις = "against" + "use") of terms. Catachresis serves ornamental purposes insofar as "misuse" of terms is intentional.

(1) The misuse sometimes originates as a "necessary metaphor," or trope invented due to a poverty of expressive options and then lexicalized out of necessity. That is, the limitation of linguistic options in a language causes words to develop multiple meanings, some of them common but some of them specialized to technical realms of discourse. Thus a necessary "misuse" occurs in the application of an expression proper to one domain

---

9. For more on irony in Paul's letters, see Reumann, "St. Paul's Use of Irony"; Spencer "Wise Fool (and the Foolish Wise)"; Holland, "Paul's Use of Irony as a Rhetorical Technique."

of discourse to a domain in which it is technically not fitting. Catachresis is especially common in metaphysical discourse, where because of the limits of language to describe transcendent realities one relies upon an extension of new meanings from old words. Thus, in Latin "wind" (*animus*) came to mean "mind"; "tasting man" (*sapiens*) came to mean "wise man"; "breath" (*spiritus*) came to mean "spirit." Where tropes become habitualized in colloquial speech and thus lexically sunk to the level of "proper signification" (*proprium*), they constitute finally what may be considered "lexicalized tropes," the weakest kind of trope. (Quintilian noted, for example, that metonymic expressions often became vulgarized, like the use of the word "Vulcan" as a designation for "fire"; *Inst.* 8.6.24–27).

Philosophers sometimes appealed to catachresis as an explanation for their inconsistency in use of terms, as they vacillated between specialized/technical meanings and public/conventional ones (e.g., Seneca, *Ben.* 2.34.3–4; 2.35.2; 5.12–17; *Ep.* 59.1). Philo of Alexandria, recognizing the "inappropriateness" of ordinary language for discussing metaphysical issues, frequently designated his language explicitly as "catachrestic" (*Cher.* 121; *Sacr.* 101; *Cain* 1.167–8; *Mut.* 1.13; *Somn.* 1.229; *Abr.* 1.120), finding recourse to catachresis necessary due both to human "weakness" (παρηγοροῦσα τὴν ἡμετέραν ἀσθένειαν, *Sac.* 1.101) and to the limitations of human language (*Opif.* 4–6). Instances of this usage are numerous. Philo observes that when God said in the Song of Moses, "Behold (ἴδετε)! Behold (ἴδετε)! It is I" (Deut 32:39), this meant "behold" only in a catachrestic sense, for naturally the *invisible God* cannot be beheld with the eyes (*Cain* 1.167–8). One also used catachresis, he suggested, when one said that God "begets" children, since the capacity for reproduction is, naturally speaking, proper only to created things (*Sac.* 1.101). Although Philo refers to "gods" other than the One God (*Opif.* 27; *Spec.* 1.19; *Aetern.* 46; *Prob.* 43–44), he notes that this language too is catachresis, since there is but one God (*Somn.* 1.229). Following Plato's lead (Plato, *Crat.* 392b; *Phaedr.* 246a), the Jewish philosopher Aristobulus coordinated the terms "human" and "mythical" as virtual synonyms. His description of Moses's language as "human" implies that Moses used the language of empirical experience only by way of accommodation; likewise, Moses's language was sometimes "mythical," being intended as a vehicle toward higher meaning (Aristobulus, *fr.* 2//Eusebius, *Praep ev.* 8.10.2).

Like Plato, Philo, and Aristobulus, Paul designates his language as non-literal, or "human" (Plato, *Crat.* 392b; *Phaedr.* 246a; Aristobulus, *fr.*

2//Eusebius, *Praep ev.* 8.10.2), in at least one passage (Rom 6:19), also noting here that he speaks in human terms out of necessity, i.e., due to our "weakness" (cf. Philo, *Sac.* 1.101). With precedent for a catachrestic use of the term "god" in the works of Jewish writers like Philo (*Somn.* 1.229), it may be too naïve a reading to see Paul referring literally to another "god" in 2 Cor 4:4 ("the god of this age," ὁ θεὸς τοῦ αἰῶνος τούτου); hence Irenaeus's appeal to solecism by transposition of τοῦ αἰῶνος τούτου is for this reason (and others), unnecessary (see below under "hyberbaton," §3.1.3.12). In 1 Cor 8:5 Paul states only that "there are those that are called gods," not that he regards them as such.

Weak metaphors are in a sense catachrestic. Quite lexicalized are sense-verbs like "see" (Rom 7:23) and "hear" (1 Cor 14:2; Gal 4:21) to mean "perceive" or "understand." Many religious terms originate as metaphors, though their figurative nature subsequently becomes weakened through use and the religious meaning becomes lexicalized: ἀπρόσκοπος ("unstumbling" → "faultless/blameless"; Phil 1:10), παράβασις ("misstep" → "transgression/sin"; Rom 2:23), or σκόλιος ("crooked" → "corrupt/bad"; Phil 2:15).

While the subject is controversial, descriptions of the Spirit in Paul's letters that utilize material language could be regarded as catachrestic, i.e., as figurative language that borrows from the empirical realm by necessity. Consider examples involving the language of "pouring" ("activities involving liquids or masses," #47), "filling" ("quantity," #59), being "in" ("extension in space," #85), and "indwelling" ("extension in space, #85). The language of "kinship" (e.g., "son," "child," "father"), "linear movement" (e.g., "fall"), and "physiological processes and states" (e.g., "drink") may in cases be considered catachrestic. See above under "Metaphor," §3.1.3.1.

Metonymies (§3.1.3.3) and synecdoches (§3.1.3.4), like metaphor, may be considered catachrestic when they are created intentionally and by necessity.

(2) Catachresis sometimes consists in a biased use of synonyms. In such cases the choice of synonyms serves to intensify the point. For instance, Paul's statement that he "robbed" other churches for wages (2 Cor 11:8) reflects a kind of hyperbolic catachresis (the term is too strong, and not the proper term); so also "terrify," i.e., because his letters are "weighty and strong" (2 Cor 10:9, 10); "bewitched" (Gal 3:1); "mutilation" in reference to people who are circumcised (Phil 3:2). Consider "whose *god* is their own belly" (Phil 3:19). Paul's description of involuntary starvation as

"fastings" draws extra attention to the situation by its originality, while also putting a positive spin on the circumstances (2 Cor 6:5). Note the active "find" for the passive "receive" in Rom 4:1.

3.1.3.10. Litotes (Lausberg, §586–88)

The expression of a superlative idea through the negation of an opposite. Litotes thus entails both emphasis and, to varying degrees, irony: emphasis in the building-up of the superlative meaning in cognitive stages, and irony through the quality of understatement.

Hope "does not disappoint" (Rom 5:5); zeal "not according to knowledge" (Rom 10:2); "not all" obeyed (Rom 10:16); love "does not work evil" toward a neighbor (Rom 13:10); "not many" were wise, etc. (1 Cor 1:26); "does not receive," i.e., "rejects" (1 Cor 2:14); God was pleased with "not many of them" (1 Cor 10:5); "a sufficient number" have died (1 Cor 11:30); "not... ignorant" (1 Cor 12:1); "not ignorant" of Satan's plans (2 Cor 2:11); "I am not lying" (2 Cor 11:31); zealous "not in a good way" (Gal 4:17); "not pleasing" to God (1 Thess 2:15); faith is "not of everyone" (2 Thess 3:2); "not idle" (2 Thess 3:7); "useless," i.e., not even physically present (Phlm 11).

3.1.3.11. Hyperbaton (Lausberg, §716–18)

The separation of two words, very closely linked syntactically, by the insertion of a sentence part that does not directly belong to this point, so as to create emphasis. See also "parenthesis" (Lausberg, §860).

Irenaeus remarks upon the difficulty of word order in Paul's letters, attributing this difficulty to "the rapidity of his discourses, and the impetus of the Spirit which is in him" (*Haer.* 3.7.2). By Irenaeus's assessment, difficult exchanges of word order would qualify less as hyperbaton than as "solecism through transposition" (see §1.2.3. above; cf. Lausberg, §505). Irenaeus, for instance, interprets ὁ θεὸς τοῦ αἰῶνος τούτου ἐτύφλωσεν τὰ νοήματα τῶν ἀπίστων (2 Cor 4:4) as meaning, not "the god of this world [i.e., Satan] has blinded the minds of the unbelievers...," but "God has blinded the minds of the unbelievers of this world...," seeing a transposition of the words τοῦ αἰῶνος τούτου. This interpretation is surely incorrect (and theologically motivated, as it alleviates Paul of "blasphemy"), though the problem he wishes to avoid is also avoided if the term "god" functions as a "catachresis" (§3.1.3.10).

There are true instances of hyperbaton in other passages. Note that in Rom 1:3–4, the words Ἰησοῦ χριστοῦ τοῦ κυρίου ἡμῶν follow τοῦ υἱοῦ αὐτοῦ in sense, but are delayed by a fairly lengthy insertion for purposes of emphasis. In 2 Cor 11:2, τῷ Χριστῷ is appositive to ἑνὶ ἀνδρὶ but is delayed to the end of the sentence for emphasis. A verb intervenes between ἴδιον and χάρισμα in 1 Cor 7:7 (ἕκαστος ἴδιον ἔχει χάρισμα); given the similarity of phrasing in v. 2 (ἕκαστος τὴν ἑαυτοῦ γυναῖκα ἐχέτω), the delay of χάρισμα perhaps serves the element of surprise: first, "let each man have his own *wife*," but then, "each one has his own [not wife but] *gift*."

3.2. In the Conjunction of Words

Ornament through the conjunction of words is achieved through "figures" (Lausberg, §600–910) and virtuous composition (§911–1054).

3.2.1. *Figures (§600–910)*

In distinction from tropes, where changes are made only to single words, figures (*figurae*), or schemes (σχήματα), involve the "shaping" (*fig-, σχημ-*) of groups of words. The name *figura* derives metaphorically from the notion of a body: figures give concrete form to verbal expression (Quintilian, *Inst.* 2.13.9; 9.1.11).

Figures are classified as either figures of speech (§604–754) or figures of thought (§755–910).

3.2.1.1. Figures of Speech (Lausberg, §604–754)

Figures of speech consist in the linguistic modification of style by means of any combination of addition, subtraction, transposition, or substitution in the conjunction of words.

3.2.1.1.1. *Epanalepsis/Geminatio (Lausberg, §616–18)*

Repetition of a particle to remind the listener of where one began.

Τούτου χάριν ἐγὼ Παῦλος ὁ δέσμιος τοῦ Χριστοῦ [Ἰησοῦ] ὑπὲρ ὑμῶν τῶν ἐθνῶν . . .

Τούτου χάριν κάμπτω τὰ γόνατά μου πρὸς τὸν πατέρα . . . (Eph 3:1, 14)

3.2.1.1.2. Anadiplosis/Reduplicatio (Lausberg, §619–20)

A kind of "repetition in contact" in which the last word or phrase of a line, clause, or sentence is repeated at the beginning of the next one for emphasis or emotive effect. See also "Climax" (§3.2.1.1.3).

Τί οὖν ἐροῦμεν; ὅτι ἔθνη τὰ μὴ διώκοντα δικαιοσύνην κατέλαβεν **δικαιοσύνην**, **δικαιοσύνην** δὲ τὴν ἐκ πίστεως, (Rom 9:30)

ἄρα ἡ πίστις ἐξ **ἀκοῆς**, ἡ δὲ **ἀκοὴ** διὰ ῥήματος Χριστοῦ. (Rom 10:17)

καὶ μὴ μόνον **ἐν τῷ παρεῖναί με πρὸς ὑμᾶς**—τεκνία μου, οὓς πάλιν ὠδίνω μέχρις οὗ μορφωθῇ Χριστὸς ἐν ὑμῖν—ἤθελον δὲ **παρεῖναι πρὸς ὑμᾶς ἄρτι**, καὶ ἀλλάξαι τὴν φωνήν μου . . . (Gal 4:18–20)

ἐταπείνωσεν ἑαυτὸν γενόμενος ὑπήκοος μέχρι **θανάτου**, **θανάτου** δὲ σταυροῦ. (Phil 2:8)

There are also pseudo-examples, the repetition being a matter of changing topical points in the discourse rather than of ornament (e.g., Rom 8:16–17; 13:2, 8; 1 Cor 6:3; 10:4; Gal 1:10; 4:4–5, 24–25; 4:31—5:1; Phil 4:18–19; 1 Thess 3:11–12).

3.2.1.1.3. Climax/Gradatio (Lausberg, §623–24)

Progressive anadiplosis.

εἰδότες ὅτι **ἡ θλῖψις ὑπομονὴν** κατεργάζεται, ἡ δὲ **ὑπομονὴ δοκιμήν**, ἡ δὲ **δοκιμὴ ἐλπίδα**.⁵ ἡ δὲ **ἐλπὶς** οὐ καταισχύνει . . . (Rom 5:3–5)

αὐτὸ τὸ πνεῦμα συμμαρτυρεῖ τῷ πνεύματι ἡμῶν ὅτι ἐσμὲν **τέκνα** θεοῦ. εἰ δὲ **τέκνα**, **καὶ κληρονόμοι· κληρονόμοι** μὲν θεοῦ, **συγκληρονόμοι** δὲ Χριστοῦ . . . (Rom 8:16–17)

οὓς **προέγνω**, καὶ **προώρισεν** . . . οὓς δὲ **προώρισεν**, τούτους **καὶ ἐκάλεσεν**· καὶ οὓς **ἐκάλεσεν**, τούτους **καὶ ἐδικαίωσεν**· οὓς δὲ **ἐδικαίωσεν**, τούτους **καὶ ἐδόξασεν**. (Rom 8:29–30)

Πῶς οὖν ἐπικαλέσωνται εἰς ὃν οὐκ **ἐπίστευσαν**; πῶς δὲ **πιστεύσωσιν** οὗ οὐκ **ἤκουσαν**; πῶς δὲ **ἀκούσωσιν** χωρὶς **κηρύσσοντος**; πῶς δὲ **κηρύξωσιν** ἐὰν μὴ **ἀποσταλῶσιν**; (Rom 10:14–15)

πάντα **ὑμῶν**, **ὑμεῖς** δὲ **Χριστοῦ**, **Χριστὸς** δὲ **θεοῦ**. (1 Cor 3:22–23)

καὶ followed by a demonstrative pronoun sometimes has a climactic effect:

ἀδελφὸς μετὰ ἀδελφοῦ κρίνεται, **καὶ τοῦτο** ἐπὶ ἀπίστων. (1 Cor 6:6)

ὑμεῖς ἀδικεῖτε καὶ ἀποστερεῖτε, **καὶ τοῦτο** ἀδελφούς. (1 Cor 6:8)

This is possibly the sense of καί also in Eph 2:8.

ὥστε οὐκέτι εἶ δοῦλος ἀλλὰ **υἱός**· εἰ δὲ **υἱός**, **καὶ κληρονόμος** διὰ θεοῦ. (Gal 4:7)

The items in 1 Cor 11:3 are climactically related but do not follow an ascending order: Θέλω δὲ ὑμᾶς εἰδέναι ὅτι **παντὸς ἀνδρὸς ἡ κεφαλὴ ὁ Χριστός** ἐστιν, **κεφαλὴ δὲ γυναικὸς ὁ ἀνήρ**, **κεφαλὴ δὲ τοῦ Χριστοῦ ὁ θεός**. (1 Cor 11:3)

τὸ δὲ κέντρον **τοῦ θανάτου ἡ ἁμαρτία**, ἡ δὲ δύναμις **τῆς ἁμαρτίας ὁ νόμος**· (1 Cor 15:56)

Cf. 1 Cor 4:7.

There are also examples involving climax of the thought:

"If [A] there is no resurrection of the dead, then [B] Christ has not been raised; and if [B] Christ has not been raised, then [C] our proclamation has been in vain and your faith has been in vain. We are even found to be misrepresenting God, because we testified of God that he raised Christ—whom he did not raise if it is true that the dead are not raised." (1 Cor 15:13–15 NRSV)

"For if [A] the dead are not raised, then [B] Christ has not been raised. If [B] Christ has not been raised, [C] your faith is futile and you are still in your sins." (1 Cor 15:16–17 NRSV)

3.2.1.1.4. Prosapodosis/Redditio (Lausberg, §625)

Repetition of words from the beginning of a colon/comma at the end of the colon/comma after a parenthesis of thought.

καὶ οἱ **ἔχοντες** γυναῖκας ὡς μὴ **ἔχοντες** ὦσιν, καὶ οἱ **κλαίοντες** ὡς μὴ **κλαίοντες**, καὶ οἱ **χαίροντες** ὡς μὴ **χαίροντες**. (1 Cor 7:29–30)

ζηλοῦσιν ὑμᾶς οὐ καλῶς, ἀλλ' ἐκκλεῖσαι ὑμᾶς θέλουσιν, ἵνα αὐτοὺς **ζηλοῦτε**· (Gal 4:17)

Χαίρετε ἐν κυρίῳ πάντοτε· πάλιν ἐρῶ, **χαίρετε**. (Phil 4:4)

3.2.1.1.5. Anaphora (Lausberg, §629)

Intermittent repetition of the beginning of a colon or comma. As with epiphora (§632), the repetition can also be relaxed by the use of synonymous expressions.

τίς ἐγκαλέσει κατὰ ἐκλεκτῶν θεοῦ; θεὸς ὁ δικαιῶν· **τίς** ὁ κατακρινῶν; Χριστὸς [Ἰησοῦς] ὁ ἀποθανών, . . . **τίς** ἡμᾶς χωρίσει ἀπὸ τῆς ἀγάπης τοῦ Χριστοῦ; (Rom 8:33–34)

ἀλλὰ λέγω, μὴ οὐκ ἤκουσαν; . . . [19] **ἀλλὰ λέγω**, μὴ Ἰσραὴλ οὐκ ἔγνω; (Rom 10:18–19)

εὐλογεῖτε τοὺς διώκοντας [ὑμᾶς], **εὐλογεῖτε** καὶ μὴ καταρᾶσθε. (Rom 12:14)

ποῦ σοφός; **ποῦ** γραμματεύς; **ποῦ** συζητητής . . . (1 Cor 1:20)

οὐ πολλοὶ σοφοὶ κατὰ σάρκα, **οὐ πολλοὶ** δυνατοί, **οὐ πολλοὶ** εὐγενεῖς· (1 Cor 1:26)

θεοῦ γάρ ἐσμεν συνεργοί, **θεοῦ** γεώργιον, **θεοῦ** οἰκοδομή ἐστε. (1 Cor 3:9)

διὰ τί οὐχὶ μᾶλλον ἀδικεῖσθε; **διὰ τί οὐχὶ μᾶλλον** ἀποστερεῖσθε; (1 Cor 6:7)

οὔτε κλέπται οὔτε πλεονέκται, **οὐ** μέθυσοι, **οὐ** λοίδοροι, **οὐχ** ἅρπαγες βασιλείαν θεοῦ κληρονομήσουσιν. (1 Cor 6:10)

Οὐκ εἰμὶ ἐλεύθερος; **οὐκ** εἰμὶ ἀπόστολος; **οὐχὶ** Ἰησοῦν τὸν κύριον ἡμῶν ἑόρακα; **οὐ** τὸ ἔργον μου ὑμεῖς ἐστε ἐν κυρίῳ; (1 Cor 9:1). Here the switch to the emphatic οὐχί in the third instance may be significant.

μὴ οὐκ ἔχομεν ἐξουσίαν φαγεῖν καὶ πεῖν; **μὴ οὐκ ἔχομεν** ἐξουσίαν ἀδελφὴν γυναῖκα περιάγειν . . . (1 Cor 9:4–5)

οἱ πατέρες ἡμῶν **πάντες** ὑπὸ τὴν νεφέλην ἦσαν **καὶ πάντες** διὰ τῆς θαλάσσης διῆλθον **καὶ πάντες** εἰς τὸν Μωϋσῆν ἐβαπτίσθησαν ἐν τῇ νεφέλῃ καὶ ἐν τῇ θαλάσσῃ **καὶ πάντες** τὸ αὐτὸ πνευματικὸν βρῶμα ἔφαγον **καὶ πάντες** τὸ αὐτὸ πνευματικὸν ἔπιον πόμα . . . (1 Cor 10:1–4)

μηδὲ εἰδωλολάτραι γίνεσθε **καθώς τινες αὐτῶν**, . . . μηδὲ πορνεύωμεν, **καθώς τινες αὐτῶν** ἐπόρνευσαν . . . μηδὲ ἐκπειράζωμεν τὸν Χριστόν, **καθώς τινες αὐτῶν** ἐπείρασαν . . . μηδὲ γογγύζετε, **καθάπερ τινὲς αὐτῶν** ἐγόγγυσαν καὶ ἀπώλοντο ὑπὸ τοῦ ὀλοθρευτοῦ. (1 Cor 10:7–10)

Διαιρέσεις δὲ χαρισμάτων εἰσίν, τὸ δὲ αὐτὸ πνεῦμα· καὶ **διαιρέσεις** διακονιῶν εἰσιν, καὶ ὁ αὐτὸς κύριος· καὶ **διαιρέσεις** ἐνεργημάτων εἰσίν, ὁ δὲ αὐτὸς θεός, ὁ ἐνεργῶν τὰ πάντα ἐν πᾶσιν. (1 Cor 12:4–6)

μὴ πάντες ἀπόστολοι; **μὴ πάντες** προφῆται; **μὴ πάντες** διδάσκαλοι; **μὴ πάντες** δυνάμεις; **μὴ πάντες** χαρίσματα ἔχουσιν ἰαμάτων; **μὴ πάντες** γλώσσαις λαλοῦσιν; **μὴ πάντες** διερμηνεύουσιν; (1 Cor 12:29–30)

οὐ ζηλοῖ, [ἡ ἀγάπη] **οὐ** περπερεύεται, **οὐ** φυσιοῦται, **οὐκ** ἀσχημονεῖ, **οὐ** ζητεῖ τὰ ἑαυτῆς, **οὐ** παροξύνεται, **οὐ** λογίζεται τὸ κακόν (1 Cor 13:4–5)

πάντα στέγει, **πάντα** πιστεύει, **πάντα** ἐλπίζει, **πάντα** ὑπομένει. (1 Cor 13:7)

δύνασθε γὰρ καθ᾽ ἕνα **πάντες** προφητεύειν, ἵνα **πάντες** μανθάνωσιν καὶ **πάντες** παρακαλῶνται, (1 Cor 14:31)

οὐ πᾶσα σὰρξ ἡ αὐτὴ σάρξ, ἀλλὰ **ἄλλη** μὲν ἀνθρώπων, **ἄλλη** δὲ σὰρξ κτηνῶν, **ἄλλη** δὲ σὰρξ πτηνῶν, **ἄλλη** δὲ ἰχθύων . . . (1 Cor 15:39)

ἄλλη δόξα ἡλίου, καὶ **ἄλλη δόξα** σελήνης, καὶ **ἄλλη δόξα** ἀστέρων· (1 Cor 15:41)

σπείρεται ἐν φθορᾷ, **ἐγείρεται ἐν** ἀφθαρσίᾳ· **σπείρεται ἐν** ἀτιμίᾳ, **ἐγείρεται ἐν** δόξῃ· **σπείρεται ἐν** ἀσθενείᾳ, **ἐγείρεται ἐν** δυνάμει· **σπείρεται** σῶμα ψυχικόν, **ἐγείρεται** σῶμα πνευματικόν. (1 Cor 15:42–44)

ποῦ σου, θάνατε, τὸ νῖκος; **ποῦ σου, θάνατε**, τὸ κέντρον; (1 Cor 15:55)

ἰδοὺ νῦν καιρὸς εὐπρόσδεκτος, **ἰδοὺ νῦν** ἡμέρα σωτηρίας. (2 Cor 6:2)

ἐν ὑπομονῇ πολλῇ, **ἐν** θλίψεσιν, **ἐν** ἀνάγκαις, **ἐν** στενοχωρίαις, **ἐν** πληγαῖς, **ἐν** φυλακαῖς, ... [plus another thirteen times]. (2 Cor 6:4–7)

διὰ τῶν ὅπλων τῆς δικαιοσύνης τῶν δεξιῶν καὶ ἀριστερῶν, [8] **διὰ** δόξης καὶ ἀτιμίας, **διὰ** δυσφημίας καὶ εὐφημίας· (2 Cor 6:7–8)

ὡς πλάνοι καὶ ἀληθεῖς, **ὡς** ἀγνοούμενοι καὶ ἐπιγινωσκόμενοι, **ὡς** ἀποθνῄσκοντες καὶ ἰδοὺ ζῶμεν, **ὡς** παιδευόμενοι καὶ μὴ θανατούμενοι, **ὡς** λυπούμενοι ἀεὶ δὲ χαίροντες, **ὡς** πτωχοὶ πολλοὺς δὲ πλουτίζοντες, **ὡς** μηδὲν ἔχοντες καὶ πάντα κατέχοντες. (2 Cor 6:8–10)

οὐδένα ἠδικήσαμεν, **οὐδένα** ἐφθείραμεν, **οὐδένα** ἐπλεονεκτήσαμεν. (2 Cor 7:2)

ἀνέχεσθε γὰρ **εἴ τις** ὑμᾶς καταδουλοῖ, **εἴ τις** κατεσθίει, **εἴ τις** λαμβάνει, **εἴ τις** ἐπαίρεται, **εἴ τις** εἰς πρόσωπον ὑμᾶς δέρει. (2 Cor 11:20)

κινδύνοις ποταμῶν, **κινδύνοις** λῃστῶν, **κινδύνοις** ἐκ γένους, **κινδύνοις** ἐξ ἐθνῶν, **κινδύνοις** ἐν πόλει, **κινδύνοις** ἐν ἐρημίᾳ, **κινδύνοις** ἐν θαλάσσῃ, **κινδύνοις** ἐν ψευδαδέλφοις, (2 Cor 11:26)

οὐκ ἔνι Ἰουδαῖος οὐδὲ Ἕλλην, **οὐκ ἔνι** δοῦλος οὐδὲ ἐλεύθερος, **οὐκ ἔνι** ἄρσεν καὶ θῆλυ· (Gal 3:28)

Εἴ τις οὖν παράκλησις ἐν Χριστῷ, **εἴ τι** παραμύθιον ἀγάπης, **εἴ τις** κοινωνία πνεύματος, **εἴ τις** σπλάγχνα καὶ οἰκτιρμοί, (Phil 2:1)

Βλέπετε τοὺς κύνας, **βλέπετε** τοὺς κακοὺς ἐργάτας, **βλέπετε** τὴν κατατομήν. (Phil 3:2)

κατὰ νόμον Φαρισαῖος, **κατὰ** ζῆλος διώκων τὴν ἐκκλησίαν, **κατὰ** δικαιοσύνην τὴν ἐν νόμῳ γενόμενος ἄμεμπτος. (Phil 3:5–6)

ὅσα ἐστὶν ἀληθῆ, **ὅσα** σεμνά, **ὅσα** δίκαια, **ὅσα** ἁγνά, **ὅσα** προσφιλῆ, **ὅσα** εὔφημα, **εἴ τις** ἀρετὴ καὶ **εἴ τις** ἔπαινος, ταῦτα λογίζεσθε· (Phil 4:8)

Μὴ οὖν τις ὑμᾶς κρινέτω ἐν βρώσει καὶ ... **μηδεὶς ὑμᾶς καταβραβευέτω** θέλων ἐν ταπεινοφροσύνῃ καὶ ... (Col 2:16, 18)

3.2.1.1.6. *Antistrophe/Epiphora* (Lausberg, §631)

A kind of "repetition at a distance" consisting in the repetition of a word or words at the end of successive clauses, sentences, or verses. The repetition can also be relaxed by the use of synonymous expressions.

Ἔτι γὰρ Χριστὸς ὄντων ἡμῶν ἀσθενῶν ἔτι κατὰ καιρὸν ὑπὲρ ἀσεβῶν **ἀπέθανεν**. μόλις γὰρ ὑπὲρ δικαίου τις **ἀποθανεῖται**· ὑπὲρ γὰρ τοῦ ἀγαθοῦ τάχα τις καὶ τολμᾷ **ἀποθανεῖν**· συνίστησιν δὲ τὴν ἑαυτοῦ ἀγάπην εἰς ἡμᾶς ὁ θεός, ὅτι ἔτι ἁμαρτωλῶν ὄντων ἡμῶν Χριστὸς ὑπὲρ ἡμῶν **ἀπέθανεν**. (Rom 5:6–8)

ἀλλὰ τὰ μωρὰ τοῦ κόσμου **ἐξελέξατο ὁ θεός**, ἵνα καταισχύνῃ τοὺς σοφούς, καὶ τὰ ἀσθενῆ τοῦ κόσμου **ἐξελέξατο ὁ θεός**, ἵνα καταισχύνῃ τὰ ἰσχυρά, καὶ τὰ ἀγενῆ τοῦ κόσμου καὶ τὰ ἐξουθενημένα **ἐξελέξατο ὁ θεός** . . . (1 Cor 1:27–28)

τί δὲ ἔχεις ὃ οὐκ **ἔλαβες**; εἰ δὲ καὶ **ἔλαβες**, τί καυχᾶσαι ὡς μὴ **λαβών**; (1 Cor 4:7)

ἕκαστος τὴν ἑαυτοῦ γυναῖκα **ἐχέτω** καὶ ἑκάστη τὸν ἴδιον ἄνδρα **ἐχέτω**. (1 Cor 7:2)

ἡ περιτομὴ **οὐδέν ἐστιν** καὶ ἡ ἀκροβυστία **οὐδέν ἐστιν** . . . (1 Cor 7:19)

καὶ ἐγενόμην τοῖς Ἰουδαίοις ὡς Ἰουδαῖος, **ἵνα Ἰουδαίους κερδήσω**· τοῖς ὑπὸ νόμον ὡς ὑπὸ νόμον, μὴ ὢν αὐτὸς ὑπὸ νόμον, **ἵνα τοὺς ὑπὸ νόμον κερδήσω**· τοῖς ἀνόμοις ὡς ἄνομος, μὴ ὢν ἄνομος θεοῦ ἀλλ' ἔννομος Χριστοῦ, **ἵνα κερδάνω τοὺς ἀνόμους**· ἐγενόμην τοῖς ἀσθενέσιν ἀσθενής, **ἵνα τοὺς ἀσθενεῖς κερδήσω**· (1 Cor 9:20–22)

Πᾶν τὸ ἐν μακέλλῳ πωλούμενον **ἐσθίετε μηδὲν ἀνακρίνοντες διὰ τὴν συνείδησιν** . . . εἴ τις καλεῖ ὑμᾶς τῶν ἀπίστων καὶ θέλετε πορεύεσθαι, πᾶν τὸ παρατιθέμενον ὑμῖν **ἐσθίετε μηδὲν ἀνακρίνοντες διὰ τὴν συνείδησιν**. ἐὰν δέ τις ὑμῖν εἴπῃ· τοῦτο ἱερόθυτόν ἐστιν, **μὴ ἐσθίετε** . . . (1 Cor 10:25, 27, 28)

Ἐὰν ταῖς γλώσσαις τῶν ἀνθρώπων λαλῶ καὶ τῶν ἀγγέλων, **ἀγάπην δὲ μὴ ἔχω, γέγονα χαλκὸς ἠχῶν ἢ κύμβαλον ἀλαλάζον**. καὶ ἐὰν ἔχω προφητείαν καὶ εἰδῶ τὰ μυστήρια πάντα καὶ πᾶσαν τὴν γνῶσιν καὶ ἐὰν ἔχω πᾶσαν τὴν πίστιν ὥστε ὄρη μεθιστάναι, **ἀγάπην δὲ μὴ ἔχω, οὐθέν εἰμι**. κἂν ψωμίσω πάντα τὰ ὑπάρχοντά μου καὶ ἐὰν παραδῶ τὸ σῶμά μου ἵνα καυχήσωμαι, **ἀγάπην δὲ μὴ ἔχω, οὐδὲν ὠφελοῦμαι**. (1 Cor 13:1–3)

ἐλάλουν **ὡς νήπιος**, ἐφρόνουν **ὡς νήπιος**, ἐλογιζόμην **ὡς νήπιος**· (1 Cor 13:11)

ὁ λαλῶν γλώσσῃ ἑαυτὸν **οἰκοδομεῖ**· ὁ δὲ προφητεύων ἐκκλησίαν **οἰκοδομεῖ**. (1 Cor 14:4)

προσεύξομαι **τῷ πνεύματι**, προσεύξομαι δὲ καὶ **τῷ νοΐ**·
ψαλῶ **τῷ πνεύματι**, ψαλῶ δὲ καὶ **τῷ νοΐ**.
(1 Cor 14:15)

ἕκαστος ψαλμὸν **ἔχει**, διδαχὴν **ἔχει**, ἀποκάλυψιν **ἔχει**, γλῶσσαν **ἔχει**, ἑρμηνείαν **ἔχει** ... (1 Cor 14:26)

Εἰ δὲ ἡ διακονία τοῦ θανάτου ἐν γράμμασιν ἐντετυπωμένη λίθοις ἐγενήθη **ἐν δόξῃ**, ..., πῶς οὐχὶ μᾶλλον ἡ διακονία τοῦ πνεύματος ἔσται **ἐν δόξῃ**; εἰ γὰρ τῇ διακονίᾳ τῆς κατακρίσεως **δόξα**, πολλῷ μᾶλλον περισσεύει ἡ διακονία τῆς δικαιοσύνης **δόξῃ**. καὶ γὰρ οὐ δεδόξασται τὸ δεδοξασμένον ἐν τούτῳ τῷ μέρει εἵνεκεν τῆς ὑπερβαλλούσης **δόξης**. εἰ γὰρ τὸ καταργούμενον διὰ **δόξης**, πολλῷ μᾶλλον τὸ μένον **ἐν δόξῃ**. (2 Cor 3:7–11)

ὅτι εἷς ὑπὲρ πάντων **ἀπέθανεν**, ἄρα οἱ πάντες **ἀπέθανον**· καὶ ὑπὲρ πάντων **ἀπέθανεν** (2 Cor 5:14–15)

Ἑβραῖοί εἰσιν; **κἀγώ**. Ἰσραηλῖταί εἰσιν; **κἀγώ**. σπέρμα Ἀβραάμ εἰσιν; **κἀγώ**. (2 Cor 11:22)

εἴτε ἐν σώματι οὐκ **οἶδα**, εἴτε ἐκτὸς τοῦ σώματος οὐκ **οἶδα**, ὁ θεὸς **οἶδεν** ... εἴτε ἐν σώματι εἴτε χωρὶς τοῦ σώματος οὐκ **οἶδα**, ὁ θεὸς **οἶδεν**
(2 Cor 12:2–3)

καὶ ἐὰν ἡμεῖς ἢ ἄγγελος ἐξ οὐρανοῦ εὐαγγελίζηται [ὑμῖν] παρ' ὃ εὐηγγελισάμεθα ὑμῖν, **ἀνάθεμα ἔστω**. ὡς προειρήκαμεν καὶ ἄρτι πάλιν λέγω· εἴ τις ὑμᾶς εὐαγγελίζεται παρ' ὃ παρελάβετε, **ἀνάθεμα ἔστω**. (Gal 1:8–9) ἐξ ἔργων νόμου τὸ πνεῦμα ἐλάβετε **ἢ ἐξ ἀκοῆς πίστεως**; . . . ὁ οὖν ἐπιχορηγῶν ὑμῖν τὸ πνεῦμα καὶ ἐνεργῶν δυνάμεις ἐν ὑμῖν, ἐξ ἔργων νόμου **ἢ ἐξ ἀκοῆς πίστεως**; (Gal 3:2, 5)

ὁ δὲ μεσίτης ἑνὸς οὐκ **ἔστιν**, ὁ δὲ θεὸς εἷς **ἐστιν**. (Gal 3:20)

ὅτι οὐκ ἔστιν ἡμῖν ἡ πάλη **πρὸς** αἷμα καὶ σάρκα, ἀλλὰ **πρὸς** τὰς ἀρχάς, **πρὸς** τὰς ἐξουσίας, **πρὸς** τοὺς κοσμοκράτορας τοῦ σκότους τούτου, **πρὸς** τὰ πνευματικὰ τῆς πονηρίας ἐν τοῖς ἐπουρανίοις. (Eph 6:12)

τινὲς μὲν καὶ διὰ φθόνον καὶ ἔριν, τινὲς δὲ καὶ δι' εὐδοκίαν **τὸν Χριστὸν κηρύσσουσιν**· . . . οἱ δὲ ἐξ ἐριθείας **τὸν Χριστὸν καταγγέλλουσιν**, οὐχ ἁγνῶς, οἰόμενοι θλῖψιν ἐγείρειν τοῖς δεσμοῖς μου. τί γάρ; πλὴν ὅτι παντὶ τρόπῳ, εἴτε προφάσει εἴτε ἀληθείᾳ, **Χριστὸς καταγγέλλεται** . . . (Phil 1:15, 17)

ὃν ἡμεῖς καταγγέλλομεν νουθετοῦντες **πάντα ἄνθρωπον** καὶ διδάσκοντες **πάντα ἄνθρωπον** ἐν πάσῃ σοφίᾳ, ἵνα παραστήσωμεν **πάντα ἄνθρωπον** τέλειον ἐν Χριστῷ· (Col 1:28)

3.2.1.1.7. Symplochē/Complexio (Lausberg, §633–34)

A kind of "repetition at a distance" consisting in a repetition of the same word or phrase at the beginning and the end of successive clauses or sentences.

ὁ κολλώμενος τῇ πόρνῃ ἓν σῶμά **ἐστιν**; **ὁ** δὲ **κολλώμενος** τῷ κυρίῳ ἓν πνεῦμά **ἐστιν**. (1 Cor 6:16–17)

ὁ σπείρων φειδομένως φειδομένως καὶ **θερίσει**, καὶ **ὁ σπείρων** ἐπ' εὐλογίαις ἐπ' εὐλογίαις καὶ **θερίσει**. (2 Cor 9:6)

3.2.1.1.8. Hendiadys

The expression of an idea by two nouns connected by "and" instead of by a noun and its qualifier. Hendiadys is a specific application of the general device of anthimeria, or the substitution of one part of speech for another (e.g., a noun for an adjective). Hendiadys sometimes comes close to synonymy (see §3.2.1.1.11).[10]

χάριν καὶ ἀποστολὴν = "the gift of apostleship" (Rom 1:5; cf. 12:3; 15:15-16; 1 Cor 3:10; 7:25; 15:10; Gal 2:9)

ὑπεροχὴν λόγου ἢ σοφίας = "a wise word," unless the two terms are roughly synonymous (1 Cor 2:1; cf. ἐν σοφίᾳ λόγου in 1:17)

πνεύματος καὶ δυνάμεως = the "powerful Spirit," unless "power" is a metonymy for "Spirit" (1 Cor 2:4). Likewise, ἐν δυνάμει καὶ ἐν πνεύματι ἁγίῳ (1 Thess 1:5).

σκληρότητά σου καὶ ἀμετανόητον καρδίαν (Rom 2:5) may be considered synonymy.

3.2.1.1.9. Paronomasia/Annominatio (Lausberg, §637-39)

A kind of relaxation of word equivalence that consists in wordplay involving words that sound alike but differ in meaning. Homoioprophoron (Lausberg, §975), or in modern parlance, alliteration, is a sub-species of paronomasia and consists in frequent repetition of the same consonant (or vowel), often the initial consonant. Alliteration, however, is often considered to be a stylistic vice (see §3.2.2.2 below).

With paronomasia, the play on words often involves variant arrangements of the same sounds; e.g., φθόνου, φόνου (Rom 1:29); ἀσυνέτους, ἀσυνθέτους (Rom 1:31); ἐσχήκαμεν, ἐστήκαμεν (Rom 5:2); ἀφθαρσίαν, ἀθανασίαν (1 Cor 15:53, 54); διακονία, δικαιοσύνης (2 Cor 3:9); ἄρρητα ῥήματα (2 Cor 12:4); ἵνα με, ἵνα μὴ (2 Cor 12:7); ἐνδυναμοῦσθε, ἐνδύσασθε, δύνασθαι (Eph 6:10, 11).

In other cases the play on words involves repetition of the same semantic root in compound form or in different parts of speech: κρίνεις, κατακρίνεις (Rom 2:1); ἀπειθοῦσι, πειθομένοις (Rom 2:8); κατεργαζομένου, ἐργαζομένῳ (Rom 2:9, 10); δίκαιοι, δικαιωθήσονται (Rom 2:13); ἠπίστησάν, ἀπιστία, πίστιν (Rom 3:3); κλάδων ἐξεκλάσθησαν (Rom 11:17); ἐξεκλάσθησαν κλάδοι (Rom 11:19); φρονεῖν, σωφρονεῖν (Rom 12:3); ὑποτασσέσθω, ἀντιτασσόμενος (Rom 13:1, 2); φόρον, φόρον, φόβον, φόβον (Rom 13:7); κρίνων, διακρινόμενος, κατακέκριται (Rom 14:22, 23); ζύμη, ζυμοῖ, ζύμην,

---

10. See discussion of the device in Bullinger, *Figures of Speech*, 657-72.

ἄζυμοι (1 Cor 5:6, 7); ἔξεστιν, ἐξουσιασθήσομαι (1 Cor 6:12); χρώμενοι, καταχρώμενοι (1 Cor 7:31); κρίμα, διακρίνων, διεκρίνομεν, ἐκρινόμεθα, κρινόμενοι, κατακριθῶμεν, κρίμα (1 Cor 11:29–34); ἀναγινώσκετε, ἐπιγινώσκετε (2 Cor 1:13); γινωσκομένη, ἀναγινωσκομένη (2 Cor 3:2); ἀπορούμενοι, ἐξαπορούμενοι (2 Cor 4:8); ἔχοντες, κατέχοντες (2 Cor 6:10); παντὶ πάντοτε πᾶσαν (2 Cor 9:8); ἐγκρῖναι, συνκρῖναι (2 Cor 10:12); συνιστανόντων, συνιᾶσιν (2 Cor 10:12); μετροῦντες, ἄμετρα, μέτρον, ἐμέρισεν, μέτρου, ἄμετρα (2 Cor 10:12–16); διάκονοι, δικαιοσύνης (2 Cor 11:15); δαπανήσω καὶ ἐκδαπανηθήσομαι (2 Cor 12:15); ἀνῆλθον, ἀπῆλθον (Gal 1:17); ὁ κλέπτων, κλεπτέτω (Eph 4:28); ἐνδυναμοῦσθε, δύνασθαι (Eph 6:10); μενῶ καὶ παραμενῶ (Phil 1:25); παρουσίᾳ, ἀπουσίᾳ (Phil 2:12); χαίρω καὶ συγχαίρω, χαίρετε καὶ συγχαίρετέ (Phil 2:17, 18); κατατομή, περιτομή (Phil 3:2, 3); περιετμήθητε περιτομῇ (Col 2:11); πάντοτε, πάντων (1 Thess 1:2); ἐργαζομένους, περιεργαζομένους (2 Thess 3:11); ἄχρηστον, εὔχρηστον (Phlm 11). The related words are often conceptually antithetical or paired in antithetical constructions (Rom 2:8; Phil 2:12; Gal 1:17; 2 Thess 3:11; Phlm 11 above).

In 1 Cor 2:13 the repetition of πνευμ- (πνεύματος, πνευματικοῖς πνευματικὰ) evokes the Corinthians' obsession with the "Spirit," and thus exudes a hint of irony.

While the list of four kinds of "flesh" in 1 Cor 15:39 clearly alludes to the genera of created things named in Gen 1:26, Paul's list substitutes πτηνός for the LXX's πετεινόν in order to create a play on the sound of κτῆνος, i.e., ἄλλη δὲ σὰρξ **κτηνῶν**, ἄλλη δὲ σὰρξ **πτηνῶν**.

In Phlm 20 ὀναίμην ("benefit") is a play on the name Ὀνήσιμος ("beneficial").

The succinctness of 1 Thess 5:15, together with its use of paronomasia (ἀντὶ, τινι) and two instances of polyptoton (see §3.2.1.1.10), reveals that this was likely a familiar proverb: μή τις κακὸν ἀντὶ κακοῦ τινι ἀποδῷ. Alliteration of both the τ and the π sounds in 1 Cor 14:32 likewise lends it a proverbial feel: πνεύματα προφητῶν προφήταις ὑποτάσσεται.

Some passages contain multiple instances of paronomasia. Rom 13:7 contains four lines, with alliteration of φ occurring in lines 1 and 3 and alliteration of τ in lines 2 and 4. In the first pair there is full paronomasia of consonants in the terms φόρον and φόβον:

τῷ τὸν φόρον τὸν φόρον, (φ)

τῷ τὸ τέλος τὸ τέλος, (τ)

τῷ τὸν φόβον τὸν φόβον, (φ)

τῷ τὴν τιμὴν τὴν τιμήν (τ)

2 Corinthians 3:2-11 contains repetition of multiple cognate groups: ἐγγεγραμμένη, ἐγγεγραμμένη, γράμματος, γράμμα, γράμμασιν; διακονηθεῖσα, διακόνους, διακονία, διακονία, διακονία, διακονία; ἱκανοί, ἱκανότης, ἱκάνωσεν; δόξῃ, δόξαν, δόξῃ, δόξα, δόξῃ, δεδόξασται, δεδοξασμένον, δόξης, δόξης, δόξῃ.

Excessive homoioprophoron (alliteration), or repetition of consonants, is considered to be a vice (Ps.-Cicero, *Rhet. Her.* 4.18; cf. Lausberg, §976). The device, however, can be considered ornamental when intentional and when other ornamental features accompany (e.g., Rom 1:30, 31; 13:7). Instances of homoioprophoron occur in Rom 1:29 (π in πεπληρωμένους πάσῃ ἀδικίᾳ πονηρίᾳ πλεονεξίᾳ), 30 (repetition of the final ς); 9:8 (τ in ταῦτα τέκνα τοῦ θεοῦ ἀλλὰ τὰ τέκνα); 13:7 (alternating repetition of φ and τ: τῷ τὸν φόρον τὸν φόρον, τῷ τὸ τέλος τὸ τέλος, τῷ τὸν φόβον τὸν φόβον, τῷ τὴν τιμὴν τὴν τιμήν); 1 Cor 3:7 (τ in ὥστε οὔτε ὁ φυτεύων ἐστίν τι οὔτε); 10:6 (κ in κακῶν, καθὼς κἀκεῖνοι); 11:4 (κ/χ in κατὰ κεφαλῆς ἔχων καταισχύνει τὴν κεφαλὴν); 11:33 (τα in ἀνεξεραύνητα τὰ κρίματα); 13:12 (π in πρόσωπον πρὸς πρόσωπον); 13:13 (alliteration of ι, π, τ, ων); 14:32 (alliteration of π); 2 Cor 5:16 (κ in καὶ ἐγνώκαμεν κατὰ σάρκα); 1 Thess 5:14 (τ/θ in νουθετεῖτε τοὺς ἀτάκτους); Rom 1:31 (the α-privative in ἀσυνέτους ἀσυνθέτους ἀστόργους ἀνελεήμονας); 2 Cor 11:20 (the ει sound in εἴ τις κατεσθίει, εἴ τις λαμβάνει, εἴ).

These examples generally occur in contexts characterized by high levels of ornament.

For instance, the alliteration in Rom 1:29 and 31 occurs amid multiple instances of paranomasia (1:29, 31); and asyndeton (1:29-31); expolitio (1:23-25). Around the alliteration in Rom 9:8 are found traductio (in both 9:6 and 7-8); pathetic polysyndeton (9:1-4); interpretatio (9:6-7); antithetical isocolon (9:8); and the thought-figures of deesis (9:1); expolitio (in both 9:6-7 and 8); and proparaskeue (9:1-5). Around 1 Cor 3:7 are found a collection of tropes (3:6-17); as well as isocolon (3:14-15); antithetical isocolon (3:17); multiple instances of tricolon (3:6-7 [x2] and 9); traductio (3:17); and the thought figures of interpretatio (3:13); interrogatio (3:16); and oxymoron (3:18). In 1 Cor 10:1-10 are found anaphora (10:1-4 and 7-10); polysyndeton (10:1-4); litotes (10:5); and isocolon (10:9-10). 1 Cor 11:1-15 contains the metaphor of the "head," semantically varied into traductio (11:4, 5); also hyperbole (11:5); isocolon (11:4-5); antimetabole (11:6); and later, aporia (11:13-14); and antithetical isocolon (11:14-15). In 1 Thess 5:14-22 there occur tricolon (5:14, 16-18); and isocolon with homoioteleuton (5:6-22). 2 Cor 11:19-29 is highly ornamental, deploying irony (11:19, 21); anaphora (11:20, 26); antistrophe (11:22); polyptoton (11:20, 29); isocolon throughout 11:21-29; homoioteleuton (11:23); tricolon (11:20, 22); and the thought-figures of interrogatio (11:22); correctio (11:16-17, 21, 23); and irony (11:19, 21).

The ornamental quality of 1 Cor 13:13 is consistent with the chapter as a whole:[11]

νυνὶ δὲ μένει	(alliteration of ν, ι)
πίστις ἐλπίς ἀγάπη	(alliteration of π)
τὰ τρία ταῦτα	(alliteration of τα)
μείζων δὲ τούτων	(alliteration of ων)

Ornamental features are also present around the alliteration in Rom 13:7; 1 Cor 11:33; 13:12; 14:32.

3.2.1.1.10. POLYPTOTON/PAREGMENON (LAUSBERG, §640-48)

Repetition of words from the same root but with different endings.

ἐξ αὐτοῦ καὶ δι' αὐτοῦ καὶ εἰς αὐτὸν (Rom 11:36); χαίρειν μετὰ χαιρόντων, καὶ κλαίειν μετὰ κλαιόντων (Rom 12:15); ἀνθέστηκεν, ἀνθεστηκότες (Rom 13:2); μηδενὶ μηδὲν (Rom 13:8); πνευματικοῖς πνευματικὰ (1 Cor 2:13); ὁ ἀροτριῶν ἀροτριᾶν (1 Cor 9:10); ἐκ πάντων πᾶσιν, (1 Cor 9:19); τοῖς Ἰουδαίοις ὡς Ἰουδαῖος, ἵνα Ἰουδαίους (1 Cor 9:20); τοῖς ἀνόμοις ὡς ἄνομος, μὴ ὢν ἄνομος (1 Cor 9:21); τοῖς ἀσθενέσιν ἀσθενής, ἵνα τοὺς ἀσθενεῖς (1 Cor 9:22); τοῖς πᾶσιν γέγονα πάντα, ἵνα πάντως (1 Cor 9:22); κἀγὼ πάντα πᾶσιν ἀρέσκω (1 Cor 10:33); προφητῶν προφήταις (1 Cor 14:32); ἐν παντὶ πάντοτε πᾶσαν (2 Cor 9:8); τίς ἀσθενεῖ καὶ οὐκ ἀσθενῶ (2 Cor 11:29); οὐ ... τὰ ὑμῶν ἀλλ' ὑμᾶς (2 Cor 12:14); οὐκ ἀπ' ἀνθρώπων οὐδὲ δι' ἀνθρώπου (Gal 1:1); εὐαγγελίζηται [ὑμῖν] παρ' ὃ εὐηγγελισάμεθα ὑμῖν (Gal 1:8); ζήσω, ζῶ, ζῇ, ζῶ, ζῶ (Gal 2:19, 20); πείθεσθαι, πεισμονή, πέποιθα (Gal 5:7, 8, 10); κατηχούμενος, κατηχοῦντι (Gal 6:6); σάρκα, σαρκὸς, and τὸ πνεῦμα, τοῦ πνεύματος (Gal 6:8); πατὴρ πάντων,

---

11. Smit, "Genre of 1 Corinthians," 205.

ὁ ἐπὶ πάντων καὶ διὰ πάντων καὶ ἐν πᾶσιν (Eph 4:6); Ἑβραῖος ἐξ Ἑβραίων (Phil 3:5); καταλάβω, κατελήμφθην, κατειληφέναι (Phil 3:12, 13); φρονεῖν, ἐφρονεῖτε (Phil 4:10); ὁ ἀδικῶν, ἠδίκησεν (Col 3:25); ὁ ἀθετῶν, ἀθετεῖ (1 Thess 4:8); καθεύδοντες, καθεύδουσιν and μεθυσκόμενοι, μεθύουσιν (1 Thess 5:7); τις, τινι and κακὸν, κακοῦ (1 Thess 5:15).

2 Corinthians 3:2–11 contains multiple instances of polyptoton: γράμματος, γράμμα, γράμμασιν; διακόνους, διακονία, διακονία, διακονία, διακονία; δόξῃ, δόξαν, δόξῃ, δόξα, δόξῃ, δόξης, δόξης, δόξῃ.

Several examples of polyptoton in 2 Corinthians involve changes of verb tense: ἐρρύσατο ἡμᾶς καὶ ῥύσεται (2 Cor 1:10); ἐτήρησα καὶ τηρήσω (2 Cor 11:9); ποιῶ καὶ ποιήσω (2 Cor 11:12).

In Rom 5:6–8, the inflected forms of the relevant verb occur invariably at the end of their respective clauses: ἀπέθανεν, ἀποθανεῖται, ἀποθανεῖν, ἀπέθανεν.

3.2.1.1.11. SYNONYMY (LAUSBERG, §649–56)

Amplification by means of words or phrases with the same or similar meaning. Synonymy counts as a kind of "word-repetition" that involves a relaxation of the equivalence of word meaning. In synonymy the synonymous words do not share complete semantic equivalency. Hence the repetition is not superfluous but includes semantic distinctions, thus serving to intensify the point. See also under Co-ordinating Accumulation (§3.2.1.1.15).

ὀργὴ καὶ **θυμός** (Rom 2:8)

σκληρότητά σου καὶ **ἀμετανόητον καρδίαν** (Rom 2:5)

ὁδηγὸν εἶναι τυφλῶν, φῶς τῶν ἐν σκότει (Rom 2:19)

παιδευτὴν ἀφρόνων, διδάσκαλον νηπίων (Rom 2:20)

With three pairs of synonymous terms: μὴ **κώμοις καὶ μέθαις**, μὴ **κοίταις καὶ ἀσελγείαις**, μὴ **ἔριδι καὶ ζήλῳ** . . . (Rom 13:13)

οἶδα καὶ πέπεισμαι (Rom 14:14)

ὁ **λόγος** μου καὶ τὸ **κήρυγμά** μου (1 Cor 2:4)

ὡς **σαρκίνοις**, ὡς **νηπίοις** ἐν Χριστῷ. (1 Cor 3:1)

περικαθάρματα τοῦ κόσμου ἐγενήθημεν, πάντων **περίψημα** (1 Cor 4:13)

With two pairs of synonymous terms: κακίας καὶ πονηρίας ... εἰλικρινείας καὶ ἀληθείας (1 Cor 5:8)

τοῖς πλεονέκταις καὶ ἅρπαξιν (1 Cor 5:10)

πᾶσαν **ἀρχὴν** καὶ πᾶσαν **ἐξουσίαν** καὶ **δύναμιν** (1 Cor 15:24)

οὐδὲ γὰρ ἐγὼ παρὰ ἀνθρώπου **παρέλαβον** αὐτό, οὔτε **ἐδιδάχθην** (Gal 1:12)

οὐκ **ἐξουθενήσατε** οὐδὲ **ἐξεπτύσατε** (Gal 4:14)

ἔρις, ζῆλος, ... διχοστασίαι, αἱρέσεις ... (Gal 5:20)

μέθαι, κῶμοι (Gal 5:21)

πάσης **ἀρχῆς** καὶ **ἐξουσίας** καὶ **δυνάμεως** καὶ **κυριότητος** (Eph 1:21)

αἰσχρότης καὶ μωρολογία ἢ εὐτραπελία (Eph 5:4)

διὰ πάσης **προσευχῆς** καὶ **δεήσεως** προσευχόμενοι ... (Eph 6:18)

ἃ καὶ **ἐμάθετε** καὶ **παρελάβετε** καὶ **ἠκούσατε** καὶ **εἴδετε** ἐν ἐμοί (Phil 4:9)

Colossians 1:16 contains two separate synonymies: (1) τὰ πάντα **ἐν τοῖς οὐρανοῖς καὶ ἐπὶ τῆς γῆς, τὰ ὁρατὰ καὶ τὰ ἀόρατα**, (2) εἴτε **θρόνοι** εἴτε **κυριότητες** εἴτε **ἀρχαὶ** εἴτε **ἐξουσίαι**.

ἀπὸ τῶν **αἰώνων** καὶ ἀπὸ τῶν **γενεῶν** (Col 1:26)

τῆς σοφίας καὶ γνώσεως (Col 2:3)

ὁσίως καὶ δικαίως καὶ ἀμέμπτως (1 Thess 2:10)

πλεονάσαι καὶ περισσεύσαι (1 Thess 3:12)

τῶν χρόνων καὶ τῶν καιρῶν (1 Thess 5:1)

ἀπὸ τῶν **ἀτόπων** καὶ **πονηρῶν** ἀνθρώπων (2 Thess 3:2)

"Signs" and "wonders" is a common collocation (a common OT idiom, e.g., Exod 7:3; Deut 4:34; Isa 8:18): ἐν δυνάμει σημείων καὶ τεράτων (Rom 15:19); σημείοις τε καὶ τέρασιν καὶ δυνάμεσιν (2 Cor 12:12); ἐν πάσῃ δυνάμει καὶ σημείοις καὶ τέρασιν (2 Thess 2:9).

Also fixed as a collocation is "fear" and "trembling": ἐν ἀσθενείᾳ καὶ ἐν φόβῳ καὶ ἐν τρόμῳ (1 Cor. 2:3); φόβου καὶ τρόμου (2 Cor 7:15; Eph 6:5; Phil 2:12).

θλίψις occurs with one or more synonyms in several passages: θλίψις . . . ἢ διωγμός (Rom 8:35); ἀνάγκῃ καὶ θλίψει (1 Thess 3:7); ἐν πᾶσιν τοῖς διωγμοῖς ὑμῶν καὶ ταῖς θλίψεσιν (2 Thess 1:4).

"Impurity" and "fornication" appear together in vice lists: ἐπὶ τῇ ἀκαθαρσίᾳ καὶ πορνείᾳ καὶ ἀσελγείᾳ (2 Cor. 12:21); πορνεία, ἀκαθαρσία (Gal 5:19).

In both Ephesians and Colossians: ψαλμοῖς καὶ ὕμνοις καὶ ᾠδαῖς πνευματικαῖς (Eph 5:19); ψαλμοῖς, ὕμνοις, ᾠδαῖς πνευματικαῖς (Col 3:16).

"Labor" and "toil" occurs in both 1 and 2 Thessalonians: τὸν **κόπον** ἡμῶν καὶ τὸν **μόχθον** (1 Thess. 2:9); ἐν **κόπῳ** καὶ **μόχθῳ** (2 Thess. 3:8).

Possibly also τοὺς δὲ ποιμένας καὶ διδασκάλους (Eph 4:11); διὰ τῆς φιλοσοφίας καὶ κενῆς ἀπάτης (Col 2:8); δοὺς παράκλησιν αἰωνίαν καὶ ἐλπίδα ἀγαθὴν (2 Thess 2:16); χάριν καὶ ἀποστολὴν (Rom 1:5; cf. 12:3; 15:15–16; 1 Cor 3:10; 7:25; 15:10; Gal 2:9).

Instances of coordination where one term is related synecdocially or metonymically to another may also apply: εἰς τὴν ἑαυτοῦ βασιλείαν καὶ δόξαν, where "glory" is a quality of the place (1 Thess 2:12); πνεύματος καὶ δυνάμεως, where "power" may be a metonymy for "Spirit" (1 Cor 2:4); likewise, ἐν δυνάμει καὶ ἐν πνεύματι ἁγίῳ (1 Thess 1:5).

On the use of synonymy in isocolon and in repetition of the thought, see below on isocolon (§3.2.1.1.22), disiunctio (§3.2.1.1.28), interpretatio (§3.2.1.1.30), and expolitio (§3.2.1.2.18).

3.2.1.1.12. *Traductio (Lausberg, §658–59)*

Repetition of the same word with different meanings.

Μηδενὶ μηδὲν **ὀφείλετε** (owe) εἰ μὴ τὸ ἀλλήλους [implicit **ὀφείλετε**, but in a modal sense, i.e., "you should"] ἀγαπᾶν (Rom. 13:8 BGT)

μηκέτι οὖν ἀλλήλους **κρίνωμεν** (condemn)· ἀλλὰ τοῦτο **κρίνατε** (make a decision) μᾶλλον . . . (Rom 14:13) σὺ πίστιν **ἔχεις** (possess); κατὰ σεαυτὸν **ἔχε** (keep). (Rom 14:22)

εἴ τις τὸν ναὸν τοῦ θεοῦ **φθείρει** (corrupts), **φθερεῖ** (destroy) τοῦτον ὁ θεός· (1 Cor 3:17)

ὁ κύριος διέταξεν τοῖς **τὸ εὐαγγέλιον** (gospel message) καταγγέλλουσιν ἐκ **τοῦ εὐαγγελίου** (proclamation of the message) ζῆν (1 Cor 9:14)

With a play on the root meaning of δοκιμ-: καθὼς **οὐκ ἐδοκίμασαν** (not see fit) τὸν θεὸν ἔχειν ἐν ἐπιγνώσει, παρέδωκεν αὐτοὺς ὁ θεὸς εἰς **ἀδόκιμον** (not approved, i.e., in a moral sense) νοῦν (Rom 1:28)

Likewise, the meaning of κόσμος changes in 1 Cor 5:10; ἀγνοεῖν in 1 Cor 14:38; ὑποτάσσειν in 1 Cor 15:27–28; νόμος in Rom 3:27; 7:14–25; 8:2–3; 1 Cor 9:20; cf. Gal 6:2; Ἰσραήλ in Rom 9:6, τέκνα and σπέρμα in 9:7–8; εἷς in Gal 3:20; σάρξ in 2 Cor 10:30; Phil 3:3–4.

A single form can have double meaning: παρεδίδετο may have two meanings ("handed over [by God's plan]," "betrayed [by Judas]") in 1 Cor 11:23; ἕως τέλους as "completely" and "to the end of the letter" in 2 Cor 1:13; σαρκί as both physical flesh and law-observance in Gal 6:13.

Paradoxical expressions can involve an implicit play on two meanings of a word: freedom/slavery in 1 Cor 9:19.

In a few cases, Paul shifts between literal and figurative meanings. "Circumcision" is sometimes literal, sometimes figurative, in Rom 2:25–29. "Freedperson," "free person," and "slave" are used in both senses in 1 Cor 7:22. Paul plays freely with the language of "sleep" in 1 Thess 4:13—5:10: from "being asleep" as death (1 Thess 4:13–15) to "being asleep" as not "being watchful/awake" for Christ's return (1 Thess 5:6–8) to "being awake" for "being alive" and "sleeping" for "being dead" (1 Thess 5:10).

3.2.1.1.13. DISTINCTIO (LAUSBERG, §660–62)

The heightening of semantic distinction, in the repetition of a word, between the normal or customary meaning of the word and the emphatic/specialized meaning of the same word.

Possibly Gal 1:6–7, εὐαγγέλιον in its normal sense of "good news" is distinguished from "the gospel" as strictly understood within Pauline discourse.

3.2.1.1.14. *Reflexio/Antanaklasis (Lausberg §663–64)*

Like irony (§3.1.3.8), reflexio consists in the repetition of a word or phrase whereby the language of one speaker is received by a second speaker in a changed sense that emphasizes the new speaker's point of view; yet, reflexio plays on meanings that both parties agree to be usual, whereas irony represents the view of the opposing party as false or nonsensical.

The repetition of γινώσκειν in 1 Cor 8:2 plays on opposing definitions of "knowing" (εἴ τις δοκεῖ ἐγνωκέναι τι, οὔπω **ἔγνω** καθὼς δεῖ **γνῶναι**). In the first instance, the word represents the audience's understanding of "knowledge" as *cognizance* regarding their liberty as believers. In the second instance, Paul redefines "knowing" in terms of deep, *situational application of the known principle*: one "knows," or understands Christian liberty, when it is worked out in action informed by the good of others.

3.2.1.1.15. *Co-ordinating Accumulation (Lausberg, §665–74)*

The addition of semantically supplementary words, which are sometimes related as polar opposites. Frequently the supplementary words consist in the enumeration of species that fall under a preceding collective term. Cf. Synonymy (§3.2.1.1.11).

"It is the power of God for salvation **to everyone who has faith, to the Jew first and also to the Greek**. (Rom 1:16 NRSV)

"There will be anguish and distress **for everyone who does evil, the Jew first and also the Greek**, but glory and honor and peace **for everyone who does good, the Jew first and also the Greek**. (Rom 2:9–10 NRSV)

"Note then the kindness and the severity of God: **toward those who have fallen severity, but toward you God's kindness**." (Rom 11:22 NRSV)

"But **to those who are the called, both Jews and Greeks**" (1 Cor 1:24 NRSV)

"We have become a spectacle **to the world, to angels and to mortals**." (1 Cor 4:9 NRSV)

3.2.1.1.16. Distributio/Diairesis (Lausberg, §675)

Division of a topic or subject into parts using isocolon (see §3.2.1.1.22).

ἔχοντες δὲ χαρίσματα κατὰ τὴν χάριν τὴν δοθεῖσαν ἡμῖν διάφορα,
    εἴτε προφητείαν κατὰ τὴν ἀναλογίαν τῆς πίστεως,
    εἴτε διακονίαν ἐν τῇ διακονίᾳ,
    εἴτε ὁ διδάσκων ἐν τῇ διδασκαλίᾳ,
    εἴτε ὁ παρακαλῶν ἐν τῇ παρακλήσει·
    ὁ μεταδιδοὺς ἐν ἁπλότητι,
    ὁ προϊστάμενος ἐν σπουδῇ,
    ὁ ἐλεῶν ἐν ἱλαρότητι.
(Rom 12:6–8)

ἀπόδοτε πᾶσιν τὰς ὀφειλάς,
    τῷ τὸν φόρον τὸν φόρον,
    τῷ τὸ τέλος τὸ τέλος,
    τῷ τὸν φόβον τὸν φόβον,
    τῷ τὴν τιμὴν τὴν τιμήν.
(Rom 13:7)

The distribution is extensive in 1 Cor 12:4–11:

Διαιρέσεις δὲ χαρισμάτων εἰσίν, τὸ δὲ αὐτὸ πνεῦμα·
καὶ διαιρέσεις διακονιῶν εἰσιν, καὶ ὁ αὐτὸς κύριος·
καὶ διαιρέσεις ἐνεργημάτων εἰσίν,
ὁ δὲ αὐτὸς θεὸς ὁ ἐνεργῶν τὰ πάντα ἐν πᾶσιν.
ἑκάστῳ δὲ δίδοται ἡ φανέρωσις τοῦ πνεύματος πρὸς τὸ συμφέρον.
    ᾧ μὲν γὰρ διὰ τοῦ πνεύματος δίδοται λόγος σοφίας,
    ἄλλῳ δὲ λόγος γνώσεως κατὰ τὸ αὐτὸ πνεῦμα,
    etc.

μὴ πάντες χαρίσματα ἔχουσιν ἰαμάτων;

μὴ πάντες γλώσσαις λαλοῦσιν;

μὴ πάντες διερμηνεύουσιν;

(1 Cor 12:30)

Οὐ πᾶσα σὰρξ ἡ αὐτὴ σάρξ·
    ἀλλὰ ἄλλη μὲν ἀνθρώπων,
    ἄλλη δὲ σὰρξ κτηνῶν,
    ἄλλη δὲ ἰχθύων,
    ἄλλη δὲ πτηνῶν.
    ἀλλ' ἑτέρα μὲν ἡ τῶν ἐπουρανίων δόξα, ἑτέρα δὲ ἡ τῶν ἐπιγείων.
    ἄλλη δόξα ἡλίου,
    καὶ ἄλλη δόξα σελήνης,
    καὶ ἄλλη δόξα ἀστέρων·

(1 Cor 15:39–41)

Αἱ γυναῖκες, ὑποτάσσεσθε . . .

Οἱ ἄνδρες, ἀγαπᾶτε . . .

Τὰ τέκνα, ὑπακούετε . . . .

Οἱ πατέρες, μὴ ἐρεθίζετε . . .

Οἱ δοῦλοι, ὑπακούετε . . .

(Col 3:18–22)

3.2.1.1.17. *Epitheton (Lausberg, §676–85)*

An attributive addition to a substantive added to complete characterization, often by referring to some defining trait.

    Especially common are epithets that identity roles or highlight the nature of relationships among believers: "Quartus the brother" (Rom 16:23); "Sosthenes the brother" (1 Cor 1:1); "Apollos the brother" (1 Cor 16:12); "Timothy the brother" (2 Cor 1:1); "Timothy the brother" (Col 1:1); "Apphia the sister" (Phlm 2); "Archippus our fellow-soldier" (Phlm 2); "Prisca and Aquila my co-workers" (Rom 16:3); "Urbanus our fellow-worker" (Rom 16:9); "Stachys my beloved" (Rom 16:9); "Timothy my fellow-worker" (Rom 16:21); "Jason and Sosipater my kinsmen" (Rom 16:21); "Aristarchus my fellow-prisoner" (Col 4:10).

Paul sometimes appends multiple epithets to a single name: "Andronichus and Junia my kinsmen and my fellow-prisoners, who also were in Christ before me" (Rom 16:7); "Epaphroditus the brother and fellow-worker and fellow-soldier of me" (Phil 2:25); "my brothers, beloved and longed for, my joy and crown" (Phil 4:1); "Epaphras our beloved fellow-slave, who is a faithful minister of Christ" (Col 1:7); "Tychicus the beloved brother and faithful minister and fellow-slave in the Lord" (Col 4:7); "Timothy our brother and co-worker" (1 Thess 3:2).

Paul often appends epithets to the names of God and Jesus, especially in prayers and benedictions; e.g., "God our Father" (1 Thess 3:11; 2 Thess 2:16); "the God of peace" (Rom 15:33; 1 Thess 5:23); "Jesus our Lord" (1 Thess 3:11), "Jesus Christ our Lord" (2 Thess 2:16); etc.

3.2.1.1.18. POLYSYNDETON (LAUSBERG §686-87)

The repeated use of conjunctions between clauses.

Extended polysyndeton occurs frequently: with εἴτε (1 Cor 3:22; Col 1:16); with οὔτε (1 Cor 6:9); with ἤ (1 Cor 5:10, 11; 14:6); with καί (Rom 9:4; 1 Cor 4:11; 13:2-3; Eph 1:21; 4:31; Phil 1:25; 1 Thess 2:15). Two blocks of polysyndeton occur in Rom 8:35 (with ἤ), 38-39 (with οὔτε). Paul varies between polysyndeton and asyndeton in 1 Cor 6:9-10; Phil 4:8-9.

Polysyndeton may be used to connote a sense of exhaustive inclusion (Rom 11:36; 1 Cor 3:22; 5:10, 11; 6:9; 7:29-30; Eph 1:21; 4:31; Col 1:16; 1 Thess 2:2); to emphasize the accumulation of items or actions (Rom 9:4; 1 Cor 4:11; 14:6; 13:2-3; 1 Thess 2:15); or to produce a sense of dramatic build-up (1 Cor 10:1-4; 13:2-3). In Gal 4:10, it perhaps indicates disgust: ἡμέρας παρατηρεῖσθε καὶ μῆνας καὶ καιροὺς καὶ ἐνιαυτούς (Gal 4:10). In several places it lends an impression that Paul is pulling examples off-handedly from what could be a much longer list of items, which he then sums up with a more comprehensive term or statement (Rom 8:38-39; 1 Cor 3:22; Phil 3:5-7, esp. if ἀλλά is not original in v. 7).

An accumulation of synonymous terms or expressions serves purposes of emphasis. See Synonymy (§3.2.1.1.11) and Co-ordinating Accumulation (§3.2.1.1.15).

3.2.1.1.19. ELLIPSIS (LAUSBERG, §690–91)

The omission of a word easily supplied. The ornamental quality of ellipsis stems from its contribution to brevity. When the omission offends clarity, however, it counts as a vice (see §1.2.2 above).

The imperatival infinitive, so-called, in reality depends upon some governing verb (as Quintilian acknowledges, commenting on the omission of the Latin *coepit* before an infinitive; see *Inst.* 9.3.58), though it is not always clear what verb should be supplied. See, e.g., Rom 12:15; Phil 3:16. Similar to imperatival infinitives, complementizers often come at the beginning of a sentence without a governing verb (ὅτι in Gal 1:20; ἵνα in 2 Cor 2:5).

The omission of εἶναι is of course conventional (BDF §127–28) in simple predications, formulas, benedictions, wishes, and many other contexts. At times an elastic verb like ἔρχεσθαι or γίνεσθαι may need to be supplied (e.g., Rom 5:15, 16, 18; 1 Cor 15:46).

"Not that ... (οὐχ ὅτι)" is conventional and ἐστίν is easily understood with this formula (2 Cor 1:24; 3:5; 7:9; Phil 3:12; 4:11, 17; 2 Thess 3:9 [x2]; cf. οὐχ οἷον δὲ ὅτι in Rom 9:6). Similar to οὐχ ὅτι are the idioms οὐ θαῦμα (2 Cor 11:14); μέγα εἰ (1 Cor 9:11; 2 Cor 11:15); εἰ δυνατόν (Rom 12:18; Gal 4:15); and οὐ καθάπερ (2 Cor 3:13). Also idiomatic is the expression οὐ μόνον δέ, ἀλλὰ καί (Rom 5:3, 11; 8:23; 9:10; cf. Wis 19:5). Ellipsis can occur after μόνον (1 Cor 7:39) or μήτι γε (1 Cor 6:3). The formula ἓν δέ in Phil 3:13 is dramatic.

The thought is often comprehensible even when the ellipsis is uncertain. Neither the subject nor the verb is clear in Rom 4:16 (διὰ τοῦτο ἐκ πίστεως), though little is lost as to the general sense, and the brevity is attractive; note also Rom 9:16 (ἄρα οὖν οὐ τοῦ θέλοντος). Something like μιμνήσκεσθε is needed before οὐ σὺ τὴν ῥίζαν βαστάζεις in Rom 11:18. The distributio (§3.2.1.1.16) in Rom 12:6–8 is highly elliptical but still comprehensible, perhaps requiring only the supplying of cognate forms; also elliptical is the distributio in Rom 13:7.

Ellipses can often be filled in by carrying over content from elsewhere in the context. In ascensive sequences, a verb can be carried over from a preceding thought, as εἰ in εἰ δὲ υἱός (Gal 4:7); in the case of καί plus a demonstrative, content can be carried over from what precedes (1 Cor 5:1; 6:6, 8; Phil 1:28); note also Phil 2:27. The ellipsis in the predicate is clear in ὁ θεὸς οἶδεν (2 Cor 11:11). An omitted prepositional phrase can be clear from the context (σὺν αὐτῇ in 1 Cor 6:16, σὺν αὐτῷ in 1 Cor

6:17). The omitted verb in Gal 3:5 is evident from ὁ ἐπιχορηγῶν. Ellipses are easily filled in when they occur in answer to a question (Rom 3:2, 27; 1 Cor 3:5; 10:19; Phil 1:18).

In 2 Thess 1:11 there is ellipsis of "and therefore in you" (Lightfoot, Notes 105): "in all them that believed, and *therefore in you*, for our testimony was believed by you." The expression of a question by τί alone is vague (e.g., Phil 1:18), though the meaning is usually clear based on the context; similarly, "what then (τί οὖν)?" (Rom 3:9; 6:15; 11:7), "what then is it (τί οὖν ἐστιν)" (1 Cor 14:15, 26), "why then (τί οὖν)?" (Gal 3:19), or "for what (τί γάρ)?" (Rom 3:3).

In Phil 1:21, Χριστός may be a metonym for a larger idea and is in that sense creative. Similar is the abbreviated expression οὕτως καὶ ἡ ἀνάστασις τῶν νεκρῶν, "so also is the resurrection of the dead" (1 Cor 15:42), which seems to mean something like, "These facts of nature provide analogies to the resurrection of the dead."

An event can stand in for the status or condition of the subject at the time they experienced it; e.g., "your calling" (τὴν κλῆσιν ὑμῶν) means, "your status when you were called" (1 Cor 1:26); as a place can stand in for one's status or condition at the time they occupied that place, " . . . who set me apart from the womb of my mother" = "from the time I was in the womb . . . " (Gal 1:15), as in English, "raised me from a boy."

For ellipsis of the thought, see the thought-figure Aposiopesis (§3.2.1.2.25).

3.2.1.1.20. ZEUGMA (LAUSBERG, §692–708)

A form of ellipsis in which an omitted part-element in a co-ordination of elements shares the same function as the remaining parallel part-element.

Like ellipsis, zeugma could count as either a virtue or a vice (Lausberg, §1063–4). Even when the omitted element requires a different form than the one used in the parallel part, the omission could be considered "complicated zeugma" (Lausberg, §700–708; cf. BDF §479.2), as opposed to vicious ellipsis; the line is not easy to draw. Many instances cited above under Solecisms, By Subtraction, §1.2.2, probably qualify as complicated zeugma; e.g., where the grammatical person changes in the ellipsis (Rom 7:17, 20; 1 Cor 7:10; 7:12; 9:25; 15:10; Gal 6:14); or the verb tense (1 Cor 13:12); or the mood (1 Cor 14:27; Eph 5:14; 1 Thess 5:4).

"Uncomplicated zeugma" (Lausberg §700–708) is too common to catalogue, and some omissions are too conventional to be considered "ornamental" (e.g., the omission of εἶναι). In parallel constructions including antitheses, comparisons, conditionals, point-counterpoint constructions, or other coordinate constructions, the omitted element is commonly identical to the remaining, parallel element; e.g., verb with embedded subject (ἐσμέν in Rom 8:17; φρονεῖτε in Col 3:2; ἐδέξασθε in 1 Thess 2:13); verbs (κατεργάζεται in Rom 5:4; εἰσῆλθεν in Rom 5:12; ἀποδιδότω in 1 Cor 7:3; δικαιωθῶμεν in Gal 2:16; etc.); predicate nominatives (τέκνα in Gal 4:31); complements (πνεῦμα in 1 Cor 16:18); verb and complement (1 Cor 7:4). The omission of the direct object (τὸν Χριστόν) after ἐπείρασαν in 1 Cor 10:9 may be explained by the fact that the text cited (LXX Num 21:5–9) refers to testing of the "Lord" (κύριος), or Yhwh; thus the omission may owe to theological propriety. The preposition is routinely omitted after the first item in a coordinated list (Eph 1:21). An adjunct alone could remain, as ἄκων in 1 Cor 9:17; πρὸς τὸν θεόν in Rom 4:2; see also Rom 4:4, 23–24; Gal 3:2.

3.2.1.1.21. ASYNDETON (LAUSBERG, §709–11)

The omission of conjunctions between words, phrases, or clauses.

The omission of καί between words in a vice list (Rom 1:29–31; 1 Cor 6:10; 2 Cor 12:20; Gal 5:19–21; Col 3:5, 8), in a virtue list (1 Cor 13:13; Gal 5:22–23; Col 3:12), in a parenetic list (Rom 12:9–13), in a list of credentials (Phil 3:5–6), in hardship lists (2 Cor 6:4–7; 11:23–29; 12:10), in a list of spiritual gifts (1 Cor 12:28). The omission of ἤ between substantives (1 Cor 3:12). Note also "one Lord, one faith, one baptism, etc." (Eph 6:4–6); "if anyone enslaves you, if anyone preys upon you, if anyone takes advantage of you, etc." (2 Cor 11:19–20). Paul varies between polysyndeton and asyndeton in 1 Cor 6:9–10; Phil 4:8–9.

Asyndeton has a variety of effects. In general, it reinforces the pathos quality created by the accumulation of items (Lausberg, §709; cf. 668). Sometimes it amplifies a sense of solemnity (Rom 9:1–3), or triumph (1 Cor 4:12–13), as the context indicates. It occurs most commonly in passages that contain other ornamental features, as in series of short assertions (1 Cor 13:4–7), exclamations (1 Cor 4:8), rhetorical questions (1 Cor 11:22; 12:29–30), or in antitheses (1 Cor 4:12–13; 15:42–44, 47–48; 2 Cor 5:17) or series of equal colons (1 Cor 1:20, 26; 4:8; 6:11; 2 Cor 7:2, 4);

such instances of asyndeton correspond with the "loose," but sometimes also the "grand," style (see §3.2.2.1 below).

3.2.1.1.22. ISOCOLON (LAUSBERG §720-54)

The coordinated juxtaposition of two or more colons or commas where the colons or commas each manifest the same sentence sequence. The equality of the colons or commas means equality with regard to number of words and of syntactic grouping but not necessarily with regard to the number of syllables or syllable quantities, and not necessarily with regard to order of elements within each colon or comma.

Isocolon can vary in the extent of equivalent structure. Isocolon involving three colons is called tricolon (see §3.2.1.1.27 below). For higher levels of isocolon see above on distributio (§3.2.1.1.16), and below on paromoiosis (§3.2.1.1.26), disiunctio (§3.2.1.1.28), antithetical isocolon (§3.2.1.1.29), and interpretatio (§3.2.1.1.30). Apart from equality of the linguistic form, isocolon may also extend to the conceptual content. See also discussion of the thought figures "antitheton" (§3.2.1.2.11) and its subclass "commutatio" (§3.2.1.2.13).

υἱοῦ αὐτοῦ [A] τοῦ γενομένου [B] ἐκ σπέρματος Δαυὶδ [C] κατὰ σάρκα,

[A] τοῦ ὁρισθέντος υἱοῦ θεοῦ [B] ἐν δυνάμει [C] κατὰ πνεῦμα ἁγιωσύνης ἐξ ἀναστάσεως νεκρῶν, Ἰησοῦ Χριστοῦ τοῦ κυρίου ἡμῶν,

(Rom 1:3-4)

[A] ὅσοι γὰρ [B] ἀνόμως [C] ἥμαρτον, [D] ἀνόμως [E] καὶ ἀπολοῦνται·

καὶ [A] ὅσοι [B] ἐν νόμῳ [C] ἥμαρτον, [D] διὰ νόμου [E] κριθήσονται·

(Rom 2:12)

[A] ὁ κηρύσσων μὴ κλέπτειν [B] κλέπτεις;

[A] ὁ λέγων μὴ μοιχεύειν [B] μοιχεύεις;

[A] ὁ βδελυσσόμενος τὰ εἴδωλα [B] ἱεροσυλεῖς;

(Rom 2:21-23)

[A] τὸ μὲν γὰρ κρίμα [B] ἐξ ἑνὸς [C] εἰς κατάκριμα,

[A] τὸ δὲ χάρισμα [B] ἐκ πολλῶν παραπτωμάτων [C] εἰς δικαίωμα.

(Rom 5:16)

[A] καρδίᾳ γὰρ [B] πιστεύεται [C] εἰς δικαιοσύνην,
[A] στόματι δὲ [B] ὁμολογεῖται [C] εἰς σωτηρίαν.
(Rom 10:10)

In Rom 11:25, the parallel elements clarify that the first line refers to the hardening of "part of Israel" rather than to "a partial hardening":

πώρωσις [A] ἀπὸ μέρους [B] τῷ Ἰσραὴλ [C] γέγονεν
ἄχρις οὗ [A] τὸ πλήρωμα [B] τῶν ἐθνῶν [C] εἰσέλθῃ
(Rom 11:25)

[A] τῇ φιλαδελφίᾳ εἰς ἀλλήλους [B] φιλόστοργοι,
[A] τῇ τιμῇ ἀλλήλους [B] προηγούμενοι,
[A] τῇ σπουδῇ [B] μὴ ὀκνηροί,
[A] τῷ πνεύματι [B] ζέοντες,
[A] τῷ κυρίῳ [B] δουλεύοντες,
[A] τῇ ἐλπίδι [B] χαίροντες,
[A] τῇ θλίψει [B] ὑπομένοντες,
[A] τῇ προσευχῇ [B] προσκαρτεροῦντες,
[A] ταῖς χρείαις τῶν ἁγίων [B] κοινωνοῦντες,
[A] τὴν φιλοξενίαν [B] διώκοντες.
(Rom 12:10–13)

[A] χαίρειν [B] μετὰ χαιρόντων,
[A] κλαίειν [B] μετὰ κλαιόντων
(Rom 12:15)

καὶ [A] ὁ ἐσθίων [B] κυρίῳ [C] ἐσθίει, [D] εὐχαριστεῖ γὰρ τῷ θεῷ·
καὶ [A] ὁ μὴ ἐσθίων [B] κυρίῳ [C] οὐκ ἐσθίει καὶ [D] εὐχαριστεῖ τῷ θεῷ.
(Rom 14:6)

[A] οὐδεὶς γὰρ ἡμῶν [B] ἑαυτῷ [C] ζῇ καὶ
[A] οὐδεὶς [B] ἑαυτῷ [C] ἀποθνῄσκει·
(Rom 14:7)

[A] ἐάν τε γὰρ ζῶμεν, [B] τῷ κυρίῳ ζῶμεν,

[A] ἐάν τε ἀποθνήσκωμεν, [B] τῷ κυρίῳ ἀποθνήσκομεν.

(Rom 14:8)

ὅτι [A] τὸ μωρὸν τοῦ θεοῦ [B] σοφώτερον τῶν ἀνθρώπων ἐστὶν

καὶ [A] τὸ ἀσθενὲς τοῦ θεοῦ [B] ἰσχυρότερον τῶν ἀνθρώπων.

(1 Cor 1:25)

ἀλλὰ [A] τὰ μωρὰ τοῦ κόσμου [B] ἐξελέξατο ὁ θεὸς [C] ἵνα καταισχύνῃ τοὺς σοφούς,

καὶ [A] τὰ ἀσθενῆ τοῦ κόσμου [B] ἐξελέξατο ὁ θεὸς [C] ἵνα καταισχύνῃ τὰ ἰσχυρά,

καὶ [A] τὰ ἀγενῆ τοῦ κόσμου καὶ τὰ ἐξουθενημένα [B] ἐξελέξατο ὁ θεός, τὰ μὴ ὄντα, [C] ἵνα τὰ ὄντα καταργήσῃ.

(1 Cor 1:27-28)

λοιδορούμενοι εὐλογοῦμεν,

διωκόμενοι ἀνεχόμεθα,

δυσφημούμενοι παρακαλοῦμεν

(1 Cor 4:12-13)

Paul responds in 1 Cor 6:14, in parallel terms, to what is likely a Corinthian slogan, cited in 6:13:

[A] τὰ βρώματα τῇ κοιλίᾳ, [B] καὶ ἡ κοιλία τοῖς βρώμασιν· [C] ὁ δὲ θεὸς καὶ ταύτην καὶ ταῦτα καταργήσει.

[A] ὁ δὲ σῶμα οὐ τῇ πορνείᾳ ἀλλὰ τῷ κυρίῳ, [B] καὶ ὁ κύριος τῷ σώματι· [C] ὁ δὲ θεὸς καὶ τὸν κύριον ἤγειρεν καὶ ἡμᾶς ἐξεγερεῖ . . .

[A] ὁ κολλώμενος τῇ πόρνῃ [B] ἓν σῶμά ἐστιν;

[A] ὁ δὲ κολλώμενος τῷ κυρίῳ [B] ἓν πνεῦμά ἐστιν.

(1 Cor 6:16-17)

[A] ἕκαστος [B] τὴν ἑαυτοῦ γυναῖκα [C] ἐχέτω

[A] καὶ ἑκάστη [B] τὸν ἴδιον ἄνδρα [C] ἐχέτω.

(1 Cor 7:2)

[A] ἡ γυνὴ [B] τοῦ ἰδίου σώματος οὐκ ἐξουσιάζει [C] ἀλλ' ὁ ἀνήρ,

[A] ὁμοίως δὲ καὶ ὁ ἀνὴρ [B] τοῦ ἰδίου σώματος οὐκ ἐξουσιάζει [C] ἀλλ' ἡ γυνή.

(1 Cor 7:4)

[A] ἑκάστῳ [B] ὡς ἐμέρισεν ὁ κύριος,

[A] ἕκαστον [B] ὡς κέκληκεν ὁ θεός ...

(1 Cor 7:17)

[A] εἴ τις ἀδελφὸς γυναῖκα ἔχει ἄπιστον [B] καὶ αὕτη συνευδοκεῖ οἰκεῖν μετ' αὐτοῦ, [C] μὴ ἀφιέτω αὐτήν·

[A] καὶ γυνὴ εἴ τις ἔχει ἄνδρα ἄπιστον [B] καὶ οὗτος συνευδοκεῖ οἰκεῖν μετ' αὐτῆς, [C] μὴ ἀφιέτω τὸν ἄνδρα.

(1 Cor 7:12-13)

[A] ἡγίασται γὰρ [B] ὁ ἀνὴρ ὁ ἄπιστος [C] ἐν τῇ γυναικὶ

[A] καὶ ἡγίασται [B] ἡ γυνὴ ἡ ἄπιστος [C] ἐν τῷ ἀδελφῷ·

(1 Cor 7:14)

[A] τί γὰρ οἶδας, [B] γύναι, [C] εἰ τὸν ἄνδρα σώσεις;

[A] ἢ τί οἶδας, [B] ἄνερ, [C] εἰ τὴν γυναῖκα σώσεις;

(1 Cor 7:16)

[A] ἡ περιτομὴ [B] οὐδέν [C] ἐστιν

[A] καὶ ἡ ἀκροβυστία [B] οὐδέν [C] ἐστιν

(1 Cor 7:19)

[A] ἐὰν δὲ καὶ γαμήσῃς, [B] οὐχ ἥμαρτες,

[A] καὶ ἐὰν γήμῃ ἡ παρθένος, [B] οὐχ ἥμαρτεν·

(1 Cor 7:28)

[A] ὁ ἄγαμος μεριμνᾷ τὰ τοῦ κυρίου, [B] πῶς ἀρέσῃ τῷ κυρίῳ·

[A] ὁ δὲ γαμήσας μεριμνᾷ τὰ τοῦ κόσμου, [B] πῶς ἀρέσῃ τῇ γυναικί,

(1 Cor 7:32-33)

[A] ὁ γαμίζων [B] καλῶς [C] ποιεῖ
[A] ὁ μὴ γαμίζων [B] κρεῖσσον [C] ποιήσει
(1 Cor 7:38)

1 Corinthians 8:8 may cite a Corinthian slogan:
οὔτε [A] ἐὰν μὴ φάγωμεν [B] ὑστερούμεθα,
οὔτε [A] ἐὰν φάγωμεν [B] περισσεύομεν.

[A] εἰ ἡμεῖς [B] ὑμῖν [C] τὰ πνευματικὰ [D] ἐσπείραμεν,
μέγα [A] εἰ ἡμεῖς [B] ὑμῶν [C] τὰ σαρκικὰ [D] θερίσομεν
(1 Cor 9:11)

1 Cor 9:19–23 presents a series of seven parallel statements, each consisting of two, balanced parts (with parenthetical additions, parallel to each other, in lines 3 and 4). The first, sixth, and seventh lines are summary statements that are unpacked in the four enclosed lines:

[1] [A] πᾶσιν ἐμαυτὸν ἐδούλωσα [B] ἵνα τοὺς πλείονας κερδήσω· ἐγενόμην . . .
[2] [A] τοῖς Ἰουδαίοις ὡς Ἰουδαῖος [B] ἵνα Ἰουδαίους κερδήσω
[3] [A] τοῖς ὑπὸ νόμον ὡς ὑπὸ νόμον . . . [B] ἵνα τοὺς ὑπὸ νόμον κερδήσω
[4] [A] τοῖς ἀνόμοις ὡς ἄνομος . . . [B] ἵνα κερδάνω τοὺς ἀνόμους ἐγενόμην . . .
[5] [A] τοῖς ἀσθενέσιν ἀσθενής [B] ἵνα τοὺς ἀσθενεῖς κερδήσω
[6] [A] τοῖς πᾶσιν γέγονα πάντα [B] ἵνα πάντως τινὰς σώσω
[7] [A] πάντα δὲ ποιῶ διὰ τὸ εὐαγγέλιον [B] ἵνα συγκοινωνὸς αὐτοῦ γένωμαι.

[A] μηδὲ ἐκπειράζωμεν τὸν Χριστόν, [B] καθώς τινες αὐτῶν ἐπείρασαν [C] καὶ ὑπὸ τῶν ὄφεων ἀπώλλυντο.
[A] μηδὲ γογγύζετε, [B] καθάπερ τινὲς αὐτῶν ἐγόγγυσαν [C] καὶ ἀπώλοντο ὑπὸ τοῦ ὀλοθρευτοῦ.
(1 Cor 10:9–10)

[A] τὸ ποτήριον τῆς εὐλογίας ὃ εὐλογοῦμεν, [B] οὐχὶ κοινωνία ἐστὶν τοῦ αἵματος τοῦ Χριστοῦ;

[A] τὸν ἄρτον ὃν κλῶμεν, [B] οὐχὶ κοινωνία τοῦ σώματος τοῦ Χριστοῦ ἐστιν;

(1 Cor 10:16)

[A] οὐ δύνασθε [B] ποτήριον κυρίου πίνειν καὶ ποτήριον δαιμονίων,

[A] οὐ δύνασθε [B] τραπέζης κυρίου μετέχειν καὶ τραπέζης δαιμονίων.

(1 Cor 10:21)

[A] πᾶς ἀνὴρ προσευχόμενος ἢ προφητεύων [B] κατὰ κεφαλῆς ἔχων [C] καταισχύνει τὴν κεφαλὴν αὐτοῦ·

[A] πᾶσα δὲ γυνὴ προσευχομένη ἢ προφητεύουσα [B] ἀκατακαλύπτῳ τῇ κεφαλῇ [C] καταισχύνει τὴν κεφαλὴν αὐτῆς·

(1 Cor 11:4-5)

[A] Τοῦτό μού ἐστιν τὸ σῶμα τὸ ὑπὲρ ὑμῶν· [B] τοῦτο ποιεῖτε εἰς τὴν ἐμὴν ἀνάμνησιν . . .

[A] Τοῦτο τὸ ποτήριον ἡ καινὴ διαθήκη ἐστὶν ἐν τῷ ἐμῷ αἵματι· [B] τοῦτο ποιεῖτε, ὁσάκις ἐὰν πίνητε, εἰς τὴν ἐμὴν ἀνάμνησιν.

(1 Cor 11:24-25)

πάντα στέγει,

πάντα πιστεύει,

πάντα ἐλπίζει,

πάντα ὑπομένει.

(1 Cor 13:7)

[A] εἴτε δὲ προφητεῖαι, [B] καταργηθήσονται·

[A] εἴτε γλῶσσαι, [B] παύσονται·

[A] εἴτε γνῶσις, [B] καταργηθήσεται.

(1 Cor 13:8)

[A] ὁ λαλῶν γλώσσῃ [B] ἑαυτὸν [C] οἰκοδομεῖ·
[A] ὁ δὲ προφητεύων [B] ἐκκλησίαν [C] οἰκοδομεῖ.
(1 Cor 14:4)

[A] προσεύξομαι τῷ πνεύματι, [B] προσεύξομαι δὲ καὶ τῷ νοΐ·
[A] ψαλῶ τῷ πνεύματι, [B] ψαλῶ δὲ καὶ τῷ νοΐ.
(1 Cor 14:15)

[A] ἢ ἀφ' ὑμῶν [B] ὁ λόγος τοῦ θεοῦ ἐξῆλθεν,
[A] ἢ εἰς ὑμᾶς μόνους [B] κατήντησεν;
(1 Cor 14:36)

1 Corinthians 15:42–49 contains five instances of isocolon (vv. 42–43, 45, 47, 48, 49):

[A] σπείρεται ἐν φθορᾷ, [B] ἐγείρεται ἐν ἀφθαρσίᾳ·
[A] σπείρεται σῶμα ψυχικόν, [B] ἐγείρεται σῶμα πνευματικόν.
[A] σπείρεται ἐν ἀσθενείᾳ, [B] ἐγείρεται ἐν δυνάμει·
(1 Cor 15:42–43)

Ἐγένετο [A] ὁ πρῶτος ἄνθρωπος Ἀδὰμ [B] εἰς ψυχὴν ζῶσαν.
[A] Ὁ ἔσχατος Ἀδὰμ [B] εἰς πνεῦμα ζῳοποιοῦν.
(1 Cor 15:45)

[A] ὁ πρῶτος ἄνθρωπος [B] ἐκ γῆς χοϊκός,
[A] ὁ δεύτερος ἄνθρωπος [B] ἐξ οὐρανοῦ.
(1 Cor 15:47)

[A] οἷος ὁ χοϊκός, [B] τοιοῦτοι καὶ οἱ χοϊκοί,
[A] καὶ οἷος ὁ ἐπουράνιος, [B] τοιοῦτοι καὶ οἱ ἐπουράνιοι.
(1 Cor 15:48)

[A] καὶ καθὼς ἐφορέσαμεν [B] τὴν εἰκόνα [C] τοῦ χοϊκοῦ,
[A] φορέσομεν καὶ [B] τὴν εἰκόνα [C] τοῦ ἐπουρανίου.
(1 Cor 15:49)

δεῖ γὰρ [A] τὸ φθαρτὸν τοῦτο [B] ἐνδύσασθαι [C] ἀφθαρσίαν
καὶ [A] τὸ θνητὸν τοῦτο [B] ἐνδύσασθαι [C] ἀθανασίαν.
(1 Cor 15:53; cf. v. 54)

[A] εἴτε δὲ θλιβόμεθα, [B] ὑπὲρ τῆς ὑμῶν παρακλήσεως καὶ σωτηρίας·
[A] εἴτε παρακαλούμεθα, [B] ὑπὲρ τῆς ὑμῶν παρακλήσεως τῆς ἐνεργουμένης ἐν ὑπομονῇ τῶν αὐτῶν παθημάτων ὧν καὶ ἡμεῖς πάσχομεν.
(2 Cor 1:6)

οὐδένα ἠδικήσαμεν,
οὐδένα ἐφθείραμεν,
οὐδένα ἐπλεονεκτήσαμεν.
(2 Cor 7:2)

ἔξωθεν μάχαι,
ἔσωθεν φόβοι.
(2 Cor 7:5)

Isocolon occurs throughout 2 Cor 11:21–29, in several distinct blocks.

[A] Ἑβραῖοί εἰσιν; [B] κἀγώ.
[A] Ἰσραηλῖταί εἰσιν; [B] κἀγώ.
[A] σπέρμα Ἀβραάμ εἰσιν; [B] κἀγώ.

[A] διάκονοι Χριστοῦ εἰσιν; παραφρονῶν λαλῶ, [B] ὑπὲρ ἐγώ·
[A] ἐν κόποις [B] περισσοτέρως,
[A] ἐν φυλακαῖς [B] περισσοτέρως,
[A] ἐν πληγαῖς [B] ὑπερβαλλόντως,
[A] ἐν θανάτοις [B] πολλάκις·
ὑπὸ Ἰουδαίων

[A] πεντάκις τεσσαράκοντα παρὰ μίαν [B] ἔλαβον,
[A] τρὶς [B] ἐραβδίσθην,

[A] ἅπαξ [B] ἐλιθάσθην,
[A] τρὶς [B] ἐναυάγησα,

[A] νυχθήμερον [B] ἐν τῷ βυθῷ πεποίηκα·
[A] ὁδοιπορίαις [B] πολλάκις,
[A] κινδύνοις [B] ποταμῶν,
[A] κινδύνοις [B] λῃστῶν,
[A] κινδύνοις [B] ἐκ γένους,
[A] κινδύνοις [B] ἐξ ἐθνῶν,
[A] κινδύνοις [B] ἐν πόλει,
[A] κινδύνοις [B] ἐν ἐρημίᾳ,
[A] κινδύνοις [B] ἐν θαλάσσῃ,
[A] κινδύνοις [B] ἐν ψευδαδέλφοις,

κόπῳ καὶ μόχθῳ,
ἐν ἀγρυπνίαις πολλάκις,
ἐν λιμῷ καὶ δίψει,
ἐν νηστείαις πολλάκις,
ἐν ψύχει καὶ γυμνότητι·
[omit v. 28]

[A] τίς ἀσθενεῖ, [B] καὶ οὐκ ἀσθενῶ;
[A] τίς σκανδαλίζεται, [B] καὶ οὐκ ἐγὼ πυροῦμαι;
(2 Cor 11:21-29)

[A] ὁ δὲ μεσίτης [B] ἑνὸς [C] οὐκ ἔστιν,
[A] ὁ δὲ θεὸς [B] εἷς [C] ἐστιν.
(Gal 3:20)

[A] οὐκ ἔνι [B] Ἰουδαῖος οὐδὲ Ἕλλην,
[A] οὐκ ἔνι [B] δοῦλος οὐδὲ ἐλεύθερος,
[A] οὐκ ἔνι [B] ἄρσεν καὶ θῆλυ·
(Gal 3:28)

[A] τὸ ζῆν [B] Χριστὸς καὶ
[A] τὸ ἀποθανεῖν [B] κέρδος.
(Phil 1:21)

[A] ἐμοὶ μὲν [B] οὐκ ὀκνηρόν,
[A] ὑμῖν δὲ [B] ἀσφαλές.
(Phil 3:1)

[A] οἱ γὰρ καθεύδοντες [B] νυκτὸς καθεύδουσιν,
[A] καὶ οἱ μεθυσκόμενοι [B] νυκτὸς μεθύουσιν·
(1 Thess 5:7)

[A] νουθετεῖτε [B] τοὺς ἀτάκτους,
[A] παραμυθεῖσθε [B] τοὺς ὀλιγοψύχους,
[A] ἀντέχεσθε [B] τῶν ἀσθενῶν,
[A] μακροθυμεῖτε [B] πρὸς πάντας.
(1 Thess 5:14)

In some examples syntactical equivalency is less exact:

In 1 Cor 2:11, some corresponding elements are transposed:
[A] τίς γὰρ οἶδεν ἀνθρώπων [B] τὰ τοῦ ἀνθρώπου [C] εἰ μὴ τὸ πνεῦμα τοῦ ἀνθρώπου τὸ ἐν αὐτῷ;
[B] τὰ τοῦ θεοῦ [A] οὐδεὶς ἔγνωκεν [C] εἰ μὴ τὸ πνεῦμα τοῦ θεοῦ.
With less exact syntactical equivalency in part [B]:

[A] ὅταν παραδιδῷ [B] τὴν βασιλείαν τῷ θεῷ καὶ πατρί,
[A] ὅταν καταργήσῃ [B] πᾶσαν ἀρχὴν καὶ πᾶσαν ἐξουσίαν καὶ δύναμιν.
(1 Cor 15:24)

[A] ἐγγεγραμμένη [B] ἐν ταῖς καρδίαις ἡμῶν,
[A] γινωσκομένη καὶ ἀναγινωσκομένη [B] ὑπὸ πάντων ἀνθρώπων·
[A] φανερούμενοι [B] ὅτι ἐστὲ ἐπιστολὴ Χριστοῦ

[A] διακονηθεῖσα [B] ὑφ' ἡμῶν,

[A] ἐγγεγραμμένη [B] οὐ μέλανι ἀλλὰ πνεύματι θεοῦ ζῶντος . . .

(2 Cor 3:2-3)

[A] ὁ εὐλογήσας [B] ἡμᾶς [C] ἐν πάσῃ εὐλογίᾳ πνευματικῇ [D] ἐν τοῖς ἐπουρανίοις [E] ἐν Χριστῷ,

καθὼς [A] ἐξελέξατο [B] ἡμᾶς [C] ἐν αὐτῷ πρὸ καταβολῆς κόσμου, εἶναι ἡμᾶς ἁγίους καὶ ἀμώμους κατενώπιον αὐτοῦ ἐν ἀγάπῃ,

[A] προορίσας [B] ἡμᾶς [C] εἰς υἱοθεσίαν [D] διὰ Ἰησοῦ Χριστοῦ [E] εἰς αὐτόν, . . .

(Eph 1:3-5)

στῆτε οὖν [A] περιζωσάμενοι [B] τὴν ὀσφὺν ὑμῶν [C] ἐν ἀληθείᾳ,

καὶ [A] ἐνδυσάμενοι [B] τὸν θώρακα [C] τῆς δικαιοσύνης,

καὶ [A] ὑποδησάμενοι [B] τοὺς πόδας [C] ἐν ἑτοιμασίᾳ τοῦ εὐαγγελίου τῆς εἰρήνης,

ἐν πᾶσιν [A] ἀναλαβόντες [B] τὸν θυρεὸν [C] τῆς πίστεως,

(Eph 6:14-16)

[A] ἀπεκδυσάμενοι [B] τὸν παλαιὸν ἄνθρωπον [C] σὺν ταῖς πράξεσιν [D] αὐτοῦ,

[A] καὶ ἐνδυσάμενοι [B] τὸν νέον τὸν ἀνακαινούμενον [C] εἰς ἐπίγνωσιν [D] κατ' εἰκόνα τοῦ κτίσαντος αὐτόν,

(Col 2:9-10)

[A] καὶ ἡ εἰρήνη τοῦ Χριστοῦ [B] βραβευέτω [C] ἐν ταῖς καρδίαις ὑμῶν, . . .

[A] ὁ λόγος τοῦ Χριστοῦ [B] ἐνοικείτω [C] ἐν ὑμῖν πλουσίως, ἐν πάσῃ σοφίᾳ

(Col 3:15, 16)

1 Thessalonians 5:16-22 contains two blocks of material, the first consisting of an adverb / adverbial phrase + a verb, and the second of a direct object / predicate complement + verb:

[A] Πάντοτε [B] χαίρετε,

[A] ἀδιαλείπτως [B] προσεύχεσθε,

[A] ἐν παντὶ [B] εὐχαριστεῖτε·

τοῦτο γὰρ θέλημα θεοῦ ἐν Χριστῷ Ἰησοῦ εἰς ὑμᾶς.

[A] τὸ πνεῦμα [B] μὴ σβέννυτε,

[A] προφητείας [B] μὴ ἐξουθενεῖτε·

[A] πάντα δὲ [B] δοκιμάζετε,

[A] τὸ καλὸν [B] κατέχετε,

[A] ἀπὸ παντὸς εἴδους πονηροῦ [B] ἀπέχεσθε.

(1 Thess 5:16–22)

Where Paul outlines multiple contingencies (which are sometimes antithetical in content), he often uses the same structure for each of them:

[A] ἐὰν δὲ ἀποθάνῃ ὁ ἀνήρ, [B] κατήργηται ἀπὸ τοῦ νόμου τοῦ ἀνδρός. [C] ἄρα οὖν ζῶντος τοῦ ἀνδρὸς μοιχαλὶς χρηματίσει· [D] ἐὰν γένηται ἀνδρὶ ἑτέρῳ·

[A] ἐὰν δὲ ἀποθάνῃ ὁ ἀνήρ, [B] ἐλευθέρα ἐστὶν ἀπὸ τοῦ νόμου, [C] τοῦ μὴ εἶναι αὐτὴν μοιχαλίδα [D] γενομένην ἀνδρὶ ἑτέρῳ.

(Rom 7:2–3)

[A] εἴ τινος τὸ ἔργον [B] μενεῖ ὃ ἐποικοδόμησεν, [C] μισθὸν λήμψεται·

[A] εἴ τινος τὸ ἔργον [B] κατακαήσεται, [C] ζημιωθήσεται, αὐτὸς δὲ σωθήσεται . . .

(1 Cor 3:14–15)

[A] εἴ τις [B] δοκεῖ ἐγνωκέναι [C] τι, [D] οὔπω ἔγνω [E] καθὼς δεῖ γνῶναι·

[A] εἰ δέ τις [B] ἀγαπᾷ [C] τὸν θεόν, [D] οὗτος ἔγνωσται [E] ὑπ' αὐτοῦ.

(1 Cor 8:2–3)

[A] εἷς θεὸς ὁ πατήρ, [B] ἐξ οὗ τὰ πάντα [C] καὶ ἡμεῖς εἰς αὐτόν,

καὶ [A] εἷς κύριος Ἰησοῦς Χριστός, [B] δι' οὗ τὰ πάντα [C] καὶ ἡμεῖς δι' αὐτοῦ.

(1 Cor 8:6)

[A] εἰ γὰρ ἑκὼν [B] τοῦτο πράσσω, [C] μισθὸν ἔχω·
[A] εἰ δὲ ἄκων [B] —, [C] οἰκονομίαν πεπίστευμαι.
(1 Cor 9:17)

[1] [A] Πᾶν τὸ ἐν μακέλλῳ πωλούμενον ἐσθίετε [B] μηδὲν ἀνακρίνοντες διὰ τὴν συνείδησιν·

...

[2] εἴ τις καλεῖ ὑμᾶς τῶν ἀπίστων καὶ θέλετε πορεύεσθαι,
[A] πᾶν τὸ παρατιθέμενον ὑμῖν ἐσθίετε [B] μηδὲν ἀνακρίνοντες διὰ τὴν συνείδησιν.
[3] ἐὰν δέ τις ὑμῖν εἴπῃ· τοῦτο ἱερόθυτόν ἐστιν,
[A] μὴ ἐσθίετε [B] δι' ἐκεῖνον τὸν μηνύσαντα καὶ τὴν συνείδησιν·
(1 Cor 10:25, 27-28)

[A] ἐὰν διαστολὴν τοῖς φθόγγοις μὴ δῷ, [B] πῶς γνωσθήσεται τὸ αὐλούμενον ἢ τὸ κιθαριζόμενον;
καὶ γὰρ [A] ἐὰν ἄδηλον σάλπιγξ φωνὴν δῷ, [B] τίς παρασκευάσεται εἰς πόλεμον;
οὕτως καὶ ὑμεῖς διὰ τῆς γλώσσης [A] ἐὰν μὴ εὔσημον λόγον δῶτε, [B] πῶς γνωσθήσεται τὸ λαλούμενον;
(1 Cor 14:7-9)

[A] Ἐὰν οὖν συνέλθῃ ἡ ἐκκλησία ὅλη ἐπὶ τὸ αὐτὸ καὶ πάντες λαλῶσιν γλώσσαις, [B] εἰσέλθωσιν δὲ ἰδιῶται ἢ ἄπιστοι, [C] οὐκ ἐροῦσιν ὅτι μαίνεσθε;
[A] ἐὰν δὲ πάντες προφητεύωσιν, [B] εἰσέλθῃ δέ τις ἄπιστος ἢ ἰδιώτης, [C] ἐλέγχεται ὑπὸ πάντων, ἀνακρίνεται ὑπὸ πάντων ...
(1 Cor 14:23-24)

Similes often come in parallel terms:

ὅμως [A] τὰ ἄψυχα φωνὴν διδόντα, εἴτε αὐλὸς εἴτε κιθάρα, [B] ἐὰν διαστολὴν τοῖς φθόγγοις μὴ δῷ, [C] πῶς γνωσθήσεται τὸ αὐλούμενον ἢ τὸ κιθαριζόμενον; ...

οὕτως καὶ [A] ὑμεῖς διὰ τῆς γλώσσης [B] ἐὰν μὴ εὔσημον λόγον δῶτε, [C] πῶς γνωσθήσεται τὸ λαλούμενον;

(1 Cor 14:7, 9)

Answers to questions often follow the structure of the question; e.g., Rom 11:1, 2; 6:1, 2; 1 Cor 12:19, 20.

In some instances synonymous expressions are substituted at the corresponding points in the colons, apparently only for the sake of variety:

In the distributio (§3.2.1.1.16) in 1 Cor 12:8–11, the first three sentences constitute an isocolon in which multiple terms are varied in constituent [A], and constituent [B] is either expressed in various synonymous ways or alternately included or omitted:

[A] ᾧ μὲν γὰρ διὰ τοῦ πνεύματος δίδοται λόγος σοφίας [B omitted], [A'] **ἄλλῳ** δὲ λόγος γνώσεως [B'] **κατὰ τὸ αὐτὸ πνεῦμα**,

[A] **ἑτέρῳ** πίστις [B] **ἐν τῷ αὐτῷ πνεύματι**, [A'] **ἄλλῳ** δὲ χαρίσματα ἰαμάτων [B'] **ἐν τῷ ἑνὶ πνεύματι**,

[A] **ἄλλῳ** δὲ ἐνεργήματα δυνάμεων [B omitted], [A'] **ἄλλῳ** [δὲ] προφητεία, ἄλλῳ [δὲ] διακρίσεις πνευμάτων [B omitted],

πάντα δὲ ταῦτα ἐνεργεῖ [B] **τὸ ἓν καὶ τὸ αὐτὸ πνεῦμα**, διαιροῦν [A] **ἰδίᾳ ἑκάστῳ** καθὼς βούλεται.

3.2.1.1.23. CHIASM (LAUSBERG, §723)

Chiasm consists in the cross-arrangement of the corresponding elements in an antithetical isocolon, the purpose of the cross-arrangment being to reinforce the antithesis (cf. Lausberg, §723; p. 322, n. 2).

A chiastic structure makes more visible the antithesis between "there is not a boast to me" and "woe it is to me" in 1 Cor 9:16:

[A] ἐὰν γὰρ εὐαγγελίζωμαι, [B] οὐκ ἔστιν μοι **καύχημα**· [C] ἀνάγκη γάρ μοι ἐπίκειται· [B] **οὐαὶ** γάρ μοί ἐστιν [A] ἐὰν μὴ εὐαγγελίσωμαι.

ὃς [A] εἰς ὑμᾶς [B] οὐκ ἀσθενεῖ [B] ἀλλὰ δυνατεῖ [A] ἐν ὑμῖν (2 Cor 13:3)

[A] ἐναρξάμενοι [B] πνεύματι [B] νῦν σαρκὶ [A] ἐπιτελεῖσθε; (Gal 3:3)

[A] Γίνεσθε [B] ὡς ἐγώ, [B] ὅτι κἀγὼ [A] ὡς ὑμεῖς. (Gal 4:12)

[A] εἰ ζῶμεν [B] πνεύματι, [B] πνεύματι [A] καὶ στοιχῶμεν. (Gal 5:25)

[A] ἐταπείνωσεν [B] ἑαυτὸν . . . διὸ καὶ ὁ θεὸς [B] αὐτὸν [A] ὑπερύψωσεν. (Phil 2:8, 9)

Black notes an extensive chiasm in Rom 12:9–13,[12] though the structure does not correspond with an antithesis:

Ἡ ἀγάπη ἀνυπόκριτος.

[A]
    [1] ἀποστυγοῦντες τὸ πονηρόν,
    [2] κολλώμενοι τῷ ἀγαθῷ,
    [B]
        [1] τῇ φιλαδελφίᾳ εἰς ἀλλήλους φιλόστοργοι,
        [2] τῇ τιμῇ ἀλλήλους προηγούμενοι,
        [3] τῇ σπουδῇ μὴ ὀκνηροί,
        [C]
            [1] τῷ πνεύματι ζέοντες,
            [2] τῷ κυρίῳ δουλεύοντες,
    [B]
        [1] τῇ ἐλπίδι χαίροντες,
        [2] τῇ θλίψει ὑπομένοντες,
        [3] τῇ προσευχῇ προσκαρτεροῦντες,
[A]
    [1] ταῖς χρείαις τῶν ἁγίων κοινωνοῦντες,
    [2] τὴν φιλοξενίαν διώκοντες.

Jeremias has shown that chiasmus involving sentence parts is plentiful in Paul's letters, and offers additional examples in Rom 2:7–10; 10:9–10; 11:22,

---

12. Black, "Pauline Love Command."

33-35; 14:7-9; 1 Cor 1:24-25; 4:10, 13b; 7:3, 22; 10:3-4; 13:2, 4; 15:50-54; Gal 5:17; Phil 1:15-16; 3:10; 4:12; Col 3:11; 1 Thess 4:15-17; Phlm 5.[13]

Not all instances of cross-arrangement can be considered ornamental. Frequently, the change of order is due only to changes of emphasis (e.g., ἐξεκλάσθησαν κλάδοι ἵνα ἐγὼ ἐγκεντρισθῶ, Rom 11:19; ζηλοῦτε τὸ προφητεύειν, καὶ τὸ λαλεῖν γλώσσαις μὴ κωλύετε, 1 Cor 14:39; δι᾽ ὑμῶν διελθεῖν εἰς Μακεδονίαν καὶ πάλιν ἀπὸ Μακεδονίας ἐλθεῖν πρὸς ὑμᾶς, 2 Cor 1:16; τὰ ἀρχαῖα παρῆλθεν, ἰδοὺ γέγονεν καινά, 2 Cor 11:7).

For instances of chiasm involving antithesis, see below under antitheton (§3.2.1.2.11).

3.2.1.1.24. *Homoioteleuton (Lausberg §725-28)*

The use of homonymous endings (not words) in successive colons. Many instances of isocolon (§3.2.1.1.22) and tricolon (§3.2.1.1.27) involve homoioteleuton. For repetition of final words, see antistrophe (§3.2.1.1.6) and symploche (§3.2.1.1.7).

ὅσοι γὰρ ἀνόμως ἥμαρτον, ἀνόμως καὶ ἀπολοῦ**νται**·
καὶ ὅσοι ἐν νόμῳ ἥμαρτον, διὰ νόμου κριθήσο**νται**·
(Rom 2:12)

ὁ κηρύσσων μὴ κλέπτειν κλέπτ**εις**;
ὁ λέγων μὴ μοιχεύειν μοιχεύ**εις**;
ὁ βδελυσσόμενος τὰ εἴδωλα ἱεροσυλ**εῖς**;
(Rom 2:21-23)

τὸ μὲν γὰρ κρίμα ἐξ ἑνὸς εἰς κατάκρι**μα**,
τὸ δὲ χάρισμα ἐκ πολλῶν παραπτωμάτων εἰς δικαίω**μα**.
(Rom 5:16)

καρδίᾳ γὰρ πιστεύεται εἰς δικαιοσύνη**ν**,
στόματι δὲ ὁμολογεῖται εἰς σωτηρία**ν**.
(Rom 10:10)

13. Jeremias, "Chiasmus in den Paulusbriefen," 145-52.

τῇ φιλαδελφίᾳ εἰς ἀλλήλους φιλόστοργ**οι**,
τῇ τιμῇ ἀλλήλους προηγούμεν**οι**,
τῇ σπουδῇ μὴ ὀκνηρ**οί**,
τῷ πνεύματι ζέοντ**ες**,
τῷ κυρίῳ δουλεύοντ**ες**,
τῇ ἐλπίδι χαίροντ**ες**,
τῇ θλίψει ὑπομένοντ**ες**,
τῇ προσευχῇ προσκαρτεροῦντ**ες**,
ταῖς χρείαις τῶν ἁγίων κοινωνοῦντ**ες**,
τὴν φιλοξενίαν διώκοντ**ες**.
(Rom 12:10–13)

εἰ ἡμεῖς ὑμῖν τὰ πνευματικὰ ἐσπείρα**μεν** . . .
εἰ ἡμεῖς ὑμῶν τὰ σαρκικὰ θερίσο**μεν**
(1 Cor 9:11)

πάντα ἔξεστιν ἀλλ᾽ οὐ πάντα συμφέρ**ει**·
πάντα ἔξεστιν ἀλλ᾽ οὐ πάντα οἰκοδομ**εῖ**.
(1 Cor 10:23)

Εἴτε οὖν ἐσθίε**τε** εἴτε πίνε**τε** εἴτε τι ποιεῖ**τε**, πάντα εἰς δόξαν θεοῦ ποιεῖ**τε**
(1 Cor 10:31)

εἴτε δὲ προφητεῖαι, καταργηθήσον**ται**·
εἴτε γλῶσσαι, παύσον**ται**·
εἴτε γνῶσις, καταργηθήσε**ται**.
(1 Cor 13:8)

σπείρεται ἐν φθορ**ᾷ**, ἐγείρεται ἐν ἀφθαρσί**ᾳ**·
σπείρεται ἐν ἀτιμί**ᾳ**, ἐγείρεται ἐν δόξ**ῃ**·
σπείρεται ἐν ἀσθενεί**ᾳ**, ἐγείρεται ἐν δυνάμει·
(1 Cor 15:42–43)

οὐδένα ἠδικήσ**αμεν**,
οὐδένα ἐφθείρ**αμεν**,
οὐδένα ἐπλεονεκτήσ**αμεν**.
(2 Cor 7:2)

ἐν κόποις περισσοτέρ**ως**,
ἐν φυλακαῖς περισσοτέρ**ως**,
ἐν πληγαῖς ὑπερβαλλόντ**ως**,
ἐν θανάτοις πολλάκι**ς**.
(2 Cor 11:23)

ὅσα ἐστὶν ἀληθῆ, ὅσα σεμνά, ὅσα δίκαια, ὅσα ἁγνά, ὅσα προσφιλῆ, ὅσα εὔφημα, εἴ τις ἀρετὴ καὶ εἴ τις ἔπαινος, ταῦτα λογίζεσ**θε**·
ἃ καὶ ἐμάθετε καὶ παρελάβετε καὶ ἠκούσατε καὶ εἴδετε ἐν ἐμοί, ταῦτα πράσσε**τε**·
(Phil 4:8–9)

εἰ γὰρ καὶ τῇ σαρκὶ ἄπ**ειμι**,
ἀλλὰ τῷ πνεύματι σὺν ὑμῖν **εἰμι**,
(Col 2:5)

οἱ γὰρ καθεύδοντες νυκτὸς καθεύδ**ουσιν**,
καὶ οἱ μεθυσκόμενοι νυκτὸς μεθύ**ουσιν**·
(1 Thess 5:7)

Note also -ν in Rom 6:19; -ει in Rom 9:18; -όντων in Rom 12:15; -μεν in Rom 14:8; -οῦ and -ων in 1 Cor 1:25; -εῖσθε in 1 Cor 6:7; -έτω in 1 Cor 7:2; -ει in 1 Cor 7:4; -εις in 1 Cor 7:16; -ου in 1 Cor 7:32–33; -ει in 1 Cor 7:38; -ω in 1 Cor 9:19–23; -μεν in 1 Cor 10:16; -ει in 1 Cor 10:23; 13:7; -μενον in 1 Cor 14:7, 9; -εν in 1 Cor 14:36; -ησόμεθα in 1 Cor 15:51; -σίαν in 1 Cor 15:53; -α in 2 Cor 4:18; -ν in Gal 6:8; -εσθαι and -ωνται in Gal 6:12, 13; -τε in 1 Thess 5:16–22.

3.2.1.1.25. HOMOIOPTOTON (LAUSBERG §729-31)

Use of the same case endings or similar sounds near each other (but not necessarily at the end of colons or commas). Excessive alliteration, however, is considered a vice; see under Paronomasia (§3.2.1.1.9), and the mention there of homoioprophoron, i.e., alliteration.

τὸ μὲν γὰρ κρί**μα** ἐξ ἑνὸς εἰς κατάκρι**μα**, τὸ δὲ χάρισ**μα** ἐκ πολλῶν παραπτωμάτων εἰς δικαίω**μα**.

(Rom 5:16)

καρδίᾳ γὰρ πιστεύεται εἰς δικαιοσύνη<u>ν</u>, στόματι δὲ ὁμολογεῖται εἰς σωτηρία<u>ν</u>.

(Rom 10:10)

εἰ δὲ τὸ παράπτω**μα** αὐτῶν πλοῦτος κόσμου καὶ τὸ ἥττη**μα** αὐτῶν πλοῦτος ἐθνῶν, πόσῳ μᾶλλον τὸ πλήρω**μα** αὐτῶν. (Rom 11:12)

τῇ φιλαδελφίᾳ εἰς ἀλλήλους φιλόστοργ**οι**,
τῇ τιμῇ ἀλλήλους προηγούμεν**οι**,
τῇ σπουδῇ μὴ ὀκνηρ**οί**,
τῷ πνεύματι ζέοντ**ες**,
τῷ κυρίῳ δουλεύοντ**ες**,
τῇ ἐλπίδι χαίροντ**ες**,
τῇ θλίψει ὑπομένοντ**ες**,
τῇ προσευχῇ προσκαρτεροῦντ**ες**,
ταῖς χρείαις τῶν ἁγίων κοινωνοῦντ**ες**,
τὴν φιλοξενίαν διώκοντ**ες**.

(Rom 12:10-13)

σπείρεται ἐν φθορ<u>ᾷ</u>, ἐγείρεται ἐν ἀφθαρσί<u>ᾳ</u>·
σπείρεται ἐν ἀτιμί<u>ᾳ</u>, ἐγείρεται ἐν δόξ<u>ῃ</u>·
σπείρεται ἐν ἀσθενεί<u>ᾳ</u>, ἐγείρεται ἐν δυνάμ<u>ει</u>·

(1 Cor 15:42-43)

τὰ γὰρ βλεπόμενα πρόσκαιρ**α**,
τὰ δὲ μὴ βλεπόμενα αἰώνι**α**.
(2 Cor 4:18)

3.2.1.1.26. PAROMOIOSIS (LAUSBERG §732)

A kind of isocolon that extends the equivalence between colons/commas to several components and also includes homoeoteleuton (Lausberg §725) and homoeoptoton (Lausberg §729).

ὅσοι γὰρ ἀνόμως ἥμαρτον, ἀνόμως καὶ ἀπολοῦ**νται**·
καὶ ὅσοι ἐν νόμῳ ἥμαρτον, διὰ νόμου κριθήσο**νται**·
(Rom 2:12)

τὸ μὲν γὰρ κρίμα ἐξ ἑνὸς εἰς κατάκρι**μα**,
τὸ δὲ χάρισμα ἐκ πολλῶν παραπτωμάτων εἰς δικαίω**μα**.
(Rom 5:16)

καρδίᾳ γὰρ πιστεύεται εἰς δικαιοσύνη**ν**,
στόματι δὲ ὁμολογεῖται εἰς σωτηρία**ν**.
(Rom 10:10)

τῇ φιλαδελφίᾳ εἰς ἀλλήλους φιλόστοργ**οι**,
τῇ τιμῇ ἀλλήλους προηγούμεν**οι**,
τῇ σπουδῇ μὴ ὀκνηρ**οί**,
τῷ πνεύματι ζέοντ**ες**,
τῷ κυρίῳ δουλεύοντ**ες**,
τῇ ἐλπίδι χαίροντ**ες**,
τῇ θλίψει ὑπομένοντ**ες**,
τῇ προσευχῇ προσκαρτεροῦντ**ες**,
ταῖς χρείαις τῶν ἁγίων κοινωνοῦντ**ες**,
τὴν φιλοξενίαν διώκοντ**ες**.
(Rom 12:10–13)

εἰ ἡμεῖς ὑμῖν τὰ πνευματικὰ ἐσπείρα**μεν** ...
εἰ ἡμεῖς ὑμῶν τὰ σαρκικὰ θερίσο**μεν**
(1 Cor 9:11)

πάντα ἔξεστιν ἀλλ' οὐ πάντα συμφέρ**ει**·
πάντα ἔξεστιν ἀλλ' οὐ πάντα οἰκοδομ**εῖ**.
(1 Cor 10:23)

εἴτε δὲ προφητεῖαι, καταργηθήσον**ται**·
εἴτε γλῶσσαι, παύσον**ται**·
εἴτε γνῶσις, καταργηθήσε**ται**.
(1 Cor 13:8)

σπείρεται ἐν φθορ**ᾷ**, ἐγείρεται ἐν ἀφθαρσίᾳ·
σπείρεται ἐν ἀτιμί**ᾳ**, ἐγείρεται ἐν δόξῃ·
σπείρεται ἐν ἀσθενεί**ᾳ**, ἐγείρεται ἐν δυνάμει·
(1 Cor 15:42–43)

οὐδένα ἠδικήσ**αμεν**,
οὐδένα ἐφθείρ**αμεν**,
οὐδένα ἐπλεονεκτήσ**αμεν**.
(2 Cor 7:2)

ἐν κόποις περισσοτέρ**ως**,
ἐν φυλακαῖς περισσοτέρ**ως**,
ἐν πληγαῖς ὑπερβαλλόντ**ως**,
ἐν θανάτοις πολλάκι**ς**.
(2 Cor 11:23)

εἰ γὰρ καὶ τῇ σαρκὶ ἄπ**ειμι**,
ἀλλὰ τῷ πνεύματι σὺν ὑμῖν **εἰμι**,
(Col 2:5)

οἱ γὰρ καθεύδοντες νυκτὸς καθεύδ**ουσιν**,
καὶ οἱ μεθυσκόμενοι νυκτὸς μεθύ**ουσιν**·
(1 Thess 5:7)

Many other examples of homoioteleuton (§3.2.1.1.24) cited above also qualify as paromoiosis.

3.2.1.1.27. TRICOLON (LAUSBERG §733)

Isocolon that consists of three colons.

[A] ὁ κηρύσσων μὴ κλέπτειν [B] κλέπτεις;
[A] ὁ λέγων μὴ μοιχεύειν [B] μοιχεύεις;
[A] ὁ βδελυσσόμενος τὰ εἴδωλα [B] ἱεροσυλεῖς;
(Rom 2:21–23)

[A] τίς ἐγκαλέσει κατὰ ἐκλεκτῶν θεοῦ; [B] θεὸς ὁ δικαιῶν·
[A] τίς ὁ κατακρινῶν; [B] Χριστὸς [Ἰησοῦς] ὁ ἀποθανών, ...
[A] τίς ἡμᾶς χωρίσει ἀπὸ τῆς ἀγάπης τοῦ Χριστοῦ; [B omitted]
(Rom 8:33–34)

ἐξ αὐτοῦ
καὶ δι' αὐτοῦ
καὶ εἰς αὐτὸν τὰ πάντα
(Rom 11:36)

μὴ κώμοις καὶ μέθαις,
μὴ κοίταις καὶ ἀσελγείαις,
μὴ ἔριδι καὶ ζήλῳ
(Rom 13:13)

[A] ποῦ σοφός; [B] ποῦ γραμματεύς; [C] ποῦ συζητητὴς
(1 Cor 1:20)

With an adjunct (< >) applying to all three colons (see Adiunctio, §743):

οὐ πολλοὶ σοφοὶ <κατὰ σάρκα>,

οὐ πολλοὶ δυνατοί,

οὐ πολλοὶ εὐγενεῖς·

(1 Cor 1:26)

[A] τὰ μωρὰ τοῦ κόσμου ἐξελέξατο ὁ θεός, [B] ἵνα καταισχύνῃ τοὺς σοφούς, καὶ

[A] τὰ ἀσθενῆ τοῦ κόσμου ἐξελέξατο ὁ θεός, [B] ἵνα καταισχύνῃ τὰ ἰσχυρά, καὶ

[A] τὰ ἀγενῆ τοῦ κόσμου καὶ τὰ ἐξουθενημένα ἐξελέξατο ὁ θεός, τὰ μὴ ὄντα, [B] ἵνα τὰ ὄντα καταργήσῃ ...

(1 Cor 1:27-28)

A series of two tricolons:

[1] [A] ἐγὼ ἐφύτευσα [B] Ἀπολλῶς ἐπότισεν [C] ἀλλὰ ὁ θεὸς ηὔξανεν

[2] [A] οὔτε ὁ φυτεύων ἐστίν τι [B] οὔτε ὁ ποτίζων [C] ἀλλ' ὁ αὐξάνων θεός

(1 Cor 3:6-7)

θεοῦ γάρ ἐσμεν συνεργοί·

θεοῦ γεώργιον,

θεοῦ οἰκοδομή ἐστε

(1 Cor 3:9)

λοιδορούμενοι εὐλογοῦμεν,

διωκόμενοι ἀνεχόμεθα,

δυσφημούμενοι παρακαλοῦμεν

(1 Cor 4:12-13)

ἀλλὰ ἀπελούσασθε,

ἀλλὰ ἡγιάσθητε,

ἀλλὰ ἐδικαιώθητε

(1 Cor 6:11)

[A] Διαιρέσεις δὲ χαρισμάτων εἰσίν, [A] τὸ δὲ αὐτὸ πνεῦμα·

[A] καὶ διαιρέσεις διακονιῶν εἰσιν, [A] καὶ ὁ αὐτὸς κύριος·

[A] καὶ διαιρέσεις ἐνεργημάτων εἰσίν, [A] ὁ δὲ αὐτὸς θεὸς ὁ ἐνεργῶν τὰ πάντα ἐν πᾶσιν.

(1 Cor 12:4-6)

μὴ πάντες χαρίσματα ἔχουσιν ἰαμάτων;

μὴ πάντες γλώσσαις λαλοῦσιν;

μὴ πάντες διερμηνεύουσιν;

(1 Cor 12:30)

[A] εἴτε δὲ προφητεῖαι, [B] καταργηθήσονται·

[A] εἴτε γλῶσσαι, [B] παύσονται·

[A] εἴτε γνῶσις, [B] καταργηθήσεται.

(1 Cor 13:8)

ἐλάλουν ὡς νήπιος,

ἐφρόνουν ὡς νήπιος,

ἐλογιζόμην ὡς νήπιος·

(1 Cor 13:11)

ὃ καὶ παρελάβετε,

ἐν ᾧ καὶ ἑστήκατε,

δι' οὗ καὶ σῴζεσθε.

(1 Cor 15:1-2)

ἄλλη δόξα ἡλίου, καὶ

ἄλλη δόξα σελήνης, καὶ

ἄλλη δόξα ἀστέρων·

(1 Cor 15:41)

[A] σπείρεται ἐν φθορᾷ, [B] ἐγείρεται ἐν ἀφθαρσίᾳ·

[A] σπείρεται ἐν ἀτιμίᾳ, [B] ἐγείρεται ἐν δόξῃ·

[A] σπείρεται ἐν ἀσθενείᾳ, [B] ἐγείρεται ἐν δυνάμει·
(1 Cor 15:42-43)

ἐν ἀτόμῳ,
ἐν ῥιπῇ ὀφθαλμοῦ,
ἐν τῇ ἐσχάτῃ σάλπιγγι·
(1 Cor 15:52)

[A] ὅτι εἷς ὑπὲρ πάντων [B] ἀπέθανεν,
[A] ἄρα οἱ πάντες [B] ἀπέθανον·
[A] καὶ ὑπὲρ πάντων [B] ἀπέθανεν
(2 Cor 5:14-15)

διὰ τῶν ὅπλων τῆς δικαιοσύνης τῶν δεξιῶν καὶ ἀριστερῶν,
διὰ δόξης καὶ ἀτιμίας,
διὰ δυσφημίας καὶ εὐφημίας·
(2 Cor 6:7-8)

οὐδένα ἠδικήσαμεν,
οὐδένα ἐφθείραμεν,
οὐδένα ἐπλεονεκτήσαμεν.
(2 Cor 7:2)

[A] ἄλλον Ἰησοῦν [B] κηρύσσει [C] ὃν οὐκ ἐκηρύξαμεν, ἤ
[A] πνεῦμα ἕτερον [B] λαμβάνετε [C] ὃ οὐκ ἐλάβετε, ἤ
[A] εὐαγγέλιον ἕτερον [B] – [C] ὃ οὐκ ἐδέξασθε,
(2 Cor 11:4)

εἴ τις κατεσθίει,
εἴ τις λαμβάνει,
εἴ τις ἐπαίρεται,
(2 Cor 11:20)

[A] Ἑβραῖοί εἰσιν; [B] κἀγώ.

[A] Ἰσραηλῖταί εἰσιν; [B] κἀγώ.

[A] σπέρμα Ἀβραάμ εἰσιν; [B] κἀγώ.

(2 Cor 11:22)

[A] οὐκ ἔνι [B] Ἰουδαῖος οὐδὲ Ἕλλην,

[A] οὐκ ἔνι [B] δοῦλος οὐδὲ ἐλεύθερος,

[A] οὐκ ἔνι [B] ἄρσεν καὶ θῆλυ·

(Gal 3:28)

[A] τίς ἐστιν ἡ ἐλπὶς [B] τῆς κλήσεως αὐτοῦ [C] -

[A] τίς ὁ πλοῦτος [B] τῆς δόξης τῆς κληρονομίας αὐτοῦ
[C] ἐν τοῖς ἁγίοις, καὶ

[A] τί τὸ ὑπερβάλλον μέγεθος [A] τῆς δυνάμεως αὐτοῦ
[C] εἰς ἡμᾶς τοὺς . . .

(Eph 1:18–19)

[A] εἷς κύριος, [B] μία πίστις, [C] ἓν βάπτισμα

(Eph 4:5)

εἷς θεὸς καὶ πατὴρ πάντων, ὁ [A] ἐπὶ πάντων καὶ [B] διὰ πάντων καὶ [C] ἐν πᾶσιν.

(Eph 4:6)

Βλέπετε τοὺς κύνας,

βλέπετε τοὺς κακοὺς ἐργάτας,

βλέπετε τὴν κατατομήν.

(Phil 3:2)

ὧν τὸ τέλος ἀπώλεια,

ὧν ὁ θεὸς ἡ κοιλία καὶ

ἡ δόξα ἐν τῇ αἰσχύνῃ αὐτῶν.

(Phil 3:19)

Πάντοτε χαίρετε,
ἀδιαλείπτως προσεύχεσθε,
ἐν παντὶ εὐχαριστεῖτε·
(1 Thess 5:16-18)

In 1 Cor 9:13-14, the third colon is introduced by a different formula:

Οὐκ οἴδατε ὅτι
    [A] οἱ τὰ ἱερὰ ἐργαζόμενοι [B] [τὰ] ἐκ τοῦ ἱεροῦ [C] ἐσθίουσιν,
    [A] οἱ τῷ θυσιαστηρίῳ παρεδρεύοντες [B] τῷ θυσιαστηρίῳ [C] συμμερίζονται;
Οὕτως καὶ ὁ κύριος διέταξεν
    [A] τοῖς τὸ εὐαγγέλιον καταγγέλλουσιν [B] ἐκ τοῦ εὐαγγελίου [C] ζῆν.

3.2.1.1.28. DISIUNCTIO (LAUSBERG, §739)

A kind of isocolon consisting of colons of synonymous predicates, as well as further clause elements (subjects, objects, adverbial designations) that are semantically different and correspond with each other syntactically, thus constituting a kind of synonymy and "accumulation" (Lausberg, §665-87). In other words, unlike interpretatio (§3.2.1.1.31), where multiple elements of the relevant colons are synonymous, disiunctio involves only one synonymous element (indicated below by formatting). Because disiunctio functions technically as an "elaboration," the variation between synonyms cannot be considered "stylistic variation" in the sense that the variation serves no purpose save the avoidance of repetition. Rather, the variation amplifies the point through accumulation.

[A] διὰ τί οὐχὶ μᾶλλον [B] **ἀδικεῖσθε**;
[A] διὰ τί οὐχὶ μᾶλλον [B] **ἀποστερεῖσθε**;
(1 Cor 6:7)

[A] Πάντα ἔξεστιν, [B] ἀλλ' οὐ πάντα **συμφέρει**.
[A] πάντα ἔξεστιν, [B] ἀλλ' οὐ πάντα **οἰκοδομεῖ**.
(1 Cor 10:23)

[A] εἴτε δὲ προφητεῖαι, [B] **καταργηθήσονται**·
[A] εἴτε γλῶσσαι, [B] **παύσονται**·
[A] εἴτε γνῶσις, [B] **καταργηθήσεται**.
(1 Cor 13:8)

[A] **προσεύξομαι** τῷ πνεύματι, [B] **προσεύξομαι** δὲ καὶ τῷ νοΐ·
[A] **ψαλῶ** τῷ πνεύματι, [B] **ψαλῶ** δὲ καὶ τῷ νοΐ.
(1 Cor 14:15)

[A] **Ἑβραῖοί** εἰσιν; [B] κἀγώ.
[A] **Ἰσραηλῖταί** εἰσιν; [B] κἀγώ.
[A] **σπέρμα Ἀβραάμ** εἰσιν; [B] κἀγώ.
(2 Cor 11:22)

[A] ἐν κόποις [B] **περισσοτέρως**,
[A] ἐν φυλακαῖς [B] **περισσοτέρως**,
[A] ἐν πληγαῖς [B] **ὑπερβαλλόντως**,
[A] ἐν θανάτοις [B] **πολλάκις**.
(2 Cor 11:23)

3.2.1.1.29. ADIUNCTIO (LAUSBERG, §743)

A kind of zeugma (§3.2.1.1.20) involving the parenthetic addition of a predicate to several colons or commata. The parenthetic element <> may be located at the beginning, at the end, or in the middle of the arrangement.

οὐ πολλοὶ σοφοὶ <κατὰ σάρκα>,
οὐ πολλοὶ δυνατοί,
οὐ πολλοὶ εὐγενεῖς·
(1 Cor 1:26)

Πάντοτε χαίρετε,
ἀδιαλείπτως προσεύχεσθε,
ἐν παντὶ εὐχαριστεῖτε·

< τοῦτο γὰρ θέλημα θεοῦ ἐν Χριστῷ Ἰησοῦ εἰς ὑμᾶς>.
(1 Thess 5:16-18)

3.2.1.1.30. ANTITHETICAL ISOCOLON (LAUSBERG, §750)

Semantic difference between the constituent elements in an isocolon where only two colons or commata are involved results in antithetical isocolon. In antithetical isocolon, the correspondences extend to the, antithetically related, conceptual content. In this way isocolon also involves the figure of thought known as antitheton (see §3.2.1.2.11).

Rom 2:7-10 contains two instances of antithetical isocolon, in vv. 7, 8 and vv. 9, 10 respectively; the two antitheses relate to each other chiastically as to their conceptual content:

[A] τοῖς μὲν καθ' ὑπομονὴν ἔργου ἀγαθοῦ δόξαν καὶ τιμὴν καὶ ἀφθαρσίαν ζητοῦσιν, [B] ζωὴν αἰώνιον· (v. 7)

[A] τοῖς δὲ ἐξ ἐριθείας καὶ ἀπειθοῦσι τῇ ἀληθείᾳ πειθομένοις δὲ τῇ ἀδικίᾳ, [B] ὀργὴ καὶ θυμός θλῖψις (v. 8)

[A] καὶ στενοχωρία ἐπὶ πᾶσαν ψυχὴν ἀνθρώπου τοῦ κατεργαζομένου τὸ κακόν, [B] Ἰουδαίου τε πρῶτον καὶ Ἕλληνος· (v. 9)

[A] δόξα δὲ καὶ τιμὴ καὶ εἰρήνη παντὶ τῷ ἐργαζομένῳ τὸ ἀγαθόν, [B] Ἰουδαίῳ τε πρῶτον καὶ Ἕλληνι· (v. 10)

[A] οὐ γὰρ οἱ ἀκροαταὶ νόμου [B] δίκαιοι παρὰ [τῷ] θεῷ,

[A] ἀλλ' οἱ ποιηταὶ νόμου [B] δικαιωθήσονται.

(Rom 2:13)

[A] οὐ γὰρ ὁ ἐν τῷ φανερῷ [B] Ἰουδαῖός ἐστιν, [C] οὐδὲ ἡ ἐν τῷ φανερῷ ἐν σαρκὶ περιτομή·

[B] ἀλλ' ὁ ἐν τῷ κρυπτῷ [B] Ἰουδαῖος, [C] καὶ περιτομὴ καρδίας ἐν πνεύματι οὐ γράμματι.

(Rom 2:28-29)

[A] τῷ δὲ ἐργαζομένῳ [B] ὁ μισθὸς οὐ λογίζεται κατὰ χάριν ἀλλὰ κατὰ ὀφείλημα·

[A] τῷ δὲ μὴ ἐργαζομένῳ, πιστεύοντι δὲ ἐπὶ τὸν δικαιοῦντα τὸν ἀσεβῆ, [B] λογίζεται ἡ πίστις αὐτοῦ εἰς δικαιοσύνην,

(Rom 4:4–5)

[A] τὸ μὲν γὰρ κρίμα [B] ἐξ ἑνὸς [C] εἰς κατάκριμα,

[A] τὸ δὲ χάρισμα [B] ἐκ πολλῶν παραπτωμάτων [C] εἰς δικαίωμα.

(Rom 5:16)

Ἄρα οὖν ὡς

[A] δι' ἑνὸς παραπτώματος [B] εἰς πάντας ἀνθρώπους [C] εἰς κατάκριμα,

οὕτως καὶ

[A] δι' ἑνὸς δικαιώματος [B] εἰς πάντας ἀνθρώπους [C] εἰς δικαίωσιν ζωῆς·

(Rom 5:18)

ὥσπερ γὰρ

[A] διὰ τῆς παρακοῆς τοῦ ἑνὸς ἀνθρώπου [B] ἁμαρτωλοὶ κατεστάθησαν οἱ πολλοί,

οὕτως καὶ

[A] διὰ τῆς ὑπακοῆς τοῦ ἑνὸς [B] δίκαιοι κατασταθήσονται οἱ πολλοί.

(Rom 5:19)

[A] ὃ γὰρ ἀπέθανεν, [B] τῇ ἁμαρτίᾳ ἀπέθανεν ἐφάπαξ·

[A] ὃ δὲ ζῇ, [B] ζῇ τῷ θεῷ.

(Rom 6:10)

[A] νεκροὺς μὲν [B] τῇ ἁμαρτίᾳ

[A] ζῶντας δὲ [B] τῷ θεῷ ἐν Χριστῷ Ἰησου

(Rom 6:11)

In Rom 6:13, isocolon is disrupted by the insertion of <ἑαυτοὺς τῷ θεῷ ὡσεὶ ἐκ νεκρῶν ζῶντας καί> in the counterpoint:

[A] μηδὲ παριστάνετε [B] τὰ μέλη ὑμῶν ὅπλα ἀδικίας [C] τῇ ἁμαρτίᾳ,

[A] ἀλλὰ παραστήσατε <ἑαυτοὺς τῷ θεῷ ὡσεὶ ἐκ νεκρῶν ζῶντας> καὶ [B] τὰ μέλη ὑμῶν ὅπλα δικαιοσύνης [C] τῷ θεῷ.

Similar wording continues in 6:19:

[A] ὥσπερ γὰρ παρεστήσατε [B] τὰ μέλη ὑμῶν δοῦλα [C] τῇ ἀκαθαρσίᾳ καὶ τῇ ἀνομίᾳ [D] εἰς τὴν ἀνομίαν,

[A] οὕτως νῦν παραστήσατε [B] τὰ μέλη ὑμῶν δοῦλα [C] τῇ δικαιοσύνῃ [D] εἰς ἁγιασμόν.
(Rom 6:19)

ἐν καινότητι πνεύματος
καὶ οὐ παλαιότητι γράμματος
(Rom 7:6)

[A] ὁ νόμος [B] πνευματικός ἐστιν·
[A] ἐγὼ δὲ [B] σάρκινός εἰμι.
(Rom 7:14)

[A] οὐ γὰρ ὃ θέλω [B] τοῦτο πράσσω,
[A] ἀλλ' ὃ μισῶ [B] τοῦτο ποιῶ.
(Rom 7:15)

τὸ γὰρ θέλειν παράκειταί μοι,
τὸ δὲ κατεργάζεσθαι τὸ καλὸν οὔ
(Rom 7:18)

[A] οὐ γὰρ ὃ θέλω [B] ποιῶ ἀγαθόν,
[A] ἀλλὰ ὃ οὐ θέλω [B] κακὸν τοῦτο πράσσω.
(Rom 7:19)

[A] τῷ μὲν νοΐ [B] δουλεύω [C] νόμῳ θεοῦ,
[A] τῇ δὲ σαρκὶ [B] — [C] νόμῳ ἁμαρτίας
(Rom 7:25)

[A] οἱ γὰρ κατὰ σάρκα ὄντες [B] τὰ τῆς σαρκὸς φρονοῦσιν,
[A] οἱ δὲ κατὰ πνεῦμα [B] τὰ τοῦ πνεύματος.
(Rom 8:5)

[A] τὸ γὰρ φρόνημα τῆς σαρκὸς [B] θάνατος,
[A] τὸ δὲ φρόνημα τοῦ πνεύματος [B] ζωὴ καὶ εἰρήνη·
(Rom 8:6)

[A] τὸ μὲν σῶμα [B] νεκρὸν [C] διὰ ἁμαρτίαν,
[A] τὸ δὲ πνεῦμα [B] ζωὴ [C] διὰ δικαιοσύνην.
(Rom 8:10)

[A] εἰ γὰρ κατὰ σάρκα [B] ζῆτε [C] μέλλετε ἀποθνήσκειν,
[A] εἰ δὲ πνεύματι [B] τὰς πράξεις τοῦ σώματος θανατοῦτε [C] ζήσεσθε.
(Rom 8:13)

[A] οὐ γὰρ ἐλάβετε [B] πνεῦμα δουλείας πάλιν [C] εἰς φόβον,
[A] ἀλλὰ ἐλάβετε [B] πνεῦμα υἱοθεσίας, [C] ἐν ᾧ κράζομεν, Αββα ὁ πατήρ·
(Rom 8:15)

[A] οὐ τὰ τέκνα [B] τῆς σαρκὸς [C] ταῦτα τέκνα τοῦ θεοῦ,
[A] ἀλλὰ τὰ τέκνα [B] τῆς ἐπαγγελίας [C] λογίζεται εἰς σπέρμα·
(Rom 9:8)

[A] ὃν θέλει [B] ἐλεεῖ,
[A] ὃν δὲ θέλει [B] σκληρύνει.
(Rom 9:18)

εἰ δὲ θέλων ὁ θεὸς ἐνδείξασθαι τὴν ὀργὴν καὶ
[A] γνωρίσαι τὸ δυνατὸν αὐτοῦ ἤνεγκεν ἐν πολλῇ μακροθυμίᾳ [B] σκεύη ὀργῆς [C] κατηρτισμένα [D] εἰς ἀπώλειαν, καὶ ἵνα
[A] γνωρίσῃ τὸν πλοῦτον τῆς δόξης αὐτοῦ [B] ἐπὶ σκεύη ἐλέους, [C] ἃ προητοίμασεν [D] εἰς δόξαν;
(Rom 9:22–23)

χαίρειν μετὰ χαιρόντων,
κλαίειν μετὰ κλαιόντων.
(Rom 10:14c, d)

[A] κατὰ μὲν τὸ εὐαγγέλιον [B] ἐχθροὶ [C] δι' ὑμᾶς,
[A] κατὰ δὲ τὴν ἐκλογὴν [B] ἀγαπητοὶ [C] διὰ τοὺς πατέρας
(Rom 11:28)

[A] ἀποθώμεθα οὖν [B] τὰ ἔργα τοῦ σκότους,
[A] ἐνδυσώμεθα [δὲ] [B] τὰ ὅπλα τοῦ φωτός.
(Rom 13:12)

[A] Ἰουδαίοις μὲν [B] σκάνδαλον, [A] ἔθνεσιν δὲ [B] μωρίαν,
[A] αὐτοῖς δὲ τοῖς κλητοῖς, Ἰουδαίοις τε καὶ Ἕλλησιν [B] Χριστὸν θεοῦ δύναμιν καὶ θεοῦ σοφίαν.
(1 Cor 1:22-24)

[A] οὐχὶ τοὺς ἔσω [B] ὑμεῖς [C] κρίνετε;
[A] τοὺς δὲ ἔξω [B] ὁ θεὸς [C] κρινεῖ.
(1 Cor 5:12-13)

The parallel structure of 1 Cor 6:6, 8 accentuates the situational irony communicated in the content. Believers look for justice among unbelievers, and commit injustice against believers:

[A] ἀλλὰ ἀδελφὸς [B] μετὰ ἀδελφοῦ κρίνεται, [C] καὶ τοῦτο [D] ἐπὶ ἀπίστων; (v. 6)
[A] ἀλλὰ ὑμεῖς [B] ἀδικεῖτε καὶ ἀποστερεῖτε, [C] καὶ τοῦτο [D] ἀδελφούς. (v. 8)

[A] Πάντα [B] μοι ἔξεστιν,
[A] ἀλλ' οὐ πάντα [B] συμφέρει.
(1 Cor 6:12)

[A] δέδεσαι [B] γυναικί, [C] μὴ ζήτει λύσιν·
[A] λέλυσαι [B] ἀπὸ γυναικός, [C] μὴ ζήτει γυναῖκα.
(1 Cor 7:27)

[A] ὁ ἄγαμος μεριμνᾷ [B] τὰ τοῦ κυρίου, [C] πῶς ἀρέσῃ [D] τῷ κυρίῳ·
[A] ὁ δὲ γαμήσας μεριμνᾷ [B] τὰ τοῦ κόσμου, [C] πῶς ἀρέσῃ [D] τῇ γυναικί,
(1 Cor 7:32-33)

ἡ γνῶσις φυσιοῖ,
ἡ δὲ ἀγάπη οἰκοδομει·
(1 Cor 8:1)

[A] εἴ τις δοκεῖ ἐγνωκέναι τι, [B] οὔπω ἔγνω καθὼς δεῖ γνῶναι·
[A] εἰ δέ τις ἀγαπᾷ τὸν θεόν, [B] οὗτος ἔγνωσται ὑπ' αὐτοῦ.
(1 Cor 8:2-3)

οὐδὲ ἡ φύσις αὐτὴ διδάσκει ὑμᾶς ὅτι
[A] ἀνὴρ μὲν ἐὰν κομᾷ [B] ἀτιμία αὐτῷ ἐστιν,
[A] γυνὴ δὲ ἐὰν κομᾷ [B] δόξα αὐτῇ ἐστιν;
(1 Cor 11:14-15)

[A] οὐ χαίρει [B] ἐπὶ τῇ ἀδικίᾳ,
[A] συγχαίρει δὲ [B] τῇ ἀληθείᾳ·
(1 Cor 13:6)

[A] ὅτε ἤμην νήπιος, [B] ἐλάλουν ὡς νήπιος, ἐφρόνουν ὡς νήπιος, ἐλογιζόμην ὡς νήπιος·
[A] ὅτε γέγονα ἀνήρ, [B] κατήργηκα τὰ τοῦ νηπίου.
(1 Cor 13:11)

[A] βλέπομεν γὰρ ἄρτι [B] δι' ἐσόπτρου ἐν αἰνίγματι,
[A] τότε δὲ [B] πρόσωπον πρὸς πρόσωπον·
(1 Cor 13:12a, b)

[A] ἄρτι γινώσκω [B] ἐκ μέρους,
[A] τότε δὲ ἐπιγνώσομαι [B] καθὼς καὶ ἐπεγνώσθην.
(1 Cor 13:12c, d)

[A] ὁ γὰρ λαλῶν γλώσσῃ [B] οὐκ ἀνθρώποις λαλεῖ ἀλλὰ θεῷ, . . .
[A] ὁ δὲ προφητεύων [B] ἀνθρώποις λαλεῖ οἰκοδομὴν καὶ παράκλησιν καὶ παραμυθίαν.
(1 Cor 14:2-3)

[A] πάντες οὐ [B] κοιμηθησόμεθα,
[A] πάντες δὲ [B] ἀλλαγησόμεθα . . .
(1 Cor 15:51)

[A] οἷς μὲν [B] ὀσμὴ ἐκ θανάτου [C] εἰς θάνατον,
[A] οἷς δὲ [B] ὀσμὴ ἐκ ζωῆς [C] εἰς ζωήν.
(2 Cor 2:16)

[A] τὰ γὰρ βλεπόμενα [B] πρόσκαιρα,
[A] τὰ δὲ μὴ βλεπόμενα [B] αἰώνια.
(2 Cor 4:18)

[A] ζῶ δὲ οὐκέτι [B] ἐγώ,
[A] ζῇ δὲ ἐν ἐμοὶ [B] Χριστός·
(Gal 2:20)

[A] ὁ δὲ μεσίτης [B] ἑνὸς οὐκ ἔστιν,
[A] ὁ δὲ θεὸς [B] εἷς ἐστιν.
(Gal 3:20)

[A] ὁ μὲν ἐκ τῆς παιδίσκης [B] κατὰ σάρκα [C] γεγέννηται,
[A] ὁ δὲ ἐκ τῆς ἐλευθέρας [B] δι' ἐπαγγελίας [C] —.
(Gal 4:23)

[A] ὅτι ὁ σπείρων εἰς τὴν σάρκα ἑαυτοῦ [B] ἐκ τῆς σαρκὸς [C] θερίσει φθοράν,

[A] ὁ δὲ σπείρων εἰς τὸ πνεῦμα [B] ἐκ τοῦ πνεύματος [C] θερίσει ζωὴν αἰώνιον.

(Gal 6:8)

[A] οὗτοι ἀναγκάζουσιν ὑμᾶς περιτέμνεσθαι, [B] μόνον ἵνα τῷ σταυρῷ τοῦ Χριστοῦ μὴ διώκωνται . . .

[A] θέλουσιν ὑμᾶς περιτέμνεσθαι [B] ἵνα ἐν τῇ ὑμετέρᾳ σαρκὶ καυχήσωνται.

(Gal 6:12, 13)

ἀνταποδοῦναι

[A] τοῖς θλίβουσιν ὑμᾶς [B] θλῖψιν

[A] καὶ ὑμῖν τοῖς θλιβομένοις [B] ἄνεσιν

(2 Thess 1:6–7)

As Johnson shows, the isocolon in Rom 1:3–4 is not antithetical.[14] See this example above under icocolon, §3.2.1.1.22.

3.2.1.1.31. *Interpretatio* (Lausberg, *§751*)

A type of isocolon in which colons are independent clauses and the clauses are conceptually synonymous with each other. Because interpretatio functions technically as an "elaboration," the variation of synonyms cannot be considered "stylistic variation" in the sense that the variation serves no purpose save the avoidance of repetition.

[1] Τί οὖν τὸ περισσὸν τοῦ Ἰουδαίου,

[2] ἢ τίς ἡ ὠφέλεια τῆς περιτομῆς;

(Rom 3:1)

[1] Ἄρα οὖν ὡς

[A] δι' ἑνὸς παραπτώματος [B] εἰς πάντας ἀνθρώπους [C] εἰς κατάκριμα, οὕτως καὶ

---

14. Johnson, "Romans 1:3–4."

[A] δι' ἑνὸς δικαιώματος [B] εἰς πάντας ἀνθρώπους [C] εἰς δικαίωσιν ζωῆς·
[2] ὥσπερ γὰρ
[A] διὰ τῆς παρακοῆς τοῦ ἑνὸς ἀνθρώπου [B] ἁμαρτωλοὶ κατεστάθησαν οἱ πολλοί,
οὕτως καὶ
[A] διὰ τῆς ὑπακοῆς τοῦ ἑνὸς [B] δίκαιοι κατασταθήσονται οἱ πολλοί.
(Rom 5:18-19)

[1] τὴν ἁμαρτίαν οὐκ ἔγνων εἰ μὴ διὰ νόμου,
[2] τήν τε γὰρ ἐπιθυμίαν οὐκ ᾔδειν εἰ μὴ ὁ νόμος ἔλεγεν, Οὐκ ἐπιθυμήσεις
(Rom 7:7)

[1] οὐ γὰρ πάντες οἱ ἐξ Ἰσραήλ, οὗτοι Ἰσραήλ·
[2] οὐδ' ὅτι εἰσὶν σπέρμα Ἀβραάμ, πάντες τέκνα ...
(Rom 9:6-7)

[1] εἰ δὲ τὸ παράπτωμα αὐτῶν πλοῦτος κόσμου καὶ
[2] τὸ ἥττημα αὐτῶν πλοῦτος ἐθνῶν ...
(Rom 11:12)

[1] εἰ δὲ ἡ ἀπαρχὴ ἁγία, καὶ τὸ φύραμα·
[2] καὶ εἰ ἡ ῥίζα ἁγία, καὶ οἱ κλάδοι.
(Rom 11:16)

[1] ὡς ἀνεξεραύνητα τὰ κρίματα αὐτοῦ
[2] καὶ ἀνεξιχνίαστοι αἱ ὁδοὶ αὐτοῦ
(Rom 11:33)

[1] ἑκάστου τὸ ἔργον φανερὸν γενήσεται, ἡ γὰρ ἡμέρα δηλώσει, ...
[2] ἑκάστου τὸ ἔργον ὁποῖόν ἐστιν τὸ πῦρ [αὐτὸ] δοκιμάσει
(1 Cor 3:13)

[1] ὃς καὶ φωτίσει τὰ κρυπτὰ τοῦ σκότους
[2] καὶ φανερώσει τὰς βουλὰς τῶν καρδιῶν·
(1 Cor 4:5)

[1] οἱ τὰ ἱερὰ ἐργαζόμενοι [τὰ] ἐκ τοῦ ἱεροῦ ἐσθίουσιν,
[2] οἱ τῷ θυσιαστηρίῳ παρεδρεύοντες τῷ θυσιαστηρίῳ συμμερίζονται;
(1 Cor 9:13)

[1] ὅτι εἰδωλόθυτόν τί ἐστιν;
[2] ἢ ὅτι εἴδωλόν τί ἐστιν;
(1 Cor 10:19)

While 1 Cor 10:21 individualizes drink and food, the point is basically the same in each line, thus emphasizing the point through "accumulation":

[1] οὐ δύνασθε ποτήριον κυρίου πίνειν καὶ ποτήριον δαιμονίων·
[2] οὐ δύνασθε τραπέζης κυρίου μετέχειν καὶ τραπέζης δαιμονίων.
(1 Cor 10:21)

[1] Διαιρέσεις δὲ χαρισμάτων εἰσίν, τὸ δὲ αὐτὸ πνεῦμα·
[2] καὶ διαιρέσεις διακονιῶν εἰσιν, καὶ ὁ αὐτὸς κύριος·
[3] καὶ διαιρέσεις ἐνεργημάτων εἰσίν, ὁ δὲ αὐτὸς θεός, ὁ ἐνεργῶν τὰ πάντα ἐν πᾶσιν.
(1 Cor 12:4–6)

[1] δεῖ γὰρ τὸ φθαρτὸν τοῦτο ἐνδύσασθαι ἀφθαρσίαν
[2] καὶ τὸ θνητὸν τοῦτο ἐνδύσασθαι ἀθανασίαν.
(1 Cor 15:53)

[1] ὅταν δὲ τὸ φθαρτὸν τοῦτο ἐνδύσηται ἀφθαρσίαν
[2] καὶ τὸ θνητὸν τοῦτο ἐνδύσηται ἀθανασίαν . . .
(1 Cor 15:54)

[1] Τὸ στόμα ἡμῶν ἀνέῳγεν ...
[2] ἡ καρδία ἡμῶν πεπλάτυνται·
(2 Cor 6:11)

[1] τίς γὰρ μετοχὴ δικαιοσύνῃ καὶ ἀνομίᾳ;
[2] ἢ τίς κοινωνία φωτὶ πρὸς σκότος;
[3] τίς δὲ συμφώνησις Χριστοῦ πρὸς Βελιάρ,
[4] ἢ τίς μερὶς πιστῷ μετὰ ἀπίστου;
[5] τίς δὲ συγκατάθεσις ναῷ θεοῦ μετὰ εἰδώλων;
(2 Cor 6:14-16)

[1] οὐ τῷ αὐτῷ πνεύματι περιεπατήσαμεν;
[2] οὐ τοῖς αὐτοῖς ἴχνεσιν;
(2 Cor 12:18)

[1] ἀλλὰ καὶ ἐὰν ἡμεῖς ἢ ἄγγελος ἐξ οὐρανοῦ [ὑμῖν] εὐαγγελίζηται παρ᾽ ὃ εὐηγγελισάμεθα ὑμῖν, ἀνάθεμα ἔστω.
ὡς προειρήκαμεν καὶ ἄρτι πάλιν λέγω·
[2] εἴ τις ὑμᾶς εὐαγγελίζεται παρ᾽ ὃ παρελάβετε, ἀνάθεμα ἔστω.
(Gal 1:8-9)

[1] τοῖς μὴ εἰδόσιν θεὸν
[2] καὶ τοῖς μὴ ὑπακούουσιν τῷ εὐαγγελίῳ
(2 Thess 1:8)

[1] ἐνδοξασθῆναι ἐν τοῖς ἁγίοις αὐτοῦ καὶ
[2] θαυμασθῆναι ἐν πᾶσιν τοῖς πιστεύσασιν
(2 Thess 1:10)

[1] ἀνελεῖ τῷ πνεύματι τοῦ στόματος αὐτοῦ καὶ
[2] καταργήσει τῇ ἐπιφανείᾳ τῆς παρουσίας αὐτοῦ
(2 Thess 2:8)

3.2.1.2. Figures of Thought (Lausberg, §755–910)

Like figures of speech (§3.2.1.1), figures of thought enhance the speaker's point by artistic means. Whereas figures of speech, however, are defined as such by their linguistic formulation, figures of thought are defined as such by their conceptual content (Lausberg, §755).

Some figures of thought are oriented toward the audience (Lausberg, §758–79), and others toward the subject matter (Lausberg, §780–910). Of those oriented toward the audience, some concern address (Lausberg, §759–75), and others questions (Lausberg, §766–79). Address of the audience functions as a figure when it serves to increase the intensity of address or to snub the audience, or when it represents a turning away from the audience. Questions become figures when they are used as devices of pathos (emotive questions) or as a means of sharpening the line of thought (interplay of question and answer, helplessness questions).

3.2.1.2.1. *Deēsis/Obsecratio* (Lausberg, §760)

Vehement supplication of either the gods or humans, often taking the form *per x* ("for the sake of *x*," in Latin; Lausberg, §760). Quintilian includes deēsis under his discussion of invention/emotions; he also remarks that an invocation to the gods "is generally thought a sign of a good conscience" (*Inst.* 6.1.33). While invocation of the gods is often sincere, deēsis is an emotive figure and can be feigned for rhetorical effect (Lausberg, §808).

God is invoked as "witness" in Rom 1:9: "For God—whom I serve with my spirit by announcing the gospel of his Son—*is my witness*" (NRSV). For the expression "God is my witness" as a classical idiom, see Novenson;[15] Quintilian, *Inst.* 5.11.42; Aristotle, *Rhet.* 1.15.13–17.

"I am *telling the truth in Christ*, I am not lying, my conscience *bearing me witness in the Holy Spirit* . . . " (Rom 9:1 NASB)

"I *appeal* to you therefore, brothers and sisters, *by the mercies of God*" (Rom 12:1 NRSV)

"I *appeal* to you, brothers and sisters, *by our Lord Jesus Christ and by the love of the Spirit*" (Rom 15:30 NRSV)

---

15. Novenson, "'God Is Witness.'"

"In what I am writing to you, *before God, I do not lie!*" (Gal 1:20 NRSV)

"Friends, *I beg you*, become as I am, for I also have become as you are." (Gal 4:12 NRSV)

"For *God is my witness*, how . . . " (Phil 1:8 NRSV)

"If then there is any encouragement in Christ, any consolation from love, any sharing in the Spirit, any compassion and sympathy . . . " (Phil 2:1 NRSV)

"*As you know and as God is our witness*, we never came with words of flattery or with a pretext for greed" (1 Thess 2:5 NRSV)

"*You are witnesses, and God also*, how pure, upright, and blameless our conduct was toward you believers" (1 Thess 2:10 NRSV)

"*I solemnly command you by the Lord* that this letter be read to all of them." (1 Thess. 5:27 NRSV)

3.2.1.2.2. *Parrhēsia/Licentia (Lausberg, §761)*

Bold speech that, though it risks turning away the audience, the speaker ultimately hopes will increase the audience's goodwill. For a discussion of parrhēsia in 2 Corinthians and Galatians, see Sampley.[16]

Paul justifies his parrhēsia in 2 Cor 3:12–13: "*Having therefore such a hope, we use great boldness in our speech*, and are not as Moses . . . " (NASB)

"We have spoken frankly to you Corinthians; our heart is wide open to you. There is no restriction in our affections, but only in yours. In return—I speak as to children—open wide your hearts also." (2 Cor 6:11–13 NRSV)

"I have spoken to you with great frankness . . . " (2 Cor 7:4 NIV)

"For we cannot do anything against the truth, but only for the truth." (2 Cor 13:8 NRSV)

"I am astonished that you are so quickly deserting the one who called you in the grace of Christ and are turning to a different gospel—" (Gal 1:6 NRSV)

---

16. Sampley, "Paul's Frank Speech."

"You foolish Galatians! Who has bewitched you? It was before your eyes that Jesus Christ was publicly exhibited as crucified! The only thing I want to learn from you is this: Did you receive the Spirit by doing the works of the law or by believing what you heard? Are you so foolish? Having started with the Spirit, are you now ending with the flesh?" (Gal 3:1 NRSV)

"But now that you have come to know God, or rather to be known by God, how can you turn back again to the weak and worthless elementary principles of the world, whose slaves you want to be once more? You observe days and months and seasons and years! I am afraid I may have labored over you in vain." (Gal 4:9–11 NRSV)

"You were running well; who prevented you from obeying the truth?" (Gal 5:7 NRSV)

3.2.1.2.3. Apostrophe (Lausberg, §762–65)

Apostrophe occurs when the speaker "turns away" from the implied audience to address a second audience.

"Therefore you are inexcusable, O man, whoever you are who judge, for in whatever you judge another you condemn yourself; for you who judge practice the same things . . . And do you think this, O man, you who judge those practicing such things, and doing the same, that you will escape the judgment of God?" (Rom 2:1, 3 NKJV)

"O man, who indeed are you, who argues with God?" (Rom 9:20)

"I am speaking to you Gentiles—inasmuch as I am an apostle to Gentiles . . ." (Rom 11:13)

"Do you (sg.) want not to be afraid of the authority?" (Rom 13:3)

"For how do you know, O wife, whether you will save your husband? Or how do you know, O husband, whether you will save your wife?" (1 Cor 7:16 NASB)

"Otherwise, if you (sg.) say a blessing with the spirit, how can anyone in the position of an outsider say the 'Amen' to your thanksgiving (1 Cor 14:16 NRSV)

"You (sg.) are no longer a slave but a son. And if a son, also an heir of God." (Gal 4:7).

3.2.1.2.4. *Erōtēsis/Interrogatio* (Lausberg, §767–70)

A question to which no answer is expected, since from the speaker's perspective the answer is self-evident. The impatient tone or emotive connotation of the question may serve to humiliate the audience.

Questions expecting "yes." Most often these are introduced by οὐ(κ): Rom 3:29b; 9:21; 1 Cor 5:2, 12b; 8:10; 9:1 (x4), 12; 10:16 (x2), 18; 14:23; 2 Cor 12:18c, d; 1 Thess 2:19; 2 Thess 2:5. Without οὐ a positive answer may still be implied (2 Cor 11:22 [x3]). In other cases the expected answer is "yes" while the question itself is sarcastic: introduced by οὐκ (1 Cor 6:5; 11:14–15); οὐκ οἴδατε ὅτι ... (Rom 6:16; 11:2; 1 Cor 3:16; 5:6; 6:2, 3, 9, 15, 16, 19; 9:13, 24), οὐκ ἐπιγινώσκετε ... ὅτι (2 Cor 13:5). Sometimes the question is laced with doubt: οὐ μνημονεύετε ὅτι ... (2 Thess 2:5).

Questions expecting "no." Most often these are introduced by μή: Rom 3:5b, 8; 9:14; 10:18; 11:1, 11; 1 Cor 9:4, 5, 8; 10:22; 11:22a; 12:29–30 (x7); 2 Cor 3:1b; 12:17. The answer "no" is sometimes evident even without the introductory μή, as when the answer is implied (Rom 4:9; 1 Cor 9:6; 11:13) or the answer is explicitly given following the question (1 Cor 10:19–20; 11:22); often the answer is given in the form μὴ γένοιτο (Rom 3:3–4, 5–6, 31; 6:1–2, 15; 7:7, 13; 9:14; 11:1, 11; 1 Cor 6:15; Gal 2:17; 3:21).

Questions having an ambiguous answer. In absence of οὐ or μή, the expected answer may be left in doubt; e.g., ἢ ἀγνοεῖτε ὅτι, ὅσοι ἐβαπτίσθημεν εἰς Χριστὸν Ἰησοῦν, εἰς τὸν θάνατον αὐτοῦ ἐβαπτίσθημεν; (Rom 6:3). When a question is sarcastic, the answer may depend upon whether one takes the perspective of the speaker or that of the audience (2 Cor 11:7, 11); so also when a question expresses indignation (2 Cor 1:17). The question may simply express astonishment (Gal 3:3, 4; 4:21), without commiting to an answer. In the series of questions in Rom 2:21–23, the addressee embodies the representative Jew in the singular (see §3.2.1.2.3 on apostrophe), so that the implied answer to the questions is "yes" for the representative, but not necessarily for everyone of the class of "Jews."

Questions in a series. Interrogatio sometimes comes in series: of two (1 Cor 6:7; 12:15–16), three (1 Cor 1:13; 9:4–6), four (1 Cor 9:1; cf. 2 Cor 12:17–18), five (Rom 2:21–23), seven (1 Cor 12:29–30). An accumulation of questions may serve to reiterate a single point (1 Cor 1:13; 6:7; 9:1) or to make complementary points (1 Cor 5:12).

Note the series of five questions that mix interrogatio and pysma (§3.2.1.2.5) in 1 Cor 11:22.

3.2.1.2.5. PYSMA/QUAESITUM (LAUSBERG, §770)

Like interrogatio, pysma is a question to which no answer is expected, since the answer is from the speaker's perspective self-evident. Whereas interrogatio, however, can be answered only by "yes" or "no," pysma requires more special answers. Often the answer is a negative expression of some kind, e.g., "I don't know," "Nowhere," "No one," "Nothing," "Not at all." In other cases the implied answer consists in a concession, e.g., "I stand corrected," "I see your point," "I suppose so."

"Then what becomes of boasting? It is excluded. By what law? By that of works? No, but by the law of faith." (Rom 3:27 NRSV)

"How can we who died to sin go on living in it?" (Rom 6:2 NRSV)

"So what advantage did you then get from the things of which you now are ashamed? The end of those things is death." (Rom 6:21 NRSV)

"For in hope we were saved. Now hope that is seen is not hope. For who hopes for what is seen?" (Rom 8:24 NRSV)

"He who did not withhold his own Son, but gave him up for all of us, will he not with him also give us everything else?" (Rom 8:32)

"Who are you to pass judgment on servants of another?" (Rom 14:4)

"For what human being knows what is truly human except the human spirit that is within?" (1 Cor 2:11 NRSV)

"If the whole body were an eye, where would the hearing be? If the whole body were hearing, where would the sense of smell be?" (1 Cor 12:17 NRSV)

"Now if Christ is proclaimed as raised from the dead, how can some of you say there is no resurrection of the dead?" (1 Cor 15:12 NRSV)

STYLE IN PAUL'S LETTERS

"Otherwise, what will those people be doing who receive baptism on behalf of the dead? If the dead are not raised at all, why are people baptized on their behalf?" (1 Cor 15:29)

"For what partnership is there between righteousness and lawlessness? Or what fellowship is there between light and darkness? What agreement does Christ have with Beliar? Or what does a believer share with an unbeliever? What agreement has the temple of God with idols?" (2 Cor 6:14-16 NRSV)

"If I love you more, am I to be loved less?" (2 Cor 12:15; cf. Gal 4:16)

"You foolish Galatians! Who has bewitched you?" (Gal 3:1)

"Now, however, that you have come to know God, or rather to be known by God, how can you turn back again to the weak and beggarly elemental spirits? How can you want to be enslaved to them again?" (Gal 4:9 NRSV)

"Have I now become your enemy by telling you the truth?" (Gal 4:16; cf. 2 Cor 12:15)

"You were running well; who prevented you from obeying the truth" (Gal 5:7 NRSV)

"But my friends, why am I still being persecuted if I am still preaching circumcision?" (Gal 5:11 NRSV)

"How can we thank God enough for you in return for all the joy that we feel before our God because of you?" (1 Thess 3:9)

Other examples include: Rom 8:31; 14:10; 1 Cor 9:7, 9; 14:6, 7, 8, 9, 16; 15:30, 32; 2 Cor 3:8; Gal 2:14; 3:5; 4:15, 21; Col 2:20.

Deliberative questions are sometimes answered immediately (1 Cor 11:22c-d; 14:15, 26). In many cases, Paul provides answers to questions that concern situational ethics; e.g., "Was anyone at the time of his call already circumcised? Let him not seek to remove the marks of circumcision. Was anyone at the time of his call uncircumcised? Let him not seek circumcision" (1 Cor 7:18); likewise, 1 Cor 7:21, 27. In Rom 7:25 Paul answers the question asked in 7:24.

Pysma is often deployed in a series. Questions may come in series of two (1 Cor 4:21; 15:29; Gal 4:9), three (1 Cor 4:7; cf. Rom 3:27), four (Rom

10:14; 1 Cor 1:20; 3:3–5), or more (five in 2 Cor 6:14–15; seven in Rom 8:31–35). A second question may offer a possible answer to the first (Rom 3:27; 1 Cor 4:21). An accumulation of questions may serve to reiterate a single point (1 Cor 1:20; 4:7; 15:29; 2 Cor 6:14–15; Gal 4:9) or may follow a climactic sequence (Rom 10:14).

Note the series of five questions that mix interrogatio (§3.2.1.2.4) and pysma in 1 Cor 11:22.

3.2.1.2.6. SUBIECTIO/AITIOLOGIA (LAUSBERG, §771–75)

Mock dialogue with question and answer (usually in a series) used to enliven the line of thought (usually called "diatribe" in today's parlance). In subiectio the opposing party is represented usually by a fictitious interlocutor who is refuted by an answer introduced by an adversative (e.g., ἀλλά); see also on apostrophe (§3.2.1.2.3). In other cases, questions may be directed toward oneself (Lausberg, §772).

The interlocutor is sometimes invoked explicitly, and is usually in the singular, as in:

"Therefore you (sg.) have no excuse ... And do you (sg.) think this, O person who judges ... " (Rom 2:1, 3)

"You (sg.) will say to me then, 'Why then does he still find fault? For who can resist his will?'" (Rom 9:19 NRSV)

"Who indeed are *you* (sg.), O person ... " (Rom 9:20).

"You (sg.) will say, 'Branches were broken off so that I might be grafted in.'" (Rom 11:19 NRSV)

"But someone (sg.) will ask, 'How are the dead raised? With what kind of body do they come?'" (1 Cor 15:35 NRSV)

Frequently Paul uses the dialogue form to move the logic of his larger argument forward, or to move it toward a clear conclusion, often for the benefit of the audience but sometimes as if addressing the questions to himself or reasoning through the matter himself. This style is especially prevalent in Romans 3 (esp. 3:1, 3[x2], 5 [x2], 6, 7, 8, 9, 27 [x3], 29, 31.[17]

"Then what advantage has the Jew? Or what is the value of circumcision?" (Rom 3:1 NRSV)

"What if some were unfaithful? Will their faithlessness nullify the faithfulness of God?" (Rom 3:3 NRSV)

"Then what becomes of our boasting? It is excluded. By what kind of law? By a law of works? No, but by the law of faith." (Rom 3:27 NRSV)

"What then are we to say? Gentiles, who did not strive for righteousness, have attained it, that is, righteousness through faith; but Israel, who did strive for the righteousness that is based on the law, did not succeed in fulfilling that law. Why not? Because they did not strive for it on the basis of faith, but as if it were based on works." (Rom 9:30–32 NRSV)

"But what does it say? 'The word is near you, on your lips and in your heart' (that is, the word of faith that we proclaim) . . . " (Rom 10:8 NRSV)

"Why then the law? It was added because . . . " (Gal 3:19 NRSV)

Several examples of such dialogue use the formula τί οὖν (Rom 3:9; 6:15; 11:7). On the formula "what then should we say?" (Rom 6:1; 7:7; 9:14, 30), see below under "Dubitatio" (§3.2.1.2.7).

The questions may be used to expose an absurdity; e.g., "And why? Because I do not love you? God knows I do!" (2 Cor 11:11 NRSV).

Other examples of subiectio include Rom 4:1, 3, 10; 10:28; 1 Cor 14:15.

3.2.1.2.7. *Aporia/Dubitatio* (Lausberg, §776–78)

Feigned oratorical helplessness conveyed in the form of a question either to the audience or to oneself about what to say next, used for the purpose of strengthening the credibility of the speaker's point of view. A related figure is communicatio (Lausberg, §779), which consists in appeal to the opinion or judgment of the audience.

---

17. See King, *Speech-in-Character*, 163–293.

"What would you prefer? Am I to come to you with a stick, or with love in a spirit of gentleness?" (1 Cor 4:21 NRSV)

"I speak as to sensible people; judge for yourselves what I say." (1 Cor 10:15 NRSV)

"Judge for yourselves: is it proper for a woman to pray to God with her head unveiled? Does not nature itself teach you that . . . " (1 Cor 11:13–14)

"The only thing I want to learn from you is this: Did you receive the Spirit by doing the works of the law or by believing what you heard?" (Gal 3:2 NRSV)

For other possible examples, see 1 Cor 11:22; 2 Cor 3:1.

The line between communicatio and subiectio (§3.2.1.2.6) is not always clear; consider:

"What then are we to say? Should we continue in sin in order that grace may abound?" (Rom 6:1 NRSV)

"What then should we say? That the law is sin? By no means!" (Rom 7:7 NRSV)

"What then are we to say? Is there injustice on God's part? By no means!" (Rom 9:14 NRSV)

"What then are we to say? Gentiles, who did not strive for righteousness, have attained it, that is, righteousness through faith . . . " (Rom 9:30 NRSV)

3.2.1.2.8. Horismos/Finitio (Lausberg, §782)

A definition of terms.

Romans 2:28–29 establishes a definition of "Jew" (Ἰουδαῖος): "For a person is not a Jew who is one outwardly, nor is true circumcision something external and physical. Rather, a person is a Jew who is one inwardly, and real circumcision is a matter of the heart—it is spiritual and not literal." (NRSV)

Romans 4:4 establishes a definition of "payment" (μισθός): "Now to one who works, wages are not reckoned as a gift but as something due" (NRSV).

3.2.1.2.9. *Synoiciosis/Conciliatio (Lausberg, §783)*

The exploitation of an argument or the terms of an opposing party in order to benefit one's own argument. Synoiciosis occurs for instance in the intentional use of obscure or ambiguous terms in order to lend the impression of agreement.

Identifying instances of synoeciosis in Paul's letters requires reconstruction of his audiences' language and viewpoints, making examples somewhat difficult to identify. In a clearer instance of the device, the terms "fools" (ἀφρόνων) and "children" (νηπίων) as descriptions of the uneducated in Rom 2:20 evidently represent the perspective of the interlocutor, though Paul himself appropriates the terms for the sake of argument. Since Paul goes on to expose the interlocutor as complicit in the same behavior as the "fools" and "children," his concession to the interlocutor's terms ultimately does greater rhetorical damage to their own status as "teachers" of these "fools" and "children."

Another example occurs in Gal 2:17. Here Paul states that, if one grants that those (i.e., "we") who are justified ἐν Χριστῷ rather than ἐξ ἔργων νόμου are, hypothetically speaking, "sinners," one must then accept the conclusion that Christ was a "servant of sin," a conclusion that presumably the audience would not wish to accept.

1 Corinthians contains at least three likely examples of synoiciosis. In 6:5 Paul grants the Corinthians' viewpoint that there may be a "wise man" among them, but in doing so causes them greater embarrassment, for no one is acting like one. Paul's appeal to a Stoic argument from "nature" in 11:14 exposes a contradiction in the Corinthians' behavior, as they themselves seem to have endorsed Stoic teachings.[18] In 15:29 Paul's rhetorical question implies, for the sake of argument, that the Corinthians' practice of baptism for the dead (ὑπὲρ τῶν νεκρῶν) is valid, though if it is valid, this undermines the Corinthians' denial of the general resurrection.

3.2.1.2.10. *Correctio/Epanorthōsis (Lausberg, §784–86)*

A correction by the speaker of what the speaker has just said. The correction may be either a semantic correction or a social correction.

---

18. See Brookins, *Corinthian Wisdom*; and Brookins, "'Natural Hair.'"

Semantic correctio. Semantic correctio comes either in the form "not *x*, but *y*" or, in its stronger form, "*x*—nay, *y*."

"To the married I give this command—not I but the Lord—that the wife should not separate from her husband." (1 Cor 7:10 NRSV)

"To the rest I say—I and not the Lord—that if any believer has a wife who is an unbeliever, and she consents to live with him, he should not divorce her." (1 Cor 7:12 NRSV)

"I worked harder than any of them—though it was not I, but the grace of God that is with me." (1 Cor 15:10 NRSV)

"For, as I can testify, they voluntarily *gave according to their means, and even beyond their means*" (2 Cor 8:3 NRSV)

"you . . . are turning to a different gospel—not that there is another gospel, but there are some who are confusing you and want to pervert the gospel of Christ." (Gal 1:6–7 NRSV)

"*I* no longer live, but *Christ* lives *in* me." (Gal 2:20)

"Did you experience so much for nothing?—if it really was for nothing." (Gal 3:4 NRSV)

"Now, however, that you have come to know God, or rather to be known by God . . . " (Gal 4:9 NRSV)

"For it is we who are the circumcision, who worship in the Spirit of God and boast in Christ Jesus and have no confidence in the flesh—*even though I, too, have confidence in the flesh.*" (Phil 3:3–4)

"Yet whatever gains I had, these I have come to regard as loss because of Christ. But [not just these things], rather, I even consider *all things* as loss, because of the surpassing value of knowing Christ Jesus my Lord." (Phil 3:7–8)

Note also statements introduced by οὐχ ὅτι, "not that" (2 Cor 1:24; 3:5; Phil 3:12; 4:11, 17; cf. Rom 9:6, οὐχ οἷον δὲ ὅτι).

Social correctio. Social correctio serves to tone down the shockingness of the speaker's assertion for the good of the audience.

STYLE IN PAUL'S LETTERS

"I wish you would bear with me in a little foolishness. Do bear with me!" (2 Cor 11:1 NRSV)

"I repeat, let no one think that I am a fool; but if you do, then accept me as a fool, so that I too may boast a little. What I am saying in regard to this boastful confidence, I am saying not with the Lord's authority, but as a fool ..." (2 Cor 11:16–17 NRSV)

"But whatever anyone dares to boast of—*I am speaking as a fool*—I also dare to boast of that." (2 Cor 11:21 NRSV)

"Are they servants of Christ? (*I speak as if insane*) I more so; in far more labors, in far more imprisonments, beaten times without number, often in danger of death." (2 Cor 11:23 NASB)

"*I have been a fool!* You forced me to it. Indeed you should have been the ones commending me, for I am not at all inferior to these super-apostles, even though I am nothing." (2 Cor 12:11 NRSV)

3.2.1.2.11. ANTITHETON (LAUSBERG, §787–807)

Antitheton consists in the opposition of contrasting words, word groups, or sentences. Cases of isocolon consisting of two colons may also exhibit antithetical conceptual content; see above on antithetical isocolon (§3.2.1.1.30).

"those who ... do not obey the truth, but obey unrighteousness" (Rom 2:8 ESV)

"For it is not the hearers of the law who are righteous in God's sight, but the doers of the law who will be justified." (Rom 2:13 NRSV)

"I do not do the good I want, but the evil I do not want is what I do." (Rom 7:19 NRSV)

"Moses writes concerning the righteousness that comes from the law, ... But the righteousness that comes from faith ..." (Rom 10:5, 6 NRSV)

"Bless those who persecute you; *bless and do not curse them*." (Rom 12:14 NRSV)

"For Jews demand signs and Greeks desire wisdom, but we proclaim Christ crucified, a stumbling block to Jews and foolishness to Gentiles, but to those who are the called, both Jews and Greeks, Christ the power of God and the wisdom of God. (1 Cor 1:22–24 NRSV)

"God's foolishness is wiser than human wisdom, and God's weakness is stronger than human strength." (1 Cor 1:25)

"For though I am free with respect to all, I have made myself a slave to all . . ." (1 Cor 9:19)

"For we know only in part, and we prophesy only in part; but when the complete comes, the partial will come to an end." (1 Cor 13:9–10)

"When I was a child, I spoke like a child, I thought like a child, I reasoned like a child; when I became an adult, I put an end to childish ways." (1 Cor 13:11)

"I would rather speak five words with my mind, in order to instruct others also, than ten thousand words in a tongue." (1 Cor 14:19 NRSV)

"Brothers and sisters, do not be children in your thinking; rather, be infants in evil, but in thinking be adults." (1 Cor 14:20)

In 1 Cor 15:50, antithetical terms are placed in direct contact: "nor does the perishable inherit the imperishable (οὐδὲ **ἡ φθορὰ τὴν ἀφθαρσίαν** κληρονομεῖ)."

"We are afflicted in every way, but not crushed; perplexed, but not driven to despair; persecuted, but not forsaken; struck down, but not destroyed . . ." (2 Cor 4:8–9)

"So if anyone is in Christ, there is a new creation: everything old has passed away; see, everything has become new!" (2 Cor 5:17)

2 Corinthians 13:3–9 develops a contrast between "weakness" and "strength" in a series of balanced lines:

ὃς εἰς ὑμᾶς οὐκ **ἀσθενεῖ** ἀλλὰ **δυνατεῖ** ἐν ὑμῖν.

καὶ γὰρ ἐσταυρώθη **ἐξ ἀσθενείας**, ἀλλὰ ζῇ **ἐκ δυνάμεως** θεοῦ.

καὶ γὰρ ἡμεῖς **ἀσθενοῦμεν** ἐν αὐτῷ, ἀλλὰ ζήσομεν σὺν αὐτῷ **ἐκ δυνάμεως** θεοῦ εἰς ὑμᾶς.

... χαίρομεν γὰρ ὅταν ἡμεῖς **ἀσθενῶμεν**, ὑμεῖς δὲ **δυνατοὶ** ἦτε·

"For through the law I died to the law, so that I might live to God." (Gal 2:19)

"Formerly, when you did not know God, you were enslaved to beings that by nature are not gods. Now, however, that you have come to know God, or rather to be known by God, how can you turn back again to the weak and beggarly elemental spirits? How can you want to be enslaved to them again?" (Gal 4:8–9)

"But if you are led by the Spirit, you are not under the Law." (Gal 5:18 NASB)

An extended antithesis between the two sons of Abraham / their mothers—or between two covenants—occurs in Gal 4:21—5:1.

"For them this is evidence of their destruction, but of your salvation." (Phil 1:28)

"who, though he was in the form of God, did not regard equality with God as something to be exploited . . . " (Phil 2:6)

"All of them are seeking their own interests, not those of Jesus Christ." (Phil 2:21)

" . . . beware of those who mutilate the flesh! For it is we who are the circumcision . . . " (Phil 3:2–3)

"Yet whatever gains I had, these I have come to regard as loss because of Christ." (Phil 3:7)

" . . . not having a righteousness of my own that comes from the law, but one that comes through faith in Christ, the righteousness from God based on faith." (Phil 3:9)

"For though I am absent in body, yet I am with you in spirit . . . " (Col 2:5)

"for you are all children of light and children of the day; we are not of the night or of darkness." (1 Thess 5:5)

"See that none of you repays evil for evil, but always seek to do good to one another and to all." (1 Thess 5:15)

The οὐ/οὐκ/μή . . . ἀλλά antithesis is ubiquitous in Paul's letters (1 Cor 1:17; 2:4, 5, 13; 5:8; Gal 4:31; Phil 3:9; etc.). More significant are examples that involve antonyms; e.g., ποτέ σοι **ἄχρηστον** νυνὶ δὲ [καὶ] σοὶ καὶ ἐμοὶ **εὔχρηστον** (Phlm 11).

Some passages contain a plethora of antitheses:

In Rom 1:19–25, there is contrast between what is "known" or "revealed" on the one hand, and the fact that their hearts were "darkened" on the other (vv. 19–21); and contrasts also in "[c]laiming to be wise, they became fools" (v. 22); the "incorruptible God" and "corruptible man" (v. 23); and "they exchanged the truth about God for a lie," "worshiped and served the creature rather than the Creator" (v. 25, NRSV).

In Rom 12:9–19: hating evil, and clinging to good (v. 9); blessing and not cursing those who persecute (v. 14); not thinking lofty thoughts but associating with the humble (v. 16); not avenging but leaving place for God's wrath (v. 19).

In Rom 8:39–39: "neither death, nor life"; "nor things present, nor things to come" (Rom 8:38–39)

A series of antitheses occurs in 1 Cor 4:10: "We are fools for the sake of Christ, but you are wise in Christ. We are weak, but you are strong. You are held in honor, but we in disrepute . . . " (NRSV)

Following nine antitheses in 2 Cor 6:8–10 are several additional antitheses in 6:14–15: antitheses between righteousness and lawlessness (6:14), between light and darkness (6:14), between Christ and Beliar (6:15), between believer and unbeliever (6:15), between the temple of God and idols (6:15).

1 Thess 5:4–8 contains a mix of conceptually overlapping antitheses: darkness and light, night and day, sleep and wakefulness, drunk and sober.

Where antithesis is strengthened by cross-arrangement of the corresponding elements the arrangement can be considered—in modern terms—as chiasm (cf. Lausberg, §723; p. 322, n.2; see also above on chiasm structured as isocolon, §3.2.1.1.23). For example:

STYLE IN PAUL'S LETTERS

[A] ἡ ἀδικία [B] ἡμῶν [B] θεοῦ [A] δικαιοσύνην συνίστησιν ... (Rom 3:5)

[A] ἡ ἀλήθεια [B] τοῦ θεοῦ [B] ἐν τῷ ἐμῷ [A] ψεύσματι ἐπερίσσευσεν. (Rom 3:7)

εἴ [A] τις [B] τὸν ναὸν τοῦ θεοῦ [C] φθείρει, [C] φθερεῖ [B] τοῦτον [A] ὁ θεός (1 Cor 3:17)

[A] πᾶσα πικρία καὶ θυμὸς καὶ ὀργὴ καὶ κραυγὴ καὶ βλασφημία [B] ἀρθήτω ἀφ' ὑμῶν σὺν πάσῃ κακίᾳ. [B] γίνεσθε εἰς ἀλλήλους [A] χρηστοί, εὔσπλαγχνοι, χαριζόμενοι ἑαυτοῖς καθὼς καὶ ὁ θεὸς ἐν Χριστῷ ἐχαρίσατο ὑμῖν.

[A] ὃς ἐν μορφῇ θεοῦ ὑπάρχων [B] οὐχ ἁρπαγμὸν ἡγήσατο τὸ εἶναι ἴσα θεῷ, [B] ἀλλὰ ἑαυτὸν ἐκένωσεν [A] μορφὴν δούλου λαβών ... (Phil 2:6–7)

[A] καυχώμενοι [B] ἐν Χριστῷ Ἰησοῦ καὶ οὐκ [B] ἐν σαρκὶ [A] πεποιθότες (Phil 3:3)

[A] μὴ ὡς ἐχθρὸν [B] ἡγεῖσθε, [B] ἀλλὰ νουθετεῖτε [A] ὡς ἀδελφόν (2 Thess 3:15)

Paradoxes entail antithesis:

"in honor and dishonor, in ill repute and good repute. We are treated as impostors, and yet are true; as unknown, and yet are well known; as dying, and see—we are alive; as punished, and yet not killed; as sorrowful, yet always rejoicing; as poor, yet making many rich; as having nothing, and yet possessing everything." (2 Cor 6:8–10 NRSV)

3.2.1.2.12. *Regressio/Epanodos (Lausberg, §798)*

The detailing resumption of each single element in a bipartite enumeration.

2 Corinthians 1:3 elaborates on the two previously named items in reverse order: "Blessed be the **God and Father** of our Lord Jesus Christ, the **Father** of mercies and the **God** of all consolation." (NRSV)

"For we are the aroma of Christ to God among **those who are being saved** and among **those who are perishing**; **to the one** a fragrance from death to death, **to the other** a fragrance from life to life." (2 Cor 2:15–16 NRSV)

In Phil 1:15–17 Paul names "some" who preach out of "envy and jealousy," and "some" who preach "with good motives" (v. 15) and then elaborates on the two groups in reverse order (vv. 16, 17, respectively).

3.2.1.2.13. *Antimetabolē/Commutatio (Lausberg, §800–803)*

Commutatio is a special type of antitheton consisting in the opposition of an idea and its converse by means of the repetition of the two word stems, with reciprocal exchange of the syntactical function of both stems in the repetition (Lausberg, §800). The relationship is chiastic either as to the arrangement of stems or as to their functions.

"remember that it is not you that support the root, but the root that supports you." (Rom 11:18 NRSV)

"Do not be overcome by evil, but overcome evil with good." (Rom 12:21 NRSV)

"Those who eat must not despise those who abstain, and those who abstain must not pass judgment on those who eat." (Rom 14:3 NRSV)

Two instances of antimetabole occur in 1 Cor 6:13 (the first instance may be a citation of a Corinthian slogan):

"'Food is meant for the stomach and the stomach for food,' ... "

"The body is meant not for fornication but for the Lord, and the Lord for the body."

Two instances of antimetabole occur in 1 Cor 7:2–4:

"For the wife does not have authority over her own body, but the husband does;"

"likewise the husband does not have authority over his own body, but the wife does."

"Was anyone at the time of his call already circumcised? Let him not reverse his circumcision. Was anyone at the time of his call uncircumcised? Let him not seek circumcision." (1 Cor 7:18)

"For whoever was called in the Lord as a slave is a freed person belonging to the Lord, just as whoever was free when called is a slave of Christ." (1 Cor 7:22 NRSV)

"For if a woman does not cover her head, let her also have her hair cut off; but if it is disgraceful for a woman to have her hair cut off or her head shaved, let her cover her head." (1 Cor 11:6 NASB)

Two instances of antimetabole occur in 1 Cor 11:8–9:

"Indeed, man was not made from woman, but woman from man." (NRSV)
"Neither was man created for the sake of woman, but woman for the sake of man." (NRSV)

"Just as woman is from the man, so also is the man from the woman." (1 Cor 11:12)

"For if *I pain you*, who is there to make me glad but *the one pained by me*?" (2 Cor 2:2)

"children ought not to lay up for their parents, but parents for their children." (2 Cor 12:14 NRSV)

"For I fear that when I come, I may find you not as I wish, and that you may find me not as you wish . . . " (2 Cor 12:20 NRSV)

"For what the flesh desires is opposed to the Spirit, and what the Spirit desires is opposed to the flesh." (Gal 5:17 NRSV)

"the world has been crucified to me, and I to the world." (Gal 6:14 NRSV)

3.2.1.2.14. OXYMORON/PARADOX (LAUSBERG, §807)

Oxymoron consists in a tight syntactic linking of contradictory terms into a unity that, as a result, acquires a strong contradictive tension. In its expanded form, the contradiction occurs at the level of thought, and is called "paradox," insofar as it is "surprising" (παράδοξος) as a fact.

Note "invisible things (τὰ ἀόρατα) . . . seen (καθορᾶται)" (Rom 1:20). "To be ambitious to be quiet (φιλοτιμεῖσθαι ἡσυχάζειν)" combines the idea of political ambition with political quietism. "The corpses (οἱ νεκροί)" will "get up incorruptible (ἐγερθήσονται)" (1 Cor 15:52).

In less compressed form, but equally paradoxical: "if we have died with Christ . . . we shall also live with him" (Rom 6:8); "whoever was called in the Lord as a slave is a freed person belonging to the Lord, just as whoever was free when called is a slave of Christ" (1 Cor 7:22 NRSV); "Christ-crucified" (1 Cor 1:23) as the "power of God" (1 Cor 1:24); "crucified the Lord of glory" (1 Cor 2:8), in which the most honored is subjected to the lowest shame; "let that person become a fool in order that they might become wise" (1 Cor 3:18); "let even those who have wives be as though they had none, and those who mourn as though they were not mourning, and those who rejoice as though they were not rejoicing, and those who buy as though they had no possessions, and those who deal with the world as though they had no dealings with it" (1 Cor 7:29–31 NRSV); "always carrying in the body the death of Jesus, so that the life of Jesus may also be made visible in our bodies" (2 Cor 4:10 NRSV); "For while we live, we are always being given up to death for Jesus's sake, so that the life of Jesus may be made visible in our mortal flesh" (2 Cor 4:11 NRSV); "we look not at what can be seen but at what cannot be seen" (2 Cor 4:18 NRSV); "being stripped we shall not be found naked" (2 Cor 5:3); "we are treated as impostors, and yet are true; as unknown, and yet are well known; as dying, and see—we are alive; as punished, and yet not killed; as sorrowful, yet always rejoicing; as poor, yet making many rich; as having nothing, and yet possessing everything" (2 Cor 6:8–10 NRSV); "the overabundance of their joy and their deep poverty overflowed into the wealth of their generosity" (2 Cor 8:2); "the Lord Jesus Christ, that though he was rich he became poor for our sake" (2 Cor 8:9); "he said to me, 'My grace is sufficient for you, for power is made perfect in weakness.' So, I will boast all the more gladly of my weaknesses, so that the power of Christ may dwell in me" (2 Cor 12:9 NRSV); "when I am weak, then I am strong" (2 Cor 12:10); "so that I might live to God; I have been crucified with Christ" (Gal 2:19); "their glory is in their shame" (Phil 3:19); "not that I seek your gifts, but I seek the profit that increases in your account" (Phil 4:17), i.e., the Philippians receive in the act of giving; "who died on our behalf, in order that . . . we might live with him" (1 Thess 5:10), i.e., Christ died and yet lives.

3.2.1.2.15. *Exclamatio (Lausberg, §809)*

Exclamatio consists in the expression of emotion by means of an isolated and intense pronouncement.

"Wretched man that I am!" (Rom 7:24)

"Thanks be to God through Jesus Christ our Lord!" (Rom 7:24 NRSV)

"Already you have all you want! Already you have become rich! Quite apart from us you have become kings! Indeed, I wish that you had become kings, so that we might be kings with you!" (1 Cor 4:8 NRSV)

"My children, for whom I am again in labor until Christ be formed in you!" (Gal 4:19 NAB)

Fourteen instances of μὴ γένοιτο, "May it never be!" (Rom 3:4, 6, 31; 6:2, 15; 7:7, 13; 9:14; 11:1, 11; 1 Cor 6:15; Gal 2:17; 3:21; 6:14).

3.2.1.2.16. SERMOCINATIO (LAUSBERG, §820–25)

The fabrication of statements, conversations, soliloquies, or unexpressed mental reflections of either historical or invented persons. Cf. prosopopoeia (Lausberg §826–9).

"But the righteousness that comes from faith says: 'Do not say in your heart, "Who will ascend into heaven?"' . . . But what does it say? 'The word is near you; on your lips and in your heart' . . . " (Rom 10:6–8 NRSV; King 2018: 88–95)

"What I mean is that each of you says, 'I belong to Paul,' or 'I belong to Apollos,' or 'I belong to Cephas,' or 'I belong to Christ.'" (1 Cor 1:12 NRSV; cf. 3:4)

"If the foot would say, 'Because I am not a hand, I do not belong to the body,' that would not make it any less a part of the body. And if the ear would say, 'Because I am not an eye, I do not belong to the body,' that would not make it any less a part of the body." (1 Cor 12:15–16 NRSV)

"For they say, 'His letters are weighty and strong, but his bodily presence is weak, and his speech contemptible.'" (2 Cor 10:10 NRSV)

"When they say, 'There is peace and security,' then sudden destruction will come upon them" (1 Thess 5:3 NRSV)[19]

---

19. So King, *Speech-in-Character*, 63–68.

In Gal 4:6 it is the Spirit (πνεῦμα) that cries out "Abba, Father!"[20]; in 1 Cor 12:3, the Spirit says "Jesus is Lord."[21]

Stowers identifies Rom 7:7–25 as prosopopoeia;[22] so also Witherington.[23]

See also sermocinatio involving a fictitious interlocutor in Subiectio/Aitiologia (§3.2.1.2.6).

3.2.1.2.17. *Prosopopoeia/Fictio Personae (Lausberg, §826–29)*

The introduction of non-personal things as persons capable of speech and other forms of personified behavior.

"*Who* will separate us from the love of Christ? Will hardship, or distress, or persecution, or famine, or nakedness, or peril, or sword? ... For I am convinced that neither death, nor life, nor angels, nor rulers, nor things present, nor things to come, nor powers, nor height, nor depth, nor anything else in all creation, will be able to separate us from the love of God in Christ Jesus our Lord." (Rom 8:35, 38 NRSV)

"But the righteousness that comes from faith says: 'Do not say in your heart, "Who will ascend into heaven?"' ... But what does it say? 'The word is near you; on your lips and in your heart' ... " (Rom 10:6–8 NRSV[24])

"If the foot would say, 'Because I am not a hand, I do not belong to the body,' that would not make it any less a part of the body. And if the ear would say, 'Because I am not an eye, I do not belong to the body,' that would not make it any less a part of the body." (1 Cor 12:15–16 NRSV)

"Love is patient; love is kind; love is not envious or boastful or arrogant or rude. It does not insist on its own way; it is not irritable or resentful; it does not rejoice in wrongdoing, but rejoices in the truth. It bears all things, believes all things, hopes all things, endures all things." (1 Cor 13:4–7 NRSV)

---

20. King, *Speech-in-Character*, 71–73.
21. King, *Speech-in-Character*, 78–81.
22. Stowers, "Romans 7:7–25 as a Speech-in-Character."
23. Witherington, *New Testament Rhetoric*, 132–52.
24. King, *Speech-in-Character*, 88–95.

STYLE IN PAUL'S LETTERS

Other examples include: Scripture "seeing beforehand" (Gal 3:8); death (Rom 5:14, 17; 1 Cor 15:26; 15:54//Hos 13:14), sin (Rom 5:21; 6:12-23; 7:8; Gal 2:17), flesh (against the Spirit in Gal 5:13-25), grace (Rom 5:21), righteousness (Rom 10:6), or creation (Rom 8:22) as actors; cf. "the power of darkness" (Col 1:13).

3.2.1.2.18. EXPOLITIO/ORATIO VARIATA (LAUSBERG, §830-42)

The elaboration of an idea either through (1) repeated *linguistic* expression of the same idea ("*saying* the same thing") or through (2) the *intellectual* development of the idea ("speaking *about* the same thing"); the boundaries between the two kinds of expolitio are fluid. Elaboration through repetition (1), also known as "epimone" (Lausberg, §835), consists in saying the same thing while changing either (a) the pronunciation or (b) the wording. The changed wording, in turn, constitutes either (i) a linguistically variable paraphrase (Lausberg, §837) or (ii) a mentally variable paraphrase (Lausberg, §838). In its short form, the change of wording using word-for-word pharaphrase is considered interpretatio (§3.2.1.1.31), or paraphrase expressed in the form of synonymous colons. While expolitio possesses a similarity to the style of Hebrew poetry, with its use of synonymous parallelism, in Paul's epistles this phenomenon is more akin to the Greek style of oratory (BDF, §489).

Synonymous repetition of the idea. Many examples consist in a series of two or more synonymous lines:

"[1] they exchanged the glory of the immortal God for images resembling a mortal human being or birds or four-footed animals or reptiles. . . .

[2] because they exchanged the truth about God for a lie and worshiped and served the creature rather than the Creator."
(Rom 1:23-25 NRSV)

Rom 2:7-8 are synonymous with 2:9-10, though the content is chiastically arranged:
"[1] [A] to those who by patiently doing good seek for glory and honor and immortality, he will give eternal life; [B] while for those who are

self-seeking and who obey not the truth but wickedness, there will be wrath and fury. (vv. 7–8)

[2] [B] There will be anguish and distress for everyone who does evil, the Jew first and also the Greek, [A] but glory and honor and peace for everyone who does good, the Jew first and also the Greek." (vv. 9, 10)

"[1] [A] What then are we to say was gained by Abraham, our ancestor according to the flesh? [B] For if Abraham was justified by works, he has something to boast about, but not before God.

[2] [A] For what does the scripture say? [B] 'Abraham believed God, and it was reckoned to him as righteousness.'"

(Rom 4:1–3)

"[1] Much more surely then, now that we have been justified by his blood, will we be saved through him from the wrath of God.

[2] For if while we were enemies, we were reconciled to God through the death of his Son, much more surely, having been reconciled, will we be saved by his life."

(Rom 5:9–10)

"[1] For since death came through a human being, the resurrection of the dead has also come through a human being;

[2] for as all die in Adam, so all will be made alive in Christ."

(1 Cor 15:21–22)

"[1] I am speaking the truth in Christ—[2] I am not lying; [3] my conscience confirms it by the Holy Spirit—I have great sorrow and unceasing anguish in my heart." (Rom 9:1–2 NRSV)

Rom 9:6–7 are roughly synonymous with 9:8:

[1] [A] For not all Israelites truly belong to Israel, and not all of Abraham's children are his true descendants; [B] but 'It is through Isaac that descendants shall be named for you.' (vv. 6–7)

τοῦτ' ἔστιν,

[2] [A] it is not the children of the flesh who are the children of God, [B] but the children of the promise are counted as descendants." (v. 8)

Rom 11:12, 15 are roughly synonymous (NRSV):

[1] [A] Now if their stumbling means riches for the world, and if their defeat means riches for Gentiles, [B] how much more will their full inclusion mean! (v. 12)

[2] [A] For if their rejection is the reconciliation of the world, [B] what will their acceptance be but life from the dead!" (v. 15)

"[1] O the depth of the riches and wisdom and knowledge of God! [2] How unsearchable are his judgments and [3] how inscrutable his ways! [4] 'For who has known the mind of the Lord? [5] Or who has been his counselor?'" (Rom 11:33–34)

"[1] that all of you be in agreement

[2] and that there be no divisions among you."

(1 Cor 1:10 NRSV)

"[1] For in the one Spirit we were all baptized into one body—Jews or Greeks, slaves or free—

[2] and we were all made to drink of one Spirit."

(1 Cor 12:13 NRSV)

In 1 Cor 13:1–3, the same idea is expressed three times, in element [C]:

[1] [A] Ἐὰν ταῖς γλώσσαις . . . , [B] ἀγάπην δὲ μὴ ἔχω, [C] γέγονα χαλκὸς ἠχῶν ἢ κύμβαλον ἀλαλάζον.

[2] [A] καὶ ἐὰν ἔχω προφητείαν . . . , [B] ἀγάπην δὲ μὴ ἔχω, [C] οὐθέν εἰμι.

[3] [A] κἂν ψωμίσω πάντα τὰ ὑπάρχοντά μου . . . , [B] ἀγάπην δὲ μὴ ἔχω, [C] οὐδὲν ὠφελοῦμαι.

(1 Cor 13:1–3)

"[1] For [A] now we see in a mirror, dimly, [B] but then we will see face to face.

[2] [A] Now I know only in part; [B] then I will know fully, even as I have been fully known. (1 Cor 13:12 NRSV)

"[1] It is sown a physical body, it is raised a spiritual body.

[2] If there is a physical body, there is also a spiritual body."

(1 Cor 15:44)

"[1] flesh and blood cannot inherit the kingdom of God,

[2] nor does the perishable inherit the imperishable."

(1 Cor 15:50 NRSV)

"[1] I was not vacillating when I intended to do this, was I?

[2] Or that which I purpose, do I purpose according to the flesh, that with me there should be yes, yes and no, no at the same time?"

(2 Cor 1:17 NASB)

"[1] [A] always carrying in the body the death of Jesus, [B] so that the life of Jesus may also be made visible in our bodies.

[2] [A] For while we live, we are always being given up to death for Jesus's sake, [B] so that the life of Jesus may be made visible in our mortal flesh."

(2 Cor 4:10–11 NRSV)

"[1] [A] So we are ambassadors for Christ, [B] since God is making his appeal through us;

[2] [A] we entreat you on behalf of Christ, [B] be reconciled to God."

(2 Cor 5:20 NRSV)

"[1] For I did not receive it from a human being—

[2] nor was I taught it . . . "

(Gal 1:12).

"[1] Live by the Spirit, I say,

[2] and do not gratify the desires of the flesh."

(Gal 5:16)

"[1] I have learned to be content with whatever I have.

[2] I know what it is to have little, and I know what it is to have plenty.

[3] In any and all circumstances I have learned the secret of being well-fed and of going hungry, of having plenty and of being in need."

(Phil 4:11–12 NRSV)

Synonymous repetition with isocolon. Where expolitio involves isocolon, parallel lines are synonymous and the device is known as Interpretatio (§3.2.1.1.31).

Repetition of the same thought. In cases there is repetition of the same idea in different words, and without the use of parallel lines or isocolon.

"Whom God put forward as a sacrifice of atonement by his blood, effective through faith (διὰ [τῆς] πίστεως ἐν τῷ αὐτοῦ αἵματι). He did this to show his righteousness (εἰς ἔνδειξιν τῆς δικαιοσύνης αὐτου), because in his divine forbearance he had passed over the sins previously committed; it was to prove at the present time that he himself is righteous (πρὸς τὴν ἔνδειξιν τῆς δικαιοσύνης αὐτοῦ) and that he justifies the one who has faith in Jesus (ἐκ πίστεως Ἰησοῦ)." (Rom 3:25–26 NRSV)

The content of 1 Cor 7:29–31 is bracketed by the virtually synonymous expressions ὁ καιρὸς συνεσταλμένος ἐστίν and παράγει ... τὸ σχῆμα τοῦ κόσμου τούτου.

1 Corinthians 15:13–18 is highly repetitive. Most redundant are the repetition of the idea in vv. 13, 16 and of the idea in vv. 14, 17:

"13 If there is no resurrection of the dead, then Christ has not been raised; 14 and if Christ has not been raised, then our proclamation has been in vain and your faith has been in vain. 15 We are even found to be misrepresenting God, because we testified of God that he raised Christ—whom he did not raise if it is true that the dead are not raised. 16 For if the dead are not raised, then Christ has not been raised. 17 If Christ has not been raised, your faith is futile and you are still in your sins. 18 Then those also who have died in Christ have perished." (NRSV)

"Be of the same mind, having the same love, being in full accord and of one mind" (Phil 2:2 NRSV)

"Not having a righteousness of my own that comes from the law, but [1] one that comes through faith in Christ, [2] the righteousness from God based on faith." (Phil 3:9 NRSV)

"In the same way, [1] husbands should love their wives as they do their own bodies.

[2] He who loves his wife loves himself." (Eph 5:28 NRSV)

"[1] seek the things that are above, where Christ is, seated at the right hand of God. [2] Set your minds on things that are above, not on things that are on earth." (Col 3:1–2 NRSV)

A repetition of thought is most extensive in Rom 5:15–21 (the gift vs. trespass; justification vs. condemnation; righteousness vs. unrighteousness; grace vs. sin; life vs. death); 6:12–21 (slaves of sin vs. slaves of Christ; law vs. grace; unrighteousness vs. righteousness); 7:15–21 (doing what he does not wish to do vs. not doing what he wishes to do).

Repetition with parallel development of the thought. Other examples involve parallel syntax but with repetition around ("talking *about*") the same topic and with development of the thought.

" . . . and not to please ourselves. Each of us must please our neighbor . . . For Christ did not please himself" (Rom 15:1–2, 3)

"[1] I know a person in Christ who fourteen years ago was caught up to the third heaven—whether in the body or out of the body I do not know; God knows. [2] And I know that such a person—whether in the body or out of the body I do not know; God knows—was caught up into Paradise and heard things that are not to be told, that no mortal is permitted to repeat." (2 Cor 12:2–4 NRSV)

"[1] when they saw that I had been entrusted with the gospel for the uncircumcised, just as Peter had been entrusted with the gospel for the circumcised [2] (for he who worked through Peter making him an apostle to the circumcised also worked through me in sending me to the Gentiles)." (Gal 2:7–8 NRSV)

"[1] Now before faith came, we were imprisoned and guarded under the law until faith would be revealed. [2] Therefore the law was our disciplinarian until Christ came, so that we might be justified by faith" (Gal 3:23–24 NRSV)

Repetition with non-parallel development of the thought. The thought can also be developed without the use of parallel syntax.

"For while we were still weak, at the right time Christ died for the ungodly. Indeed, rarely will anyone die for a righteous person—though perhaps for a good person someone might actually dare to die. But God proves his love for us in that while we still were sinners Christ died for us." (Rom 5:6–8)

"For rulers are not a terror to good conduct, but to bad. Do you wish to have no fear of the authority? Then do what is good, and you will receive its approval; for it is God's servant for your good. But if you do what is wrong, you should be afraid, for the authority does not bear the sword in vain! It is the servant of God to execute wrath on the wrongdoer." (Rom 13:3–4 NRSV)

Romans 14:1–10 elaborates, with varying levels of redundancy, the fact that God will judge/receive both those who "eat" and those who "do not eat."

"[1] For whoever was called in the Lord as a slave is a freed person belonging to the Lord, just as whoever was free when called is a slave of Christ. [2] You were bought with a price; do not become slaves of human masters." (1 Cor 7:22–23 NRSV)

"What you sow does not come to life unless it dies. And as for what you sow, you do not sow the body that is to be, but a bare seed, perhaps of wheat or of some other grain. But God gives it a body as he has chosen, and to each kind of seed its own body." (1 Cor 15:36–38 NRSV)

"Yet we know that a person is justified not by the works of the law but through faith in Jesus Christ. And we have come to believe in Christ Jesus, so that we might be justified by faith in Christ, and not by doing the works of the law, because no one will be justified by the works of the law." (Gal 2:16 NRSV)

"[1] God chose you as the first fruits for salvation through sanctification by the Spirit and through belief in the truth. [2] For this purpose he called you through our proclamation of the good news, so that you may obtain the glory of our Lord Jesus Christ." (2 Thess 2:13–14)

3.2.1.2.19. Simile/Similitudo (Lausberg, §843–47)

The use of comparison to clarify the matter at hand by appealing to more familiar experiences of natural and human life (but not to historically fixed events). Comparison characterized by maximum level of familiarity are hackneyed and cannot be considered ornamental. For the similar device of "allegory" (§3.1.3.2) see above under tropes (§3.1.3).

"For as in one body we have many members, and not all the members have the same function, so we, who are many, are one body in Christ, and individually we are members one of another." (Rom 12:4–5)

"Do you not know that those who are employed in the temple service get their food from the temple, and those who serve at the altar share in what is sacrificed on the altar? *In the same way*, the Lord commanded that those who proclaim the gospel should get their living by the gospel." (1 Cor 10:13–14 NRSV)

1 Corinthians 15:36–49 weaves together allegory and simile. Following the allegory of the seed (vv. 36–38), Paul develops a single simile in two parts (which itself contains further allegory in vv. 45–49): just as there are various kinds of bodies within the created order (1 Cor 15:39–42), (1) "so also" (οὕτως) are there multiple (or two) types of human body (15:42–44); and (2) "so also" (οὕτως) is there a distinction between the earthly body, like Adam's, and the heavenly body, like Christ's (15:45–49).

In Gal 4:1–7, Paul says that, just as heirs are like slaves when they are still minors (both being overseen by a guardian), so also, believers were enslaved to the spirits of the world while young but have now been redeemed.

In Rom 5:12–21; 1 Cor 15:22 Paul compares (the epochs of) Adam/Christ.

There are many shorter similes: shining "as stars in the world" (Phil 2:15); "shown as if reflected in a mirror" (2 Cor 3:18); heirs/minors as slaves (Gal 4:1–3); Paul being received "as an angel of God" (Gal 4:14); "like a nurse tenderly caring for her own children" (1 Thess 2:7 NRSV); "like a father with his children" (1 Thess 2:11 NRSV); "like a thief" (1 Thess 5:2, 4); "sudden destruction will come upon them, as labor pains come upon a pregnant woman" (1 Thess 5:3 NRSV); "the husband is the head of the wife just as Christ is the head of the church" (Eph 5:23).

STYLE IN PAUL'S LETTERS

3.2.1.2.20. *Proparaskeuē/Praeparatio (Lausberg, §854–55)*

Proparaskeuē occurs when the speaker prepares the audience for certain (usually shocking) lines of argument.

In Rom 9:1–5, Paul solemnly asserts that he has sincere love for his fellow Israelites and emphasizes his conviction that manifold salvation privileges still belong to them. These assurances are made in preparation for what will appear, to non-believing Jews, to be a shocking discourse about God's present wrath toward Israel.

3.2.1.2.21. *Concessio (Lausberg, §856)*

A confession of the validity of one or another of an opponent's arguments.

In Gal 1:17 Paul concedes that, although he did not learn his gospel from any human being (1:16), he did visit Jerusalem and meet with those who were apostles before him.

3.2.1.2.22. *Parenthesis/Interpositio (Lausberg, §860)*

The insertion into a sentence of a clause that is distinct from, though not unrelated, to the subject. As with hyperbaton (§3.1.3.12), the resulting cyclical structure creates tension that stands in need of resolution. Parenthesis is sometimes involved in correctio (§3.2.1.2.10).

"And why not say (as some people slander us by saying that we say), 'Let us do evil so that good may come'? Their condemnation is deserved!" (Rom 3:8 NRSV)

"I am speaking the truth in Christ—I am not lying; my conscience confirms it by the Holy Spirit—I have great sorrow and unceasing anguish in my heart." (Rom 9:1–2 NRSV)

"Even before they had been born or had done anything good or evil—so that God's purpose of election might continue, not by works but by his call—she was told, 'The older shall serve the younger.'" (Rom 9:11–12)

"But to me it is of little consequence that I should be evaluated by you or by any human court. So far from that, I do not even evaluate myself (for I am not aware of anything regarding myself, though I am not justified by this fact); rather, the one evaluating me is the Lord." (1 Cor 4:3–4)

"To the married I give this command—not I but the Lord—that the wife should not separate from her husbanad—and if she does separate, let her remain unmarried or else be reconciled to her husband—and that the husband should not divorce his wife." (1 Cor 7:10–11)

"To those under the law I became as one under the law (though I myself am not under the law) so that I might win those under the law. To those outside the law I became as one outside the law (though I am not free from God's law but am under Christ's law) so that I might win those outside the law." (1 Cor 9:20–21 NRSV)

"And spirits of prophets are subject to prophets (for God is not a God of disorder but of peace), just as in all the churches of the saints." (1 Cor 14:32–33)

" . . . through which also you are being saved (for what other reason did I preach to you?), if you hold fast, unless you believed heedlessly." (1 Cor 15:2)

"Now, I urge you, brothers and sisters—you know the household of Stephanas, that it is, as it were, a first-fruit of Achaia, and that they have appointed themselves for ministry to the saints—I urge *you* also to be subject to such people as these." (1 Cor 16:15–16)

"In return (I speak as to children) open wide your hearts also." (2 Cor 6:13)

" . . . though I did regret it—for I see that that letter caused you sorrow, though only for a while—I now rejoice." (2 Cor 7:8–9 NASB)

"But whatever anyone dares to boast of (I am speaking as a fool) I also dare to boast of that." (2 Cor 11:21 NRSV)

"Are they servants of Christ? (I speak as if insane) I more so; in far more labors, in far more imprisonments, beaten times without number, often in danger of death." (2 Cor 11:23 NASB)

"And I know that such a person—whether in the body or out of the body I do not know; God knows—was caught up into Paradise and heard things that are not to be told." (2 Cor 12:3 NRSV)

"And from those who were supposed to be acknowledged leaders (what they actually were makes no difference to me; God shows no partiality)—these very leaders contributed nothing to me." (Gal 2:6 NRSV)

"God . . . even when we were dead through our trespasses, made us alive together with Christ—by grace you have been saved—and raised us up with him and seated us with him in the heavenly places in Christ Jesus." (Eph 2:4–6 NRSV)

"for you were formerly darkness, but now you are light in the Lord; walk as children of light (for the fruit of the light consists in all goodness and righteousness and truth), trying to learn what is pleasing to the Lord." (Eph 5:8–10 NASB)

"If with Christ you died to the elemental spirits of the world, why, as if you were still alive in the world, do you submit to regulations—'Do not handle, Do not taste, Do not touch (referring to things that all perish as they are used)—according to human precepts and teachings?" (Col 2:20–22 ESV)

"For never at any time did we become sycophantic (as you well know), nor opportunistic (as God is our witness), as we did not seek renown from any human being." (1 Thess 2:5)

"As for us, brothers and sisters, although we became separated from you for a short time (in person, not in heart) we longed with great eagerness to see you face to face." (1 Thess 2:17)

"for what is our hope or joy or crown of boasting (is it not indeed you?) when we stand before our Lord Jesus upon his coming?" (1 Thess 2:19)

In Eph 3:1, a parenthesis begins but grows so long that the sentence trails into anacoluthon, to resume its original structure in v. 14. In this case, the digression cannot be considered ornamental (see similar examples under discussion of anacoluthon in §1.2.1.2 and §1.2.4.4). In other cases, the parenthesis is more an afterthought than a strategic insertion ("and I was hindered until now" in Rom 1:13; "for I am going through Macedonia" in 1 Cor 16:5). Nor are parentheses ornamental when their purpose is interpretive, as in Rom 10:6–7.

3.2.1.2.23. SENTENTIA/GNOMĒ (LAUSBERG, §872–79)

A sentence that expresses an idea that has generic application and is widely regarded as true, thus also having authority as a proof.

Traditional gnomai. Paul's letters contain some probable examples of traditional gnomai, though their nature as gnomai is difficult to determine where external parallels are lacking.

"Nothing beyond what is written." (1 Cor 4:6 NRSV)

"Many members, but one body." (1 Cor 12:20)

"Spirits of prophets are subject to prophets." (1 Cor 14:32)

"Bad company corrupts good character." (1 Cor 15:33 NIV; Menander, *Thais* 187.1/218.1)

Paul sometimes puts gnomai into the mouth of an interlocutor:

"Do not handle, Do not taste, Do not touch" (Col 2:21 NRSV)

Paul sometimes uses OT quotations as pointed conclusions:

"Let the one who boasts boast in the Lord." (1 Cor 1:31; 2 Cor 10:17; Jer 9:22–23)

"Let us eat and drink, for tomorrow we die." (1 Cor 15:32; LXX Isa 22:13; cf. Eccl 2:24; 3:12)

Original gnomai. Holloway has shown that Paul frequently devises "pointed" gnomai of his own:[25]

(1) Many examples are formulated in paradoxical terms (on paradox, see §3.2.1.2.14):

"for if you live according to the flesh, you will die; but if by the Spirit you put to death the deeds of the body, you will live." (Rom 8:13 NRSV)

"So do not let your good be spoken of as evil." (Rom 14:16 NRSV)

"so that no one might boast in the presence of God" (1 Cor 1:29 NRSV)

---

25. Holloway, "Paul's Pointed Prose."

"If you think that you are wise in this age, you should become fools so that you may become wise." (1 Cor 3:18 NRSV)

"For the wisdom of this world is foolishness with God." (1 Cor 3:19 NRSV)

"For though I am free with respect to all, I have made myself a slave to all, so that I might win more of them." (1 Cor 9:19 NRSV)

(2) Many examples involve antithesis (Rom 2:13; 14:17; 1 Cor 4:20; 7:9; 8:1b; 10:12; 14:33; 2 Cor 3:6) or parallelism (Rom 2:12; 4:25; 6:3; 6:20; 1 Cor 3:17; 2 Cor 9:6; Gal 6:8). On antithesis and parallelism see also §3.2.1.1.30; 3.2.1.2.11 (antithesis) and 3.2.1.1.22, 23, 27, 28 (parallelism) above.

"For it is not the hearers of the law who are righteous in God's sight, but the doers of the law who will be justified." (Rom 2:13 NRSV)

"For the kingdom of God is not food and drink but righteousness and peace and joy in the Holy Spirit." (Rom 4:17 NRSV)

"For the kingdom of God is not food and drink but righteousness and peace and joy in the Holy Spirit." (1 Cor 4:20 NRSV)

"For it is better to marry than to be aflame with passion." (1 Cor 7:9 NRSV)

"Knowledge puffs up, but love builds up." (1 Cor 8:1 NRSV)

"So if you think you are standing, watch out that you do not fall." (1 Cor 10:12 NRSV)

"for God is a God not of disorder but of peace." (1 Cor 14:33 NRSV)

"for the letter kills, but the Spirit gives life." (2 Cor 3:6 NRSV)

"All who have sinned apart from the law will also perish apart from the law, and all who have sinned under the law will be judged by the law." (Rom 2:12 NRSV)

"who was handed over to death for our trespasses and was raised for our justification." (Rom 4:25 NRSV)

"Do you not know that all of us who have been baptized into Christ Jesus were baptized into his death?" (Rom 6:3 NRSV)

"When you were slaves of sin, you were free in regard to righteousness." (Rom 6:20 NRSV)

"If anyone destroys God's temple, God will destroy that person." (1 Cor 3:17 NRSV)

"the one who sows sparingly will also reap sparingly, and the one who sows bountifully will also reap bountifully." (2 Cor 9:6 NRSV also in Gal 6:8)

(3) There are also several paronomastic examples (1 Cor 3:17; 8:2–3; 9:22; Rom 3:26; 12:3; 14:22; 2 Cor 10:3); on paronomasia, see §3.2.1.1.9.

"it was to prove at the present time that he himself is righteous and that he justifies the one who has faith in Jesus." (Rom 3:26 NRSV)

"For by the grace given to me I say to everyone among you not to think of yourself more highly than you ought to think, but to think with sober judgment." (Rom 12:3 NRSV)

"The faith that you have, have as your own conviction before God." (Rom 14:22 NRSV)

"If anyone destroys God's temple, God will destroy that person." (1 Cor 3:17 NRSV)

"Anyone who claims to know something does not yet have the necessary knowledge" (1 Cor 8:2 NRSV)

"To the weak I became weak, so that I might win the weak." (1 Cor 9:22 NRSV)

"Indeed, we live as human beings, but we do not wage war according to human standards" (2 Cor 10:3 NRSV)

(4) Paul often deploys gnomai as concluding summaries, or clausulae (Rom 3:26b; 5:8; 1 Cor 9:22c–d; 10:12; 2 Cor 12:10b–c).

3.2.1.2.24. PARALEPSIS/PRAETERITIO (LAUSBERG, §882–86)

Paralepsis occurs when the speaker draws attention to something while pretending to pass it over.

"otherwise, if some Macedonians come with me and find that you are not ready, we would be humiliated—to say nothing of you—in this undertaking." (2 Cor 9:4 NRSV)

"But Timothy's worth you know, how like a son with a father he has served with me in the work of the gospel." (Phil 2:22 NRSV)

"For it is we who are the circumcision, who worship in the Spirit of God and boast in Christ Jesus and have no confidence in the flesh—even though I, too, have confidence in the flesh." (Phil 3:3–4)

"Now concerning love of the brothers and sisters, you do not need to have anyone write to you" (1 Thess 4:9 NRSV). Paul goes on to discuss the subject in vv. 10–12.

"Now concerning the times and the seasons, brothers and sisters, you do not need to have anything written to you." (1 Thess 5:1 NRSV); the subject is then discussed in vv. 2–11.

"I say nothing about your owing me even your own self." (Phlm 19 NRSV)

3.2.1.2.25. APOSIOPESIS/RETICENTIA (LAUSBERG, §887–88)

The omission of the expression of an idea, where the omission is made known by breaking off a sentence already begun. The break may indicate that the audience already knows what would have been said; it may serve to evade objection; or it may be merely emotive.

"I did not write these things that it may be done in my case. For I would rather die than—No one shall nullify my right to boast!" (1 Cor 9:15)

In 2 Thess 2:4, Paul is drawn into a long appositive, which cuts off at the end of the verse. The curtailment, however, does not reflect anacoluthon.[26] Rather, Paul has initiated a review of his previous teachings in v. 4, and promptly cuts it off in v. 5 because he expects his brief prelude to be sufficient to jog his audience's memory ("do you not *remember*" in v. 5): "For if the rebellion does not come first and the man of lawlessness is not revealed—the son of destruction, the one who opposes and exalts himself above everything named as a divinity or object of worship, so that he sits

---

26. Contra Robertson, *Grammar of the Greek New Testament*, 1203.

in the Temple of God in order to display himself as being a god . . . " One must clearly supply in the apodosis something like "the Day of the Lord will not come." Paul does not so much digress in elaborating on the man of lawlessness as he does assume the audience's easy recollection of an earlier teaching, as if to say: "For unless the apostasy comes first—do you not remember discussing this when I was with you?"

Likewise, the protasis in Rom 9:22 remains unresolved. However, Paul may may intend through the premise stated in the protasis only to offer a suggestion, while deliberately refusing to complete the thought due to its provocative nature: "And if God, wanting to show his wrath and to make his power known, endured with much longsuffering vessels of wrath prepared for destruction, and did so in order to make known the riches of his glory upon vessels of mercy, which he prepared beforehand for glory—" Paul's final omission of the apodosis is undoubtedly meant to provoke reflection ("What if God . . . ?").

The μέν clause in Rom 7:12 is never resolved with a correlate δέ: "*On the one hand* (μέν), the Law is holy, and the commandment holy and just and good—". Is Paul implicitly contrasting the "Law" with "Sin" (i.e., on the one hand the Law is good, while sin is bad)? Or does the correlate idea come in the next chapter, and more specifically in 8:3: "what was *impossible* for the Law because *it was weak through the flesh* . . . " (Rom 8:3). If Paul is already thinking this far ahead in the argument, the μέν in 7:12 would suggest that his remark about the Law as "holy, just, and good" will require further qualification; i.e., the Law is holy, but it is too weak to overcome the problem of sin. Perhaps Paul deemed so direct a contrast to be too provocative to risk, and so makes strategic use of aposiopesis.

3.2.1.2.26. Hysteron Proteron (Lausberg, §891–92)

An inversion of logical or temporal order in such a way as puts the conclusion before the premise.

Paul says that Christ "hands over the kingdom to God and the Father" before stating that Christ "abolishes every rule and authority and power" (1 Cor 15:24). Paul refers to God's "children" (Rom 8:21) although they still await their "adoption" (Rom 8:23).

3.2.1.2.27. Irony (Lausberg, §902–4)

Speech in which the speaker either feigns ignorance or feigns agreement with the audience, ultimately in order to expose or ridicule their views as incorrect or absurd. The force of the irony may be in low-evidence (as when it is hidden) or in high-evidence (as when it openly exposes the incorrectness or absurdity of the audience's opinion). In distinction from the trope "irony" (§3.1.3.8), which concerns the use of an individual word in a way opposite its meaning, irony as a figure of thought (§3.2.1.2) extends the irony to whole sentences, passages, or even the whole cause.

"Already you have all you want! Already you have become rich! Quite apart from us you have become kings! Indeed, I wish that you had become kings, so that we might be kings with you!" (1 Cor 4:8 NRSV)

"We do not dare to classify or compare ourselves with some of those who commend themselves." (2 Cor 10:12 NRSV)

"For you gladly put up with fools, being wise yourselves!" (2 Cor 11:19 NRSV)

"But whatever anyone dares to boast of—*I am speaking as a fool*—I also dare to boast of that." (2 Cor 11:21 NRSV)

"How have you been worse off than the other churches, except that I myself did not burden you? *Forgive me this wrong*!" (2 Cor 12:13 NRSV)

In Gal 2:15, there is irony in the use of antithesis between "we Jews" and "sinners from the Gentiles."

"Having begun by the Spirit, are you now being perfected by the flesh?" (Gal 3:3 NASB)

For more on irony in Paul's letters, see Reumann, "St. Paul's Use of Irony" and Spencer, "Wise Fool (and the Foolish Wise)."

3.2.1.2.28. Periphrasis (Lausberg, §907)

As a thought-figure, periphrasis consists in the expression of an idea by the substitution of a more expansive description. Where the description relies on a more specific paraphrase, it may be considered synecdochic. See also the trope "periphrasis" (§3.1.3.9), as well as "antonomasia" (§3.1.3.7).

"Bear the sword" = avenge (Rom 13:4); "twinkling of an eye" = an instant (1 Cor 15:52); not to let "the sun go down on" = let time expire (Eph 4:26); "knee might bend" = worship (Phil 2:10).

3.2.2. Composition (Lausberg, §911–1054)

The rhetorical theory of "composition" concerns the syntactic-formation of clauses. This area of style encompasses both the theory of sentences (Lausberg, §912–947) and the theory of word order (Lausberg §948–1054).

3.2.2.1. Styles of Composition (Lausberg, §912–47)

Analysis of sentences considers the variable degrees of sentence elaboration, or "style" (λέξις) of linking ideas together syntactically. Rhetoricians typically described three styles: the loose style (Lausberg, §916–20), the running style (§921–22), and the complicated style (§923–47). For alternative classifications, see Cicero, *Or.* 3.199, 212, 177; Ps.-Cicero, *Rhet. Her.* 4.11–16; Demetrius, *Eloc.* 240–304.

The basic units of expression include the period, the colon, and the comma.

The period (Lausberg, §923–47) is the largest thought-unit of a sentence. Some rhetoricians defined the period as that which could be uttered in a single breath, or alternatively, as the largest unit that the audience could understand. Periodic sentences are complex and deploy hypotaxis with subordination sometimes to the third or fourth degree.

The next largest thought-unit is the colon (Lausberg, §928–34). A colon comprises a whole clause (main or subordinate) or word group and so in a sense expresses a complete thought; though as part of the period the colon is not fully independent syntactically. On the juxtaposition of multiple equivalent colons, see "Isocolon" (§3.2.1.1.22).

The shortest thought-unit is the comma (Lausberg, §935–40). A comma is a chopped-off piece of a sentence, which in itself does not express a complete thought. The comma is subordinate to the colon and therefore a part of it.

No single style characterizes Paul's letters as a whole, nor any single letter of Paul. It may be said that certain of Paul's epistles gravitate more toward one style than the others. In general, Paul's more "personal" letters (1 Thessalonians, 2 Thessalonians) exhibit a looser style of composition, and his "formal," more diplomatic, letters a more complex style (1–2 Corinthians, Romans). However, a piece of literature need not maintain a consistent style. Using an alternative classification (the "subdued," "temperate," and "exalted" styles), St. Augustine notes that Paul moves between styles (*de Doctr. Chr.* 4.20.39–44), sometimes using multiple styles within a single passage (*de Doctr. Chr.* 4.7.12–13; breaking down 2 Cor 11:16–30, for example). The general rule is that style should correspond, and thus change, with the content (Quintilian, *Inst.* 9.4.138).

3.2.2.1.1. *The Loose Style (§916–20)*

Characterizing the loose style is the juxtaposition of *syntactically independent, equivalent* commas and colons. The loose style is the least premeditated, most spontaneous, and generally characterizes casual conversation. Thus, it is also common in dialectical discourse, as in questioning witnesses or, when simulating debate, in diatribe.

The simplest sentences in Paul's letters usually involve antitheses (Rom 6:23; 7:14, 15, 17, 18, 19, 20, 25; 8:5, 6, 10; 9:6–8, 16; 11:18; 13:12; 1 Cor 4:12–13; 7:18; 11:8–12; 15:42–44, 47–48; 2 Cor 4:18; 5:7, 17; 6:12; 12:14; Gal 2:20; 4:7; 5:16, 17; 6:15; Phil 1:21; 2:21); series of succinct assertions (1 Cor 13:4–7), exclamations (1 Cor 4:8), rhetorical questions (1 Cor 11:22; 12:29–30; 2 Cor 6:14–16), or complementary pairs (Col 3:18–21); or isocolon with multiple colons (1 Cor 1:20, 26; 4:8; 6:11; 2 Cor 6:11; 7:2, 4).

Paratactic style in Paul's letters is normally achieved through coordination. Asyndeton is more exceptional, and is generally limited to passages that exhibit additional ornamental features (Rom 12:6–16; 1 Cor 1:26; 4:8, 12–13; 6:11; 12:29–30; 13:4–7; 15:40–58; 16:13–14; 2 Cor 6:11).

Holloway has shown that "pointed" gnomai (see §3.2.1.2.23), after the style of the Roman declamatory schools, are a common feature of Paul's style, particularly in his letters to the Roman and Corinthian churches.[27] Longer stretches of pointed clauses, in the loose style (Rom 7:7–25; 9:14–20; 11:11–16; 12:6–16; 13:1–14; 14:13–23; 1 Cor 15:40–48; Gal 2:18–21; 3:15–22; 5:21–26), are common in more polemical sections (2 Cor 7:2–4;

---

27. Holloway, "Paul's Pointed Prose."

11:1–12:21; Gal 3:1–14; 5:7–12), in the use of diatribe or inner dialogue (Rom 7:7–25; 9:14–20; 11:11–16; Phil 1:21–24), and in general, amid intermittent question and answer (Rom 7:7–25; 9:14–20; 11:11–16; 1 Cor 7:18, 21; Gal 3:15–22; 5:7–12). Otherwise, pointed sentences appear in Paul's letters more sporadically (Rom 8:8, 17, 24–25; 11:6–7; 1 Cor 1:20, 26; 4:8, 12–13; 2 Cor 5:20; Eph 4:4–6; Phil 4:4–5), being interwoven into sections characterized more generally by a running style.

Sections of a polemical or diatribal nature are often characterized by a high degree of ornament; see for example under "Interrogatio" (§3.2.1.2.4), "Pysma" (§3.2.1.2.5), and "Subiectio" (§3.2.1.2.6). Fittingly, Quintilian recommends the use of short colons and commas for "fierce, insistent, pugnacious speaking" (*Inst.* 9.4.126). As such, Paul's style may be loose in its degree of elaboration while also exhibiting notable ornament. Thus the alternative classification of style into "simple," "middle," and "grand" (Ps.-Cicero, *Rhet. Her.* 4.11–16), where ornament is a defining factor, may sometimes offer a more apt description of a passage. For instance, while isocolon (§3.2.1.1.22) may involve "loose" syntax, it also constitutes an artistic feature less characteristic of the casual nature of the loose style. Thus, where ornamental elements are prominent, the style could be described as "middle" (e.g., Rom 12:6–16; 13:7–8, 12–14) or even "grand" (1 Cor 15:40–58).

Literary "forms" as understood in the vein of form criticism can be correlated with the theory of style in some respects. For instance, the loose style, though often elevated, commonly characterizes parenetic sections (Rom 12:9–17; 14:13–23; 1 Cor 7:18–23; 15:33–34; 16:13–14; 2 Cor 13:11; Col 4:2; 1 Thess 5:12–22).

3.2.2.1.2. The Running Style (§921–22)

The running style consists in the linking of clauses in the natural order of their contents by means of parataxis (through the use of coordinating conjunctions) or minimal hypotaxis (the subordination of clauses). It is called the "running" style because the thought proceeds, as it were, in a straight line, and lacks a branching out of the connected ideas.

Paul's longer sentences typically are not periodic but, even when they involve multiple subordinate clauses, run on in more linear fashion, without deeply embedded levels of subordination and without the kind of circular structure that resolves the main point at the end of the sentence.

Note long, non-periodic sentences in: 1 Cor 1:4-8; 2 Cor 1:3-7; Eph 1:3-14 (cf. Robbins 1986); 1:15-21; 3:1-7, 8-12, 14-18; 4:11-16, 20-24; 5:18-24; 6:5-8, 14-20; Phil 3:8-11; Col 1:3-8, 9-20; 2 Thess 1:3-10 [12]. Moderately long sentences appear in Rom 3:22b-26; 4:16-17; Eph 2:14-16; Phil 1:3-7, 12-14, 18-20, 27-28; 2:1-4, 14-16; Col 2:1-3; 1 Thess 1:2-5; Phlm 4-6. Some longer sentences consist largely in strings of relative clauses (Col 3:5-7; and with a long appositive in Rom 1:1-7; Phlm 10-13), appositional phrases (Rom 2:5-8; Col 1:24-29; 1 Thess 2:14-16; with participial phrases in Col 2:10-15, 18-19; 4:2-4), participial phrases (2 Cor 3:2-3; 4:8-10; 10:4-5; with purposes clauses in Col 4:2-4), or infinitive phrases (1 Thess 4:3-7). The enumeration of items, occurrences, or behaviors is sometimes responsible for protraction (Rom 12:6-13; 2 Cor 4:8-11; 6:3-10; 11:24-27). A long genitive absolute precedes the main clause in 1 Thess 3:6-8. Longer sentences often become derailed into anacoluthon (2 Cor 8:18-21; Rom 5:12-18; 12:6-8; 15:23-28; Eph 2:1-5; 3:1-14; Col 1:9-23; cf. Kirby 1987 on the structure of Rom 5:12).

Examples above illustrate how common longer sentences are in the proems of Paul's letters (1 Cor 1:4-8; Eph 1:3-14; 1 Thess 1:2-5; Col 1:3-8; 2 Thess 1:3-10).

3.2.2.1.3. *The Periodic Style (Lausberg, §923-47)*

The periodic style is characterized by complex sentences structured hyotactically, with subordination of clauses extending sometimes to the third or fourth degree, and the main point coming at the end of the sentence (the "clausula"). The resulting sentence structure is called a "period" because the unfolding of the thought forms, as it were, a circle. The effect of this structure is the building up of tension that is resolved only at the end of the sentence, where the main idea is completed. This type of composition is well suited to proems and epilogues, and for amplifying one's main point (Quintilian, *Inst.* 9.4.128). The periodic style is also fitting when speaking on lofty subjects (Quintilian, *Inst.* 9.4.136).

Galatians contains two examples of lengthy periodic sentences that reserve the main point for the end:

ὅτε δὲ εὐδόκησεν ὁ ἀφορίσας με ἐκ κοιλίας μητρός μου καὶ καλέσας διὰ τῆς χάριτος αὐτοῦ ἀποκαλύψαι τὸν υἱὸν αὐτοῦ ἐν ἐμοὶ ἵνα εὐαγγελίζωμαι αὐτὸν ἐν τοῖς ἔθνεσιν, εὐθέως οὐ προσανεθέμην σαρκὶ καὶ αἵματι, οὐδὲ ἀνῆλθον εἰς Ἱεροσόλυμα πρὸς τοὺς πρὸ ἐμοῦ ἀποστόλους, ἀλλὰ **ἀπῆλθον εἰς Ἀραβίαν, καὶ πάλιν ὑπέστρεψα εἰς Δαμασκόν**. (Gal 1:15–17)

ἀλλὰ τοὐναντίον ἰδόντες ὅτι πεπίστευμαι τὸ εὐαγγέλιον τῆς ἀκροβυστίας καθὼς Πέτρος τῆς περιτομῆς, ὁ γὰρ ἐνεργήσας Πέτρῳ εἰς ἀποστολὴν τῆς περιτομῆς ἐνήργησεν καὶ ἐμοὶ εἰς τὰ ἔθνη, καὶ γνόντες τὴν χάριν τὴν δοθεῖσάν μοι, Ἰάκωβος καὶ Κηφᾶς καὶ Ἰωάννης, οἱ δοκοῦντες στῦλοι εἶναι, **δεξιὰς ἔδωκαν ἐμοὶ καὶ Βαρναβᾷ κοινωνίας** . . . (Gal 2:7–9)

Complex sentences with a periodic structure, including placement of the main point at the end, occur elsewhere occasionally. While periodic (circular) in structure, these sentences, however, generally do not have multiple levels of clause subordination:

Εἰ δὲ **σὺ** Ἰουδαῖος ἐπονομάζῃ καὶ ἐπαναπαύῃ νόμῳ καὶ καυχᾶσαι ἐν θεῷ καὶ γινώσκεις τὸ θέλημα καὶ δοκιμάζεις τὰ διαφέροντα κατηχούμενος ἐκ τοῦ νόμου, πέποιθάς τε σεαυτὸν ὁδηγὸν εἶναι τυφλῶν, φῶς τῶν ἐν σκότει, παιδευτὴν ἀφρόνων, διδάσκαλον νηπίων, ἔχοντα τὴν μόρφωσιν τῆς γνώσεως καὶ τῆς ἀληθείας ἐν τῷ νόμῳ· ὁ οὖν διδάσκων ἕτερον **σεαυτὸν οὐ διδάσκεις**; (Rom 2:17–21)

Romans 3:21–26 is a single sentence that circles back topically to where it started: Νυνὶ δὲ χωρὶς νόμου δικαιοσύνη θεοῦ πεφανέρωται . . . εἰς τὸ εἶναι αὐτὸν δίκαιον καὶ δικαιοῦντα τὸν ἐκ πίστεως Ἰησοῦ.

Romans 3:38–39 also has a periodic structure: **πέπεισμαι** γὰρ **ὅτι** οὔτε θάνατος οὔτε ζωὴ οὔτε ἄγγελοι οὔτε ἀρχαὶ οὔτε ἐνεστῶτα οὔτε μέλλοντα οὔτε δυνάμεις οὔτε ὕψωμα οὔτε βάθος οὔτε τις κτίσις ἑτέρα **δυνήσεται ἡμᾶς χωρίσαι ἀπὸ τῆς ἀγάπης τοῦ θεοῦ τῆς ἐν Χριστῷ Ἰησοῦ τῷ κυρίῳ ἡμῶν**.

Though cumbersome, the syntax of 1 Cor 5:3–5 is ultimately resolved, the demonstrative τοῦτο (v. 3) representing a left-dislocation that is finally resumed with τὸν τοιοῦτον (v. 5)—a scheme not uncommon among the best orators (cf. Cicero, *Fin.* 3.21; *cum . . . cum*).

Philippians has several examples of sentences with a periodic structure:

Ὥστε, ἀγαπητοί μου, **καθὼς πάντοτε ὑπηκούσατε**, μὴ ὡς ἐν τῇ παρουσίᾳ μου μόνον ἀλλὰ νῦν πολλῷ μᾶλλον ἐν τῇ ἀπουσίᾳ μου, μετὰ φόβου καὶ τρόμου **τὴν ἑαυτῶν σωτηρίαν κατεργάζεσθε**· (Phil 2:12)

Τὸ λοιπόν, ἀδελφοί, **ὅσα** ἐστὶν ἀληθῆ, **ὅσα** σεμνά, **ὅσα** δίκαια, **ὅσα** ἁγνά, **ὅσα** προσφιλῆ, **ὅσα** εὔφημα, εἴ **τις ἀρετὴ** καὶ **εἴ τις ἔπαινος**, **ταῦτα λογίζεσθε**· (Phil 4:8)

ἃ καὶ ἐμάθετε καὶ παρελάβετε καὶ ἠκούσατε καὶ εἴδετε ἐν ἐμοί, **ταῦτα πράσσετε**· (Phil 4:9)

While interpreters frequently characterize the long sentence of Eph 1:3-14 as awkward, Robbins argues that the sentence accords with "the principles of Greek rhetoric as explained by the ancient rhetoricians themselves and exemplified in classical literature";[28] according to Robbins's analysis the sentences breaks down into eight periodic sentences. Robertson lists as periodic Rom 1:1-7; 11:33-36; Eph 1:3-14; he also cites Rom 12:6-8; 2 Cor 8:18-21; Col 1:9-23, though he notes that these sentences ultimately break away into anacoluthon.[29] Snyman considers Rom 8:32 to be periodic.[30]

Other passages contain longer sentences that exhibit a more exalted, or ornamental, style, but that do not suspend the main point to the end, i.e., do not have a "periodic" structure. Note for instance Rom 8:28-39; 2 Cor 6:2-11; Gal 4:10-20.

3.2.2.2. Word Order (Lausberg §948-1054)

Included in discussion of word order are the matters of syntax (Lausberg, §950-53), euphony (§954-76), and rhythm (§977-1054).

Quintilian's discussion of word order focuses primarily on the avoidance of compositional vices. For instance, Quintilian describes as infelicitous "a long series of words with similar cadences, terminations, and inflections (*Inst.* 9.4.42; cf. Lausberg, §965). Pertinent in Paul's letters are passages like Col 3:7, which contains four successive words, representing three different parts of speech, that have homonymous endings: περιεπατήσα**τέ** πο**τε** ὅ**τε** ἐζῆ**τε** (Col 3:7).

---

28. Robbins, "Composition of Eph 1:3-14," 677.
29. Robertson, *Grammar of the Greek New Testament*, 433-34.
30. Snyman, "Style and Meaning in Romans 8:31-39."

Likewise, "the last syllable of the preceding word and the first of the following word should not be the same" (Quintilian, *Inst.* 9.4.41). But note 2 Cor 11:20: εἴ τις κατεσθί<u>ει</u>, <u>εἴ</u> τις λαμβάν<u>ει</u>, <u>εἴ</u>.

Excessive repetition of the same consonant is also to be avoided (Ps.-Cicero, *Rhet. Her.* 4.18). Passages that exhibit this quality where ornament is otherwise lacking, where no pattern exists, or where the repetition does not serve rhetorical propriety in the context would qualify under this vice. Perhaps Eph 3:20 would qualify under this description; i.e., ν in τὴν δύναμιν τὴν ἐνεργουμένην ἐν ἡμῖν. Yet, this phenomenon, in many cases qualifies under the subcategory of paronomasia known as homoioprophoron/alliteration (Lausberg, §975); see §3.2.1.1.9 above.

BIBLIOGRAPHY

Anderson, R. Dean. *Glossary of Greek Rhetorical Terms*. Contributions to Biblical Exegesis and Theology 24. Leuven: Peeters, 2000.
Berlin, Adele. *The Dynamics of Biblical Parallelism*. Grand Rapids: Eerdmans, 1985.
Betz, Hans D. *Galatians*. Hermeneia. Philadelphia: Fortress, 1979.
Black, David Alan. "The Pauline Love Command: Structure, Style, and Ethics in Romans 12:9–21." *Filologia Neotestamentaria* 2 (1989) 3–22.
Blass, F., et al., eds. *A Greek Grammar of the New Testament and Other Early Christian Literature*. Chicago: Chicago University Press, 1961.
Boring, M. Eugene. "The Language of Universal Salvation in Paul." *Journal of Biblical Literature* 105 (1986) 269–92.
Botha, Jan. "Style in the New Testament: The Need for Serious Reconsideration." *Journal for the Study of the New Testament* 14 (1991) 71–86.
Brookins, Timothy A. *Corinthian Wisdom, Stoic Philosophy, and the Ancient Economy*. Society for New Testament Studies Monograph Series 159. Cambridge: Cambridge University Press, 2014.
———. "'Natural Hair': A 'New Rhetorical' Assessment of 1 Cor 11:14–15." In *Paul and the Greco-Roman Philosophical Tradition*," edited by Andrew Pitts and Joseph Dodson, 173–98. Library of New Testament Studies. Edinburgh: T. & T. Clark, 2017.
Bullinger, E. W. *Figures of Speech Used in the Bible*. Repr. Grand Rapids: Baker, 1968.
Burke, Trevor J. *Family Matters: A Socio-Historical Study of Kinship Metaphors in 1 Thessalonians*. Journal for the Study of the New Testament Supplments 247. London: T. & T. Clark, 2003.
Campbell, Constantine R. *Advances in the Study of Greek: New Insights for Reading the New Testament*. Grand Rapids: Zondervan, 2015.
Caragounis, Chrys C. *The Development of Greek and the New Testament: Morphology, Syntax, Phonology, and Textual Transmission*. Grand Rapids: Baker Academic, 2006.
Cicero. *On the Orator: Book 3. On Fate. Stoic Paradoxes. Divisions of Oratory*. Translated by H. Rackham. Loeb Classical Library 349. Cambridge, MA: Harvard University Press, 1942.
Classen, C. Joachim. "St. Paul's Epistles and Ancient Greek and Roman Rhetoric." *Rhetorica* 10 (1992) 319–44.
Cosby, Michael R. "Paul's Persuasive Language in Romans 5." In *Persuasive Artistry: Studies in New Testament Rhetoric in Honor of George A. Kennedy*, edited by Duane F. Watson, 209–26. Sheffield: Sheffield Academic, 1991.
Cranfield, C. E. B. *The Epistle to the Romans 1–8*. International Critical Commentary. Edinburgh: T. & T. Clark, 1975.

BIBLIOGRAPHY

Daube, D. "Rabbinic Methods of Interpretation and Hellenistic Rhetoric." *Hebrew Union College Annual* 22 (1949) 239–64.

de Jonge, Casper C. "Style (lexis), Ancient Theories of." In *Encyclopedia of Ancient Greek Language and Linguistics*, edited by Georgios K. Giannakis, 326–31. Leiden: Brill, 2014.

Eriksson, Anders. "Special Topics in 1 Corinthians 8–10." In *The Rhetorical Interpretation of Scripture: Essays from the 1996 Malibu Conference*, edited by Stanley E. Porter, 272–301. Novum Testamentum Supplements 180. Sheffield: Sheffield Academic, 1999.

Estes, Douglas. *Questions and Rhetoric in the Greek New Testament: An Essential Reference Resource for Exegesis*. Grand Rapids: Zondervan, 2016.

Fairweather, J. "The Epistle to the Galatians and Classical Rhetoric: Parts 1 & 2." *Tyndale Bulletin* 45 (1994) 1–38.

Finlan, Stephen. *The Background and Content of Paul's Cultic Atonement Metaphors*. Academia Biblica 19. Atlanta: Society of Biblical Literature, 2004.

Fitzmyer, Joseph A. *Romans*. Anchor Bible 33. New Haven, CT: Yale University Press, 1993.

Gaventa, Beverly Roberts. *Our Mother Saint Paul*. Louisville, KY: Westminster John Knox, 2007.

Given, Mark D. "Paul and Rhetoric: A *Sophos* in the Kingdom of God." In *Paul Unbound: Other Perspectives on the Apostle*, edited by Mark D. Given, 175–200. Grand Rapids: Baker Academic, 2021.

Heylen, Victor Leonard. "Les Métaphores et les Métonymies dans les Épîtres Pauliniennes." *Ephemerides Theologicae Lovanienses* 12 (1935) 253–90.

Hidary, Richard. *Rabbis and Classical Rhetoric: Sophistic Education and Oratory in the Talmud and Midrash*. Cambridge: Cambridge University Press, 2017.

Hogeterp, Albert L. A. *Paul and God's Temple: A Historical Interpretation of Cultic Imagery in the Corinthian Correspondence*. Bible et terre sainte 2. Leuven: Peeters, 2006.

Holland, Glen. "Paul's Use of Irony as a Rhetorical Technique." In *The Rhetorical Analysis of Scripture*. Journal for the Study of the New Testament Supplements 146, edited by Stanley E. Porter and Thomas H. Olbricht, 234–48. Sheffield: Sheffield Academic Press, 1997.

Holloway, Paul A. "Paul's Pointed Prose: The 'Sententia' in Roman Rhetoric and Paul." *Novum Testamentum* 40 (1998) 32–53.

Howson, John Saul. *The Metaphors of St. Paul*. Strahan, 1868.

Hughes, Frank W. "The Rhetoric of Letters." In *The Thessalonians Debate: Methodological Discord or Methodological Synthesis?*, edited by Karl P. Donfried and Johannes Beutler, 194–240. Grand Rapids: Eerdmans, 2000.

Hughes, Frank W., and Robert Jewett. *The Corinthian Correspondence: Redaction, Rhetoric, and History*. Minneapolis: Fortress Academic, 2021.

Jeremias, Joachim. "Chiasmus in den Paulusbriefen." *Zeitschrift für die neutestamentlich Wissenschaft und die Kunde älteren Kirche* 49 (1958) 139–56.

Jewett, Robert. "The Rhetorical Function of Numerical Series in Romans." In *Persuasive Artistry: Studies in New Testament Rhetoric in Honor of George A. Kennedy*. Journal for the Study of the New Testament Supplements 50, edited by Duane F. Watson, 227–45. Sheffield: Sheffield Academic, 1991.

Johnson, Nathan C. "Romans 1:3–4: Beyond Antithetical Parallelism." *Journal of Biblical Literature* 136 (2017) 467–90.

Judge, E. A. "Paul's Boasting in Relation to Contemporary Professional Practice." *Australian Biblical Review* 16 (1968) 37–50.

Keach, Benjamin. *Τροποσχημαλογία. Tropes and Figures*. London: John Darby for John Hancock I/II & Bernard Alsop, 1682.

Kennedy, George. *Classical Rhetoric and Its Christian and Secular Tradition from Ancient to Modern Times*. 2nd ed. Chapel Hill, NC: University of North Carolina Press, 1999.

———. *New Testament Interpretation through Rhetorical Criticism*. Chapel Hill, NC: University of North Carolina Press, 1984.

King, Justin D. *Speech-in-Character, Diatribe, and Romans 3:1–9: Who's Speaking When and Why It Matters*. Leiden: Brill, 2018.

Kirby, John T. "The Syntax of Romans 5:12: A Rhetorical Approach." *New Testament Studies* 33 (1987) 283–86.

Klauck, Hans-Josef. *Ancient Letters and the New Testament: A Guide to Context and Exegesis*. Waco, TX: Baylor University Press, 2006.

Lakoff, George, and Mark Johnson. *Metaphors We Live By*. Chicago: The University of Chicago Press, 2003.

Lampe, Peter. "Rhetorical Analysis of Pauline Texts: Methodological Reflections." In *Paul and Rhetoric*, edited by J. Paul Sampley and Peter Lampe, 3–21. New York: T. & T. Clark, 2010.

Lanham, Richard A. *A Handlist of Rhetorical Terms*. 2nd ed. Oakland: University of California Press, 2012.

Lausberg, Heinrich. *Handbuch der literarischen Rhetorik: Eine Grundlegung der Literaturwissenschaft*. 2nd ed. Ismaning: Max Huber Verlag, 1973.

———. *Handbook of Literary Rhetoric: A Foundation for Literary Study*. Edited by David E. Orton and R. Dean Anderson. Tranlsated by Matthew T. Bliss, Annemiek Jansen, and David E. Orton. Leiden: Brill, 1998.

Levison, John R. "Did the Spirit Inspire Rhetoric?" In *Persuasive Artistry*, edited by Duane F. Watson, 25–40. Sheffield: Sheffield Academic, 1991.

Lightfoot, J. B. *Notes on Epistles of St. Paul*. London, 1904.

Louw, Johannes P., and Eugene A. Nida, eds. *Greek-English Lexicon of the New Testament Based on Semantic Domains*. 2 vols. New York: United Bible Societies, 1988.

MacDonald, Michael J. *Glossary of Greek and Latin Rhetorical Terms*. The Oxford Handbook of Rhetorical Studies. Oxford: Oxford University Press, 2017.

Mack, Burton. *Rhetoric and the New Testament*. Minneapolis: Fortress, 1990.

Marshall, Peter. *Enmity in Corinth: Social Conventions in Paul's Relations with the Corinthians*. Wissenschaftliche Untersuchungen zum Neuen Testament 2:23. Tübingen: Mohr Siebeck, 1987.

Martin, Josef. *Antike Rhetorik: Technik und Methode*. Handbuch der Altertumswissenschaft, II.3. Münich: Beck, 1974.

Martin, Troy W. "Invention and Arrangement in Recent Pauline Rhetorical Studies." In *Paul and Rhetoric*, edited by J. Paul Sampley and Peter Lampe, 48–118. New York: T. & T. Clark, 2010.

Mengestu, Abera M. *God as Father in Paul: Kingship Language and Identity Formation in Early Christianity*. Eugene, OR: Pickwick, 2013.

Mihaila, Corin. *The Paul-Apollos Relationship and Paul's Stance toward Greco-Roman Rhetoric*. Library of New Testament Studies 402. London: T. & T. Clark, 2009.

Morgan, Teresa. *Literate Education in the Hellenistic and Roman Worlds*. Cambridge: Cambridge University Press, 1998.

BIBLIOGRAPHY

Muilenburg, James. "Form Criticism and Beyond." *Journal of Biblical Literature* 88 (1969) 1–18.

Murphy-O'Connor, Jerome. *Paul the Letter-Writer: His World, His Options, His Skills.* Collegeville: Liturgical, 1995.

Norden, E. *Antike Kunstprosa.* 2 vols. Repr. Stüttgart: Teubner, 1958.

Novenson, Matthew V. "'God Is Witness': A Classical Rhetorical Idiom in Its Pauline Usage." *Novum Testamentum* 52 (2010) 355–75.

Olbricht, Thomas H. "An Aristotelian Rhetorical Analysis of 1 Thessalonians." In *Greeks, Romans, and Christians: Essays in Honor of Abraham J. Malherbe,* edited by David L. Balch et al., 216–36. Minneapolis: Fortress, 1990.

———. "The Flowering of Rhetorical Criticism in America." In *The Rhetorical Analysis of Scripture,* edited by Stanley E. Porter and Thomas H. Olbricht, 79–102. Sheffield: Sheffield Academic, 1997.

———. "Rhetorical Criticism in Biblical Commentaries." *Currents in Biblical Research* 7 (2008) 11–36.

Parsons, Mikeal C. and Michael Wade Martin. *Ancient Rhetoric and the New Testament: The Influence of Elementary Greek Composition.* Waco, Tx.: Baylor University Press, 2018.

Perelman, Chaim, and L. Olbrechts-Tyteca. *The New Rhetoric. A Treatise on Argumentation.* Translated by J. Wilkinson and P. Weaver. Notre Dame: University of Notre Dame Press, 1971.

Porter, Stanley E. *Idioms of the Greek New Testament.* Second Edition. Biblical Languages: Greek 2. Sheffield: Sheffield Academic, 1994.

———. *Linguistic Analysis of the Greek New Testament: Studies in Tools, Methods, and Practice.* Grand Rapids: Baker Academic, 2015.

———, ed. *Handbook of Classical Rhetoric in the Hellenistic Period (330 B.C.–A.D. 400).* Leiden: Brill, 1997.

Porter, Stanley E., and Thomas H. Olbricht, eds.. *Rhetoric and the New Testament: Essays from the 1992 Heidelburg Conference.* Journal for the Study of the New Testament Supplemental Series 90. Sheffield: Sheffield Academic, 1993. Reprinted in Library of New Testament Studies. London: T. & T. Clark, 2001.

———. *The Rhetorical Analysis of Scripture: Essays from the 1995 London Conference.* Journal for the Study of the New Testament Supplemental Series 146. Sheffield: Sheffield Academic, 1997.

Porter, Stanley E., and Dennis L. Stamps, eds. *The Rhetorical Interpretation of Scripture: Essays from the 1996 Malibu Conference.* Novum Testamentum Supplements 180. Sheffield: Sheffield Academic, 1999.

Reed, Jeffrey T. "The Epistle." In *Handbook of Classical Rhetoric in the Hellenistic Period: 330 B.C.–A.D. 400,* edited by Stanley E. Porter, 171–93. Leiden: Brill, 2001.

Reumann, John. "St. Paul's Use of Irony." *Lutheran Quarterly* 7 (1955) 140–45.

Robbins, Charles J. "The Composition of Eph 1:3–14." *Journal of Biblical Literature* 105 (1986) 677–87.

Roberts, Alexander and James Donaldson, eds. *The Ante-Nicene Fathers. 1885–1887.* 10 vols. Repr. Peabody, MA: Hendrickson, 1994.

Robertson, A. T. *A Grammar of the Greek New Testament in the Light of Historical Research.* 4th ed. Nashville: Broadman, 1934.

Rolland, Philippe. "L'antithese de Rm 5–8." *Biblica* 69 (1988) 396–400.
Rowe, Galen O. "Style." In *Handbook of Classical Rhetoric in the Hellenistic Period: 330 B.C.–A.D. 400*, edited by Stanley E. Porter, 121–58. Boston; Leiden: Brill, 2001.
Sampley, J. Paul. "Paul, His Opponents in 2 Corinthians 10–13, and the Rhetorical Handbooks." In *The Social World of Formative Christianity and Judaism: Essays in Tribute to Howard Clark Kee*, edited by Jacob Neusner et al., 162–77. Philadelphia: Fortress, 1988.

———. "Paul's Frank Speech with the Galatians and the Corinthians." In *Philodemus and the New Testament World*, edited by J. T. Fitzgerald et al., 295–321. Leiden: Brill, 2004.

Sampley, J. Paul, and Peter Lampe, eds. *Paul and Rhetoric*. New York: T. & T. Clark, 2010.
Schellenberg, Ryan S. *Rethinking Paul's Rhetorical Education: Comparative Rhetoric and 2 Corinthians 10–13*. Early Christianity and Its Literature 10. Atlanta: Society of Biblical Literature, 2013.
Schmeller, Thomas. "Dissimulatio artis? Paulus und die antike Rhetorik." *New Testament Studies* 66 (2020) 500–520.
Schreiner, Thomas R. *Romans*. Baker Exegetical Commentary on the New Testament. Grand Rapids: Baker Academic, 1998.
Senft, Christophe. *La Première Épître de Saint Paul aux Corinthiens*. Commentaire du Nouveau Testament. 2nd ed. Geneva: Labor et Fides, 1990.
Slings, S. R. "Figures of Speech and their Lookalikes." In *Grammar as Interpretation*, edited by E. J. Bakker, 169–214. Leiden: Brill, 1997.
Smit, Joop. "The Genre of 1 Corinthians in the Light of Classical Rhetoric." *Novum Testamentum* 33 (1991) 193–216.
Smith, Richard Upsher. *A Glossary of Terms in Grammar, Rhetoric, and Prosody for Readers of Greek and Latin: a vade mecum*. Mundelein, IL: Bolchazy-Carducci, 2011.
Smyth, Herbert Werner. *Greek Grammar*. Cambridge, MA: Harvard University Press, 1920.
Snyman, Andris H. "Style and Meaning in Romans 8:31–9." *Neotestamentica* 18 (1984) 94–103.
Spencer, Aída Besançon. "The Wise Fool (and the Foolish Wise): A Study of Irony in Paul." *Novum Testamentum* 23 (1981) 349–60.
Stowers, Stanley K. "Apostrophe, προσωποποιία, and Paul's Rhetorical Education." In *Early Christianity and Classical Culture: Comparative Studies in Honor of Abraham J. Malherbe*, edited by John T. Fitzgerald et al., 351–69. Leiden: Brill, 2003.

———. "Romans 7:7–25 as a Speech-in-Character (προσοποποιία)." In *Paul in his Hellenistic Context*, edited by Troels Engberg-Pederson, 180–202. Minneapolis: Fortress, 1995.

Turner, N. *A Grammar of New Testament Greek. Vol. 4. Style*. Edinburgh: T. & T. Clark, 1976.
Volkmann, Richard. *Die Rhetorik der Griechen und Römer in systematischer Übersicht*. 3rd ed. Hildescheim: Olms, 1963.
Wanamaker, Charles A. *The Epistles to the Thessalonians*. The New International Greek Testament Commentary. Grand Rapids: Eerdmans, 1990.
Watson, Duane F. "The New Testament and Greco-Roman Rhetoric: A Bibliographical Update." *Journal of the Evangelical Theological Society* 33 (1990) 513–24.

BIBLIOGRAPHY

———. "The New Testament and Greco-Roman Rhetoric: A Bibliography." *Journal of the Evangelical Theological Society* 31 (1988) 465–72.

———. "The Role of Style in the Pauline Letters: From Ornamentation to Argumentative Strategies." In *Paul and Rhetoric*, edited by J. Paul Sampley and Peter Lampe, 119–39. London: T. & T. Clark, 2010.

Watson, Duane F., and Alan J. Hauser, eds. *Rhetorical Criticism of the Bible: A Comprehensive Bibliography with Notes History and Method*. Leiden: Brill, 1994.

Weiss, Johannes. "Beiträge zur paulinischen Rhetoric." In *Theologische Studien in Honor of Bernard Weiss*, 165–247. Göttingen: Vandenhoeck & Ruprecht, 1897.

Williams, David. *Paul's Metaphors: Their Context and Character*. Grand Rapids: Eerdmans, 2003.

Winter, Bruce W. "Rhetoric." In *The Dictionary of Paul and His Letters*, edited by Gerald F. Hawthorne and Ralph P. Martin, 820–22. Downers Grove, IL: InterVarsity, 1993.

Witherington, Ben, III. *New Testament Rhetoric: An Introductory Guide to the Art of Persuasion in and of the New Testament*. Eugene, OR: Cascade, 2009.

Witmer, Stephen E. "θεοδίδακτος 1 Thessalonians 4.9: A Pauline Neologism." *New Testament Studies* 52 (2006) 239–50.

Wuellner, Wilhelm H. "Paul as Pastor: The Function of Rhetorical Questions in First Corinthians." In *L' Apôtre Paul: Personnalité, Style et Conception Du Ministère*, edited by A. Vanhoye, 49–77. Leuven: Peeters, 1986.

———. "Paul's Rhetoric of Argumentation in Romans: An Alternative to the Donfried-Karris Debate over Romans." *Catholic Biblical Quarterly* 38 (1976) 330–51.

AUTHOR INDEX

Anderson, R. Dean, 21, 22

Berlin, Adele, 11
Betz, Hans D., 6, 7
Black, David Alan, 7, 8, 131
Blass, F., 5, 23
Boring, M. Eugene, 26
Botha, J. E., 1, 17
Brookins, Timothy A., 165
Bullinger, E. W., 4, 8, 21, 102
Burke, Trevor J., 11

Campbell, Constantine R., 18
Caragounis, Chrys C., 45
Classen, C. Joachim, 5, 6, 7, 8, 10
Cosby, Michael R., 7
Cranfield, C. E. B., 13

Daube, David, 16
Donaldson, James, 14

Eriksson, Anders, 7
Estes, Douglas, 11

Fairweather, J., 5
Finlan, Stephen, 11
Fitzmyer, Joseph A., 25, 27

Gaventa, Beverly Roberts, 11
Given, Mark D., 7, 9

Hauser, Alan J., 4, 5, 6
Heylen, Victor Leonard, 5
Hidary, Richard, 16
Hogeterp, Albert L. A., 11
Hock, Ronald, 12

Holland, Glen, 7
Holloway, Paul A., 7, 188, 195
Howson, John Saul, 4
Hughes, Frank W., 7, 9

Jeremias, Joachim, 5, 132
Jewett, Robert, 7
Johnson, Mark, 22
Johnson, Nathan C., 11, 152
de Jonge, Casper C., 10
Judge, E. A., 5

Keach, Benjamin, 4
Kennedy, George, 5, 6, 9, 12, 16
King, Justin D., 7, 163, 175, 176
Kirby, John T., 197
Klauck, Hans-Josef, 9, 10, 11, 21

Lakoff, George, 22
Lampe, Peter, 6, 9, 10
Lanham, Richard A., 21, 22
Lausberg, Heinrich, 10–11, 18–20, 21, 22
Levison, John R., 7, 12
Lightfoot, J. B., 30
Litfin, Duane, 2, 12
Louw, Johannes P., 19, 50, 66, 77, 85

MacDonald, Michael J., 21, 22
Mack, Burton, 2, 5
Marshall, Peter, 13
Martin, Dale 12
Martin, Josef, 10
Martin, Michael, 12
Martin, Troy W., 9
Mengestu, Abera M., 11
Mihaila, Corin, 13

AUTHOR INDEX

Morgan, Teresa, 4
Muilenberg, James, 5–6, 8
Murphy-O'Connor, Jerome, 9, 12

Neyrey, Jerome, 12
Nida, Eugene A., 19, 50, 66, 77, 85
Norden, E., 10
Novenson, Matthew V., 7, 156

Olbrechts-Tyteca, L., 11
Olbricht, Thomas H., 5, 6, 7

Parsons, Michael, 12
Perelman, Chaim, 11
Plummer, Alfred, 5
Porter, Stanley E., 6, 7, 8, 9, 10, 16, 47

Reed, Jeffrey T., 9, 10
Reumann, John, 5, 193
Robbins, Charles J., 7, 197, 199
Roberts, Alexander, 14
Robertson, A. T., 5, 23, 191
Rolland, Philippe, 11
Rowe, Galen O., 8, 10, 22

Sampley, J. Paul, 6, 7, 157

Schellenberg, Ryan S., 12, 16
Schmeller, Thomas, 7
Schneider, Norbert, 5
Schreiner, Thomas R., 27
Senft, Christophe, 47
Slings, S. R., 18
Smit, Joop, 105
Smith, Richard Upsher, 22
Smyth, Herbert Werner, 23
Snyman, Andris H., 7, 8, 199
Spencer, Aida Besançon, 7, 8, 193
Stamps, Dennis L., 6, 9
Stowers, Stanley K., 7, 176

Turner, Nigel, 5

Volkmann, Richard, 10

Wanamaker, Charles A., 7, 26
Watson, Duane F., 4, 5, 6, 7, 8, 9
Weiss, Johannes, 5, 12
Williams, David, 11
Winter, Bruce W., 13
Witherington, Ben, 7, 9, 12, 176
Witmer, Stephen E., 49
Wuellner, Wilhelm H., 6, 11

SUBJECT INDEX

accumulation, 116, 143, co-ordinating accumulation, 106, 110, 113
adiunctio, 139, 144–45
allegory, 66–77, 174
alliteration, 102, 104, 135, 200, see also "homoiopropheron"
anacoluthon, 30, 42–44, 187, 197, 199
anadiplosis (reduplicatio), 94
anaphora, 96–98
antimetabole (commutatio), 172–73
antistrophe (epiphora), 99–101, 132
antithetical isocolon, see "isocolon"
antitheton, 117, 145, 167–71, 172, 189
antonomasia, 87–88, 194
aporia (dubitatio), 163–64
aposiopesis (reticentia), 44, 115, 191–92
apostrophe, 158–59, 162
archaism, 48
Aristotle, 2, 13
arrangement (dispositio), see "parts of rhetoric"
art of rhetoric, the (ars, τέχνη), 13
artificial rhetoric, see "art of rhetoric"
asyndeton, 113, 116–17, 195
Augustine, 4, 14, 195
authorship, disputed and undisputed letters, 20, 25
barbarism, 29

Bede, 4

Caecilius, 3
catachresis, 49, 85, 87, 89–92
chiasm, 130–32, 170
Cicero, 2, 13, 28

clarity (perspicuitas), see "virtues (stylistic virtue)"
climax (gradatio), 94–95
colon, 117, 132, 138, 143, 145, 152, 177, 194, 195, 196
comma, 117, 145, 194, 195, 196
communicatio, 163, 164
commutatio, 117
complicated zeugma, see "zeugma"
composition, 3, 194–200, style of, 194–99
conceptual metaphor theory, 22
concessio, 185
co-ordinating accumulation, see "accumulation"
correctio (epanorthosis), 165–67, 185
correctness (Latinitas, ἑλληνισμός), see "virtues (stylistic virtue)"
Crassus, 13, 22, 28

deēsis (obsecratio), 156–57
deliberative speech, see "genus"
delivery (pronuntiatio), see "parts of rhetoric"
Demetrius, of Phaleron, 2
diatribe, 162, 195, 196
Dionysius, of Halicarnuss, 3
diplomatic letters, 9, 21, 24, 195
discourse analysis, 17–18
disiunctio, 108, 117, 143–44
disputed letters, see "authorship"
distinctio, 109
distributio (diairesis), 111–12, 114, 117

education, of Paul, 12–13, 15, 16, 24
elementary exercises, 12
ellipsis, 30–38, 114–15

SUBJECT INDEX

epanalepsis (geminatio), 93–94
epideictic speech, see "genus"
epimone, 177
epiphora, see "antistrophe"
epistolography (epistolary theory), 8–10
epitheton, 112–13
erōtēsis (interrogatio), 159–60, 196
euphony, 199
exclamatio, 174–75
exemplum, 7
expolitio, 108, 177–83, see also "epimone"

figures, 3, 93–194, figures of speech, 3, 93–155, 156, figures of thought, 3, 156–94
forensic speech, see "genus"
form criticism, 25, 196

genus, speech types (deliberative, epideictic, and forensic), 7

hendiadys, 101–2
homoioprophoron, 102, 104, 132, 200
homoioptoton, 135–36
homoioteleuton, 132–34, 138
horismos (finitio), 164
hyperbaton, 91, 92–93, 185
hyperbole, 50, 87, 105
hysteron proteron, 192

imitation, of rhetoric, 13, 14, 15
inartificial rhetoric, 13
interpretatio, 108, 117, 143, 152–55, 177
interrogatio, see "erōtēsis"
invention (inventio), see "parts of rhetoric"
irony, as trope, 88–89, 109, as figure of thought, 193
isocolon, 108, 111, 117–30, 132, 138, 143, 145, 146, 152, 194, 196, antithetical isocolon, 117, 145–52

Jerusalem, 12

left-dislocation, 40, 42, 43
lexicalized tropes, 22, 49, 50, 77, 85, 89
litotes, 92

Melanchthon, Phillip, 4, 6
memory (memoria), see "parts of rhetoric"
metaphor, 3, 50–66, necessary metaphor, 89
metaplasmos, 29
metonymy, metonym, 3, 77–84, 108, 115
Middle Ages, 10

nature (natural rhetoric), 13, 14, 15
necessary metaphor, see "metaphor"
neologism, 48–49
New Rhetoric, 11

onomatopoeia, 48
ornament (ornatus), see "virtues (stylistic virtue)"
oxymoron (paradox), 173–74, 188

paradox, 109, 171, 188, see also "oxymoron"
paralepsis (praeteritio), 190–91
parenesis, parenetic style, 25, 196
parenthesis (interpositio), 92, 185–87
paromoiosis, 117, 136–38
paronomasia (annominatio), 102–5, 135, 190, 200
parrhēsia (licentia), 157–58
parts of rhetoric, 3, 10, arrangement (dispositio), 6–7, 8, 10, delivery (pronuntiatio), 2, invention (inventio), 6–7, 8, 10, memory (memoria), 2, style (elocutio), 1, 5–8, 10
period, 194, 197, periodic style (see "composition, style of")
periphrasis, as trope, 89, 194, as figure of thought, 193–94
pleonasm, 29–30
pointed sentences, 188, 195, 196
polyptoton (paregmenon), 105–6
polysyndeton, 113, 116
practice, of rhetoric, 13, 14, 15
proofs, artificial and inartificial, 7
proparaskeue (praeparatio), 185
propriety (aptum), see "virtues (stylistic virtue)"

SUBJECT INDEX

prosapodosis (redditio), 96
prosopopoeia (fictio personae), 175, 176–77
Pseudo-Aristotle, 2
Pseudo-Cicero, 2
pysma (quaesitum), 160–62, 196

Quintilian, 2, 3, 10, 14, 18, 19

reflexio (antanaklasis), 88, 110
Reformers, the, 4
regressio (epanodos), 171–72
rhetorical criticism, 4–10

semantic domain, 50, 66, 77, 85
Semitisms, 30
sententia (gnomē), 188–90, 195
sermocinatio, 65, 175–76
simile (similitudo), 174
solecism, 29–44, 115
style of composition
    complicated style (periodic style), 194
    exalted style (grand style), 195
    grand style (exalted style), 117, 196
    loose style, 117, 194, 195–96
    middle style (temperate style), 196,
    periodic style (complicated style), 197–99
    running style, 194, 196–97
    simple style (subdued style), 196
    subdued style (simple style), 195
    temperate style (middle style), 195
subiectio (aetiologia), 162–63, 176, 196

symploche (complexio), 101, 132
synecdoche, 3, 84–86, 108, 194
synoiciosis (conciliatio), 165
synonymy, 106–8, 110, 113
syntactical analysis, 17–18

Tarsus, 12
Theophrastus, 3
theory, of rhetoric, 14, 15
topoi, 7
traductio (antanaklasis), 34, 108–9
tricolon, 117, 132, 138–43
tropes, 3, 48, 49–93, 174

uncomplicated zeugma, see "zeugma"
universal rhetoric, 11

vices (stylistic vice), 15, 28, 29, 30, 42, 44, 102, 104, 114, 115, 135, 200
virtues (stylistic virtue), 3, 9, 17, 18, 19, 22, 28, 30, 45, 47, 115, clarity (perspicuitas), 3, 9, 17–18, 19, 44–47, correctness (Latinitas), 3, 17–18, 19, 22, 28, ornament (ornatus), 3, 9, 17–18, 19, 22, 47–200, propriety (aptum), 3, 9, 19

word order, 199–200

zeugma, 30, 115, complicated zeugma, 24, 27, 30, 115, uncomplicated zeugma, 116

SCRIPTURE INDEX

Old Testament

Genesis
1:26	103

Exodus
7:3	107

Leviticus
18:22	48
20:13	48

Numbers
21:5–9	116

Deuteronomy
25:4	73
32:35	58
32:39	90
4:34	107

2 Kings
17:12	49

Psalms
8:6	58, 64
68:23	70

Ecclesiastes
2:24	188
3:12	188

Isaiah
8:18	107
22:13	188
43:6	53
54:13	49
64:3	43, 85
65:16e	43

Jeremiah
9:22–23	188

Hosea
13:14	26, 177

Malachi
1:2–3	84

New Testament

Mark
14:29	44

Luke
1:37	39

SCRIPTURE INDEX

John

10:28	39

Acts

9:30	15
22:3	12
26:4	12

Romans

1:1–7	197, 199
1:1	57, 58
1:3–4	93, 117, 152
1:3	79
1:5	81, 102, 108
1:7	52
1:9	60, 61, 156
1:13	33, 50, 187
1:14	62
1:16	69, 110
1:18–3:8	24
1:19–25	170
1:19–21	170
1:20	173
1:21	32
1:22	170
1:23–25	104, 177
1:23	29, 170
1:24	79
1:25	170
1:27	54, 62
1:28	109
1:29–31	104, 116
1:29	102, 104
1:30	104
1:31	102, 104
2	56
2:1	102, 158, 162
2:3	54, 158, 162
2:4	61
2:5–8	197
2:5	63, 88, 102, 106
2:6	32, 58
2:7–10	131, 145
2:7–8	177
2:7	145, 178
2:8	33, 42, 102, 103, 106, 145, 167, 178
2:9–10	110, 177
2:9	78, 102, 145, 178
2:10	102, 145, 178
2:11	64
2:12	117, 132, 136, 189
2:13	61, 64, 102, 145, 167, 189
2:14–15	70
2:14	81
2:15–29	109
2:15	61
2:17–21	198
2:17	56
2:19	68, 70, 106
2:20	52, 106, 165
2:21–23	117, 132, 138, 159
2:23	91
2:25	79
2:26	79, 85
2:27	81, 85
2:28–29	145, 164
2:29	61
3:1	152, 163
3:2	115
3:3–4	159
3:3	102, 115, 163
3:4	175
3:5–6	159
3:5	163, 171
3:5b	159
3:6	77, 163, 175
3:7	63, 163, 171
3:8	159, 163, 185
3:9	39, 57, 64, 115, 163
3:20	39, 61, 79
3:21–26	198
3:22b–26	197
3:24	58, 61, 64
3:25–26	181
3:25	27, 65, 74, 78, 81, 82, 84
3:26	190
3:26b	190

SCRIPTURE INDEX

3:27	109, 115, 160, 161, 162, 163	5:17	57, 177
		5:18–19	153
3:29	163	5:18	25, 26, 43, 114, 146
3:29b	159	5:19	146
3:30	85	5:21	57, 177
3:31	159, 163, 175	6:1–2	159
3:38–39	198	6:1	62, 130, 163, 164
4:1–3	178	6:2–11	70
4:1	53, 79, 92, 163	6:2	64, 160, 175
4:2	37, 116	6:3	65, 159, 189
4:3	61, 163	6:4	56, 60, 75
4:4–5	146	6:5	63
4:4	116, 164	6:6	55
4:5	61	6:8	41, 174
4:6	61	6:10	146
4:9	82, 85, 159	6:11	64, 146
4:10	79, 163	6:12–23	71, 177
4:11	52, 57, 79	6:12–21	182
4:12	68, 79	6:13	51, 61, 146
4:13	82	6:14	57, 64
4:16–17	197	6:15	57, 64, 115, 159, 163, 175
4:16	82, 114		
4:17	189	6:16	159
4:19	87	6:17	35
4:23–24	116	6:18–19	50
4:25	26, 27, 37, 60, 189	6:18	71
5	7	6:19	61, 79, 82, 91, 134, 147
5:2	54, 55, 102		
5:3–5	4, 94	6:20	71, 189, 190
5:3	114	6:21	50, 160
5:4	116	6:22	38, 50, 61
5:5	60, 65, 92	6:23	62, 195
5:6–8	99, 106, 183	7:1–6	71
5:6	60	7:2–3	128
5:8	74, 190	7:2	57
5:9–10	178	7:4–13	70
5:9	78, 82	7:4	50
5:10	58	7:6	147
5:11	58, 114	7:7–25	7, 76, 195, 196
5:12–21	184	7:7	27, 47, 84, 153, 159, 163, 164, 175
5:12–18	43, 197		
5:12	43, 116, 197	7:8	69, 177
5:14	57, 84, 88, 177	7:8b	47
5:15–21	182	7:11	55, 69
5:15	43, 114	7:12	27, 192
5:16	114, 117, 132, 135, 136, 146	7:13	42, 44, 159, 175
		7:14–25	109

215

SCRIPTURE INDEX

Romans (continued)

7:14	57, 62, 64, 71, 147, 195	8:31	161
7:15–21	182	8:32	160, 199
7:15	147, 195	8:33–34	96, 138
7:17	32, 64, 115, 195	8:35–37	72
7:18	64, 86, 147, 195	8:35	63, 78, 108, 113, 176
7:19	147, 167, 195	8:38–39	113, 170
7:20	32, 64, 115, 195	8:38	176
7:22	64	8:39	63
7:23	75, 91	9:1–9	24
7:24	38, 161, 175	9:1–5	104, 185
7:25	147, 161, 195	9:1–4	104
8:1	64	9:1–3	116
8:2–3	109	9:1–2	178, 185
8:2	71	9:1	104, 156
8:3	42, 43, 192	9:2	79
8:4	54, 79	9:3	79, 87
8:5	79, 148, 195	9:4	53, 113
8:6	79, 80, 148, 195	9:5	53, 79
8:7	58, 79	9:6–8	195
8:8	79, 196	9:6–7	104, 153, 178
8:9	61, 65, 79	9:6	39, 104, 109, 114, 166
8:10	64, 80, 148, 195	9:7–13	52
8:11	65	9:7–8	104, 109
8:12	62, 79, 148, 188	9:7	82
8:14	53	9:8	39, 104, 148, 178
8:15–17	68, 75	9:10	53, 114
8:15	37, 53, 148	9:11–12	185
8:16–17	94	9:13	84
8:16	53	9:14–20	195, 196
8:17	116, 196	9:14	64, 159, 163, 164, 175
8:20–21	71	9:16	54, 114, 195
8:21–23	53	9:18	63, 134, 148
8:21	53, 56, 192	9:19	162
8:22	69, 177	9:20	158, 162
8:23	37, 42, 58, 59, 60, 114, 192	9:21–22	72
8:24–25	196	9:21	67, 159
8:24	56, 80, 160	9:22–23	148
8:27	57, 61	9:22	27, 192
8:28–39	199	9:30–32	163
8:29–30	94	9:30	94, 163, 164
8:29	52, 53, 68, 75, 85	9:32	69
8:31–39	7	10:1	69, 79
8:31–35	162	10:2	92
		10:4	37

10:5	167	12:3	42, 102, 108, 190
10:6–8	175, 176	12:4–5	51, 67, 184
10:6–7	187	12:5	64
10:6	167, 177	12:6–17	42
10:8	163	12:6–16	195, 196
10:9	79	12:6–13	197
10:9–10	131	12:6–8	43, 111, 114, 197, 199
10:10	69, 79, 118, 132, 135, 136	12:6	42
10:12	61	12:9–21	21
10:14–15	95	12:10–13	118, 133, 135, 136
10:14	162	12:14	96, 167, 170
10:14c	149	12:15	105, 114, 118, 134
10:14d	149	12:16	170
10:16	92	12:18	114
10:17	47, 94	12:19	41, 43, 58, 170
10:18–19	96	12:19a	47
10:18	159	12:20	47
10:19	47	12:21	172
10:28	163	13:1–14	195
11:1	130, 159, 175	13:1	78, 81, 102
11:2	130, 159	13:2	81, 94, 102, 105, 183
11:6–7	196	13:3–4	
11:7	63, 80, 115, 163	13:3	81, 158
11:10	70	13:4	194
11:11–16	195, 196	13:5	37, 84
11:11	54, 69, 159, 175	13:7–8	196
11:12	61, 135, 153, 179	13:7	102, 103, 104, 105, 111, 114
11:13	158		
11:14	79	13:8	34, 94, 105, 108
11:15	58, 77, 179	13:10	62, 80, 92
11:16–24	66, 72	13:11	35, 42, 56, 69, 70, 80, 83
11:16	59, 60, 153		
11:17	102	13:12–14	196
11:18	114, 172, 195	13:12–13	68
11:19	102, 132, 162	13:12	60, 64, 75, 149, 195
11:22	42, 110, 131	13:13	54, 82, 106, 138
11:25	25, 63, 118	13:14	60
11:28	53, 149	14:1–10	183
11:32	58	14:1	56
11:33–36	199	14:3	172
11:33–35	132	14:4	61, 68, 69, 160
11:33–34	179	14:5	64
11:33	61, 153	14:6	118
11:36	105, 113, 138	14:7–9	132
12:1	60, 74, 85, 156	14:7	118
12:2	83	14:8	119, 134

SCRIPTURE INDEX

Romans *(continued)*

14:9	71
14:10	75, 161
14:13–23	25, 195, 196
14:13	108
14:14	106
14:15	77
14:16	188
14:17	77, 189
14:19	59
14:20	55, 59
14:21	85
14:22	102, 109, 190
14:23	102
15:1–2	182
15:2	59
15:3	182
15:8	60
15:13	62, 63
15:14	62
15:15–16	102, 108
15:16	60, 74
15:19	62, 107
15:20	73
15:23–28	43, 197
15:23–24	43
15:24	62
15:27	60, 62
15:28	50, 57
15:30	156
15:33	113
16:1	53
16:3	112
16:4	78, 86
16:5	37, 59, 60
16:7	113
16:9	112
16:13	53
16:18	42, 78
16:20	57, 64, 69, 88
16:21	113
16:23	112
16:25–27	43
16:26	70

1 Corinthians

1:1	112
1:2	53, 81
1:4–8	197
1:5	47, 61
1:7	47
1:8	36
1:10	81, 179
1:12	175
1:13	84, 159, 160
1:15	39
1:16	78
1:17–2:10	7
1:17	12, 85, 102, 170
1:18	39, 85
1:20	96, 116, 138, 162, 195, 196
1:21	77, 88
1:22–24	149, 168
1:23	174
1:24–25	132
1:24	110, 174
1:25	35, 88, 118, 134, 168
1:26	92, 96, 115, 116, 139, 144, 195, 196
1:27–28	99, 119, 139
1:29	39, 86, 188
1:30	27, 39, 58, 61, 80, 81, 82, 84
1:31	35, 188
2:1–5	12
2:1	102
2:2	39
2:3	108
2:4	83, 102, 106, 108, 170
2:4a	35
2:5	170
2:8	88, 174
2:9	35, 43, 85
2:11	126, 160
2:12	77
2:13	103, 105, 170
2:14	39, 89, 92
2:15	39, 89

3:1	26, 33, 39, 52, 86, 106	4:15	71, 87
3:2	46, 67	4:18	39, 64
3:2a–b	34	4:19	35, 64
3:2c	35	4:20	189
3:3–5	162	4:21	71, 161, 162, 164
3:3	54	5:1	35, 44, 87, 114
3:4–5	47	5:2	64, 159
3:4	175	5:3–5	40, 198
3:5–23	24	5:3	88
3:5	28, 42, 60, 115	5:5	79, 83, 88
3:6–17	104	5:6–8	74
3:6–9	66, 72	5:6	67, 103, 159
3:6–7	104, 139	5:7	74, 82, 103
3:7	104	5:8	51, 107, 170
3:8	39, 47, 62	5:9	39
3:9	51, 96, 104, 139	5:10	35, 107, 109, 113
3:9–15	66, 67	5:11	86, 113
3:9b	47	5:12–13	149
3:10–15	73	5:12	88, 160
3:10	59, 102, 108	5:12b	159
3:12	116	6:2	45, 77, 78, 159
3:13	39, 104, 153	6:3	94, 114, 159
3:14–15	104, 128	6:4	88
3:16–17	67	6:5	88, 159, 165
3:16	104, 159	6:6	46, 95, 114, 149
3:17	39, 51, 104, 109, 171, 189, 190	6:7	61, 86, 96, 134, 143, 159, 160
3:18	38, 104, 174, 189	6:8	95, 114, 149
3:19	39, 88, 189	6:9–10	113, 116
3:22–23	95	6:9	45, 48, 62, 113, 159
3:22	113	6:10	62, 96, 116
4:1	54, 59, 60	6:11	116, 139, 195
4:2	59	6:12	103, 149
4:3–4	186	6:13	119, 172
4:3	46	6:14	119
4:5	68, 154	6:15–17	52, 66, 67
4:6	64, 84, 188	6:15	84, 159, 175
4:7	95, 99, 161, 162	6:16–17	101, 119
4:8	57, 61, 88, 116, 175, 193, 195, 196	6:16	114, 159
		6:17	115
4:9	73, 78, 110	6:19	45, 51, 159
4:10	88, 132, 170	6:20	71
4:11	87, 113	7:1	39
4:12–13	116, 119, 139, 195, 196	7:2–4	172
		7:2	99, 119, 134
		7:3	116, 132
4:13	63, 74, 88, 107	7:4	116, 120, 134

SCRIPTURE INDEX

1 Corinthians *(continued)*

7:5	84, 88
7:7	93
7:8	35
7:9	54, 89
7:10–11	186
7:10	32, 115, 166
7:12–13	120
7:12	32, 115, 166
7:14	120
7:15	37, 53, 57
7:15ab	47
7:15c	47
7:15d	47
7:16	80, 86, 120, 134, 158
7:17	54, 120
7:18–23	25, 196
7:18	79, 161, 172, 195, 196
7:19	34, 79, 99, 120
7:21	161, 196
7:21ab	47
7:22–23	183
7:22	37, 47, 57, 71, 72, 109, 132, 173, 174
7:23	57, 71, 72
7:24	64
7:25	102, 108
7:27	150, 161
7:28	79, 120
7:29–31	174, 181
7:29–30	96, 113
7:29	35, 44
7:31	77, 103
7:32–33	120, 134, 150
7:35	71
7:36	31
7:37	41, 43, 63
7:38	121, 134
7:39	114
8:1	45, 59, 64, 150, 189
8:1b	189
8:2–3	128, 150, 190
8:2	110, 190
8:5–6	44
8:5	91
8:6	65, 128
8:7	56, 61, 63
8:8	121
8:9	47, 51, 56, 89
8:10	56, 59, 89, 159
8:11	47, 56
8:12	33, 42, 42, 84
8:13	51, 77, 87
9:1–27	89
9:1	59, 97, 159, 160
9:2	44, 57
9:4–6	159
9:4–5	97
9:4	159
9:5	32, 159
9:6	159
9:7	161
9:8	159
9:9	39, 73, 161
9:10	47, 72, 105
9:11	114, 121, 133, 137
9:12	32, 159
9:13–14	143
9:13	154, 159
9:14	109
9:15	39, 191
9:16	130
9:17	59, 116, 129
9:19–23	121, 134
9:19	71, 105, 109, 168, 189
9:20–22	99
9:20–21	186
9:20	57, 64, 105, 109
9:21	105
9:22	86, 105, 190
9:22c	190
9:22d	190
9:24–25	54, 73, 75
9:24	78, 159
9:25	32, 51, 115
9:26–27	73
9:27	87
10:1–10	104
10:1–4	97, 104, 113
10:1	39, 52

SCRIPTURE INDEX

10:3–4	132	11:8–9	173
10:4	39, 94	11:9	47
10:5	92, 104	11:10	47
10:7–10	97, 104	11:12	65, 173
10:7	32	11:13–14	164
10:8	54	11:13	105, 159
10:9–10	104, 121	11:14–15	105, 150, 159
10:9	27, 31, 116	11:14	105, 165
10:11	65	11:17	31
10:12	54, 189, 190	11:18	38, 40
10:13–14	184	11:18a	47
10:13	55	11:19	47, 89
10:14–22	45	11:20	39, 47
10:14	49, 54	11:21	87
10:15	88, 164	11:22	45, 53, 116, 159, 160, 162, 195
10:16–17	51	11:22a	159
10:16	77, 78, 82, 122, 134, 159	11:22c	161
10:17	51	11:22d	161
10:18	159	11:23	109
10:19–20	159	11:24–25	122
10:19	115, 154	11:24	51
10:20	46	11:25	78
10:21	78, 122, 154	11:28	46
10:22	45, 89, 159	11:29–34	103
10:23	59, 133, 134, 137, 143	11:29	36
		11:30	46, 92
10:25	99, 129	11:32	77
10:26	39	11:33	104, 105
10:27–28	129	12:1	92
10:27	99	12:3	176
10:28	99	12:4–11	111
10:31	133	12:4–6	97, 140, 154
10:32	53	12:4	39
10:33	105	12:6	79
11:1–15	104	12:8–11	130
11:1	35	12:12–27	52, 66, 67
11:2–16	24	12:12	84
11:2	31, 164	12:13	56, 65, 179
11:3	52, 95	12:14	52
11:4–5	122	12:15–17	52
11:4	31, 86, 104, 105	12:15–16	159, 175, 176
11:5	86, 87, 105	12:15	39
11:6	87, 105, 173	12:17	160
11:7	39	12:18	52
11:7b	47	12:19	52, 130
11:8–12	195	12:20	52, 130, 188

SCRIPTURE INDEX

1 Corinthians *(continued)*

12:21	39
12:22	46, 52
12:23	65
12:25	52
12:26	52
12:27	52
12:28	79, 116
12:29–30	97, 116, 159, 195
12:29	79
12:30	112, 140
12:31	54
13:1–3	100, 179
13:1	51, 78, 79
13:2–3	113
13:2	87, 132
13:4–7	116, 176, 195
13:4–5	97
13:4	64, 132
13:6	150
13:7	97, 122, 134
13:8	122, 133, 137, 140, 144
13:9–10	168
13b	132
13:11	52, 100, 140, 150, 168
13:12	32, 70, 85, 104, 105, 115, 179
13:12a	150
13:12b	150
13:12c	151
13:12d	151
13:13	104, 116
14:2–3	151
14:2	46, 79, 91
14:2d	47
14:3	36, 39, 59, 89
14:4	39, 59, 100, 123
14:5	29, 59, 123
14:6	113, 161
14:7–9	129
14:7	130, 134, 161
14:8	161
14:9	40, 130, 134, 161
14:11	59
14:12	59, 79
14:14	50
14:15	100, 115, 144, 161, 163
14:16	158, 161
14:17	59
14:18	79
14:19	87, 168
14:20	52, 168
14:23–24	129
14:23	159
14:25	64
14:26	79, 100, 115, 161
14:27	32, 33, 115
14:31	97
14:32–33	186
14:32	79, 103, 104, 105, 188
14:33	45, 189
14:34–35	45
14:36	45, 123, 134
14:38	31, 109
14:39	132
15:1–2	140
15:1	55
15:2	29, 186
15:3	60, 84
15:8	56
15:9	53
15:10	32, 102, 108, 115, 166
15:12	27, 64, 160
15:13–18	181
15:13–15	95
15:13	64, 181
15:14	181
15:16–17	95
15:16	181
15:17	64, 181
15:20	59, 60
15:21–22	178
15:21	32, 33
15:22	184
15:23	59, 60, 76
15:24	33, 107, 126, 192
15:26	177
15:27–28	109

15:27	58, 64
15:28	58, 64
15:29	161, 162, 165
15:30	161
15:32	33, 38, 50, 72, 73, 161, 188
15:33–34	25, 196
15:33	188
15:34	56
15:35–38	66, 72
15:35	162
15:36–49	184
15:36–38	183, 184
15:36–37	75
15:39–56	24
15:39–42	66, 184
15:39–41	112
15:39	97, 103
15:40–58	195, 196
15:40–48	195
15:41	97, 140
15:42–49	123
15:42–44	72, 97, 116, 184, 195
15:42–43	123, 133, 135, 137, 141
15:42	59, 115
15:43	59
15:44	59, 89, 180
15:45–49	184
15:45	46, 123
15:46	46, 89, 114
15:47–48	116, 195
15:47	76, 77, 123
15:48	32, 123
15:49	60, 123
15:50–54	132
15:50	80, 86, 168, 180
15:51	39, 134, 151
15:52	141, 173, 194
15:53	60, 102, 124, 134, 154
15:54–57	72
15:54–56	67
15:54	21, 26, 60, 102, 124, 154, 177
15:55	98
15:56	95
16:2	87
16:3	37
16:5	187
16:9	72, 76, 83
16:12	39, 112
16:13–14	25, 195, 196
16:13	56, 61, 75
16:15–16	186
16:15	59, 60
16:18	116
16:21	79

2 Corinthians

1:3–7	197
1:3	171
1:6	69, 124
1:8–9	46
1:8	65
1:9	82
1:10	106
1:12	79
1:13	103, 109
1:14	81
1:16	132
1:17	79, 159, 180
1:21	58, 60
1:22	57, 62, 64
1:23	61, 78
1:24	114, 166
2:2	173
2:4	87
2:5	65, 114
2:6	81
2:7	56
2:10	32, 85
2:11	88, 92
2:12	76
2:13	56, 78
2:14	58, 63
2:15–16	171
2:15	63
2:16	63, 151
2:17	35, 62, 64
3:1	32, 164
3:1b	159

SCRIPTURE INDEX

2 Corinthians *(continued)*

3:2–11	104, 106
3:2–3	66, 70, 127, 197
3:2	103
3:3	51, 67
3:5	114, 166
3:6–7	86
3:6	60, 189
3:7–11	100
3:8	161
3:9	102
3:12–13	157
3:13	114
3:14	30, 63
3:15	30, 84
3:18	184
4:2	54
4:3–6	66, 70
4:3	64
4:4	38, 91, 92, 67, 76
4:8–11	197
4:8–10	197
4:8–9	168
4:8	103
4:10–11	180
4:10	87, 174
4:11	174
4:15	62
4:16	64
4:18	134, 136, 151, 174, 195
5:1	29, 89
5:2–4	73
5:2	51
5:3	174
5:4	56, 65
5:5	62
5:6	42, 43, 65, 66
5:7	54, 195
5:8	51, 60, 95, 66
5:9	65, 66
5:10	75
5:12	41, 42
5:14–15	100, 141
5:14	74
5:15	34, 74
5:16	104
5:17	59, 64, 82, 116, 168, 195
5:18	58
5:19	58, 77
5:20	58, 180, 196
5:21	27, 60, 84
6:2–11	199
6:2	69, 98
6:3–10	197
6:3	51
6:4–7	98, 116
6:4	60
6:5	92
6:7–8	98, 141
6:7	51, 61
6:8–10	98, 170, 171, 174
6:9	41, 43
6:10	61, 103
6:11–13	157
6:11	64, 155, 195
6:12	78, 195
6:13	53, 186
6:14–16	155, 161, 195
6:14–15	162, 170
6:14	59, 170
6:15	170
6:16	51
6:18	53
7:1	61, 74
7:2–4	195
7:2	98, 116, 124, 134, 137, 141, 195
7:3	64
7:4	62, 116, 157, 195
7:5	41, 42, 64, 86, 124
7:8–9	186
7:9	114
7:10	69
7:13	30, 56
7:15	78, 108
8:2	62, 76, 174
8:3	166
8:7	35, 63
8:8	76
8:9	61, 174
8:16	64

SCRIPTURE INDEX

8:18–21	43, 197, 199	11:19	89, 105, 193
8:20	42	11:20	57, 98, 104, 105, 141, 200
9:3	62	11:21	89, 105, 167, 186, 193
9:4	191		
9:6	72, 101, 189, 190	11:21–29	105, 124, 125
9:7	79	11:22	33, 82, 100, 105, 142, 144, 159
9:8	63, 103, 105		
9:10	72	11:23	60, 87, 105, 134, 137, 144, 167, 186
9:11	42, 61		
9:13	42	11:23–29	116
9:12	60	11:24–27	197
9:14	62, 64	11:26–27	33
10–13	24	11:26	98, 105
10:1	43	11:28	55
10:2	54	11:29	54, 105, 55, 61
10:3–6	75	11:31	92
10:3	190	12:1	43
10:4–5	197	12:2–4	182
10:7	78, 85	12:2–3	100
10:8	55, 59	12:3	186
10:9	87, 89, 91	12:4	102
10:10	12, 65, 87, 89, 91, 175	12:5a	47
		12:5b	47
10:12–16	103	12:6	38, 47
10:12	89, 103, 193	12:7	51, 64, 102
10:17	188	12:9	64, 65, 174
10:30	109	12:10	116, 174
11:1–12:21	196	12:10b	190
11:2	70, 93	12:10c	190
11:4	84, 141	12:11	89, 167
11:5	89	12:12	107
11:6	12, 32	12:13	56, 89, 193
11:7	132, 159	12:14	56, 105, 173, 195
11:8	87, 91	12:15	62, 78, 103, 161
11:9	56, 62, 106	12:16	65, 89
11:1	167	12:17–18	159
11:10	81	12:17	40, 159
11:11	114, 159, 163	12:18	54, 68, 155
11:12	32, 106	12:18c	159
11:14	88, 114	12:18d	159
11:15	103, 114	12:19	59, 64
11:16–12:13	7	12:20	116, 173
11:16–30	195	12:21	108
11:16–17	105, 167	13:3–9	168
11:18	79	13:3	130
11:19–29	24, 105	13:5	63, 64, 159
11:19–20	116		

SCRIPTURE INDEX

2 Corinthians (continued)

13:6–7	63
13:8	34, 157
13:10	55, 59
13:11	25, 196

Galatians

1–2	7
1:1	105
1:4	83
1:6–9	46
1:6–7	109, 166
1:8–9	100, 155
1:6	157
1:8	87, 105
1:10	46, 94
1:12	107, 180
1:14	41
1:15–17	198
1:15	115
1:16	85, 185
1:17	103, 185
1:20	37, 114, 157
1:21	15
2:2	54
2:4	53, 71, 72
2:5	29
2:6	43, 85, 88, 187
2:7–9	198
2:7	82, 85, 88
2:8	85
2:9	35, 83, 89, 102, 108
2:10	30, 35
2:11	85
2:12	88
2:14	54, 161
2:15	193
2:16	39, 79, 86, 116, 183
2:17	159, 165, 175, 177
2:18–21	195
2:18	55, 59
2:19	55, 105, 169, 174
2:20	105, 151, 166, 195
3:1–14	196
3:1	91, 158
3:2	62, 101, 116, 164
3:3	79, 131, 159, 193
3:4	159, 166
3:5	101, 115, 161
3:7	52
3:8	81, 177
3:11	64
3:13	27, 58, 60, 81, 84
3:15–22	195, 196
3:15	50
3:16	82
3:18	62
3:19	36, 40, 79, 115, 163
3:20	101, 109, 125, 151
3:21	159, 175
3:22–23	71
3:22	64
3:23–24	182
3:23	57, 64, 80
3:24	37
3:26	64
3:27	65
3:28	98, 125, 142
3:29	62, 82
4:1–7	62, 68, 71, 75, 184
4:1–3	184
4:4–5	94
4:4	57, 64, 69
4:5	53, 57, 62, 64
4:6	65, 176
4:7	95, 114, 159, 195
4:8–9	71, 169
4:9	161, 162, 166
4:9–11	158
4:10–20	199
4:10	83, 86, 113
4:12	157
4:13	86
4:14	86, 107, 184
4:15	87, 114, 161
4:16	89, 161
4:17	92, 96
4:18–20	94
4:19	32, 36, 52, 53, 69, 175
4:21–5:1	66, 68, 75, 169

4:21	57, 64, 91, 131, 159, 161
4:22–5:1	71, 72
4:22	88
4:23	79, 88, 151
4:24–25	94
4:25	76
4:26	53, 76
4:28	53
4:29	79
4:31–5:1	94
4:31	53, 88, 116, 170
5:1	61
5:4	54
5:6	34, 79
5:7–12	196
5:7	54, 105, 158, 161
5:8	105
5:9	67
5:10	105
5:11	51, 161
5:12	87
5:13–25	177
5:13	79
5:15	55, 56
5:16	54, 79, 180, 195
5:17	58, 79, 132, 173, 195
5:18	57, 64, 169
5:19–21	116
5:19	61, 79, 108
5:20	49, 107
5:21–26	195
5:21	62, 107
5:22–23	116
5:22	50
5:24	69
5:25	54, 131
6:1	32
6:2	65, 109
6:5	65
6:6	105
6:7–9	72
6:8	105, 134, 152, 189, 190
6:10	52
6:12	78, 85, 134, 152
6:13	86, 109, 134, 152
6:14	14, 32, 55, 78, 85, 115, 173, 175
6:15	34, 79, 195
6:16	54, 64
6:18	42

Ephesians

1:3–14	197, 199
1:3–5	127
1:4	63
1:6	88
1:7	61, 72, 78, 82
1:13	69
1:14	58
1:15–21	197
1:18–19	142
1:18	61, 75
1:21	81, 107, 113, 116
1:22–23	52, 67
1:22	52, 58, 64
2:1–5	40, 43, 197
2:2	51, 53, 54, 77, 83
2:4–6	187
2:4	61
2:7	61
2:8	95
2:10	54, 59
2:11	30, 85
2:13	78, 92
2:12	30
2:14–16	197
2:16	52
2:19	53, 59
2:20–22	67
3:1–14	197
3:1–7	197
3:1	43, 94, 187
3:2	59
3:6	52
3:7	41
3:8–12	197
3:8	61
3:14–18	197
3:14	43, 94, 187
3:16	61, 64

SCRIPTURE INDEX

Ephesians *(continued)*

3:17	50, 59, 64
3:20	200
4:1	54
4:4–6	196
4:4	52
4:5	142
4:6	106, 142
4:17	54
4:11–16	197
4:11	108
4:12	52
4:14	68
4:15	52, 67
4:16	59
4:18	54, 63
4:20–24	197
4:22	76
4:23	29
4:24	76
4:25	52
4:26	194
4:27	88
4:28	103
4:29	34, 39, 59
4:30	36, 57, 58
4:31	113
5:1	53
5:2	54, 74
5:3	34
5:4	107
5:5	42, 62
5:6	53
5:8–10	187
5:8	53, 54, 68, 182
5:14	115
5:15	54
5:18–24	197
5:18	62
5:19–21	42
5:19	108
5:22–32	70
5:23	52, 67, 69, 184
5:24	33
5:26–27	74
5:27	41, 63
5:28	79
5:33	35
6:4–6	116
6:5–8	197
6:5	33, 41, 42, 108
6:10–17	75
6:10	102, 103
6:11–18	66, 72
6:11–14	69
6:11	88, 102
6:12	85, 101
6:13	83
6:14–20	197
6:14–16	127
6:18	56, 107
6:22	79

Philippians

1:1	57
1:3–7	197
1:6	36
1:7	64
1:8	61, 78, 157
1:10	69
1:11	50
1:11	62
1:12–14	197
1:13	37
1:14	78
1:15	101
1:15–17	172
1:15–16	132
1:15	172
1:16	172
1:17	78, 101, 172
1:18–20	197
1:18–19	47
1:18	47, 115
1:21	84, 115, 126, 195
1:22	50, 79
1:23	55
1:24	79
1:25	103, 113
1:27–28	197
1:27	43, 54, 61, 75
1:28	69, 114, 169

SCRIPTURE INDEX

1:29–30	42	3:16	54, 114
1:30	58	3:17	54
2:1–4	197	3:18	54, 85
2:1	41, 78, 98, 157	3:19	77, 78, 84, 91, 142, 174
2:2	181		
2:6–7	171	3:20	42, 53, 69, 84
2:6	169	3:21	36, 58, 64
2:7	62	4:1	51, 61, 78, 80, 82, 83, 113
2:8	94, 131		
2:9	131	4:3	57
2:10	86, 194	4:4–5	196
2:11	86	4:4	96
2:12	69, 79, 103, 108, 198	4:5	84
		4:7	58
2:14–16	197	4:8–9	113, 116, 134
2:15	61, 63, 91, 184	4:8	98, 199
2:16	54, 83	4:9	107, 199
2:17	34, 74, 103	4:10	31, 34, 106
2:18	103	4:11–12	181
2:21	169, 195	4:11	65, 114, 166
2:22	52, 53, 191	4:12	132
2:23	38	4:15	32
2:25	40, 60, 61, 113	4:17	72, 76, 114, 166, 174
2:27	64, 65, 114		
2:30	60, 64, 78	4:18–19	94
3:1	126	4:18	61, 74
3:2–3	169	4:19	42, 61
3:2	50, 79, 87, 91, 103, 142	4:23	78

Colossians

3:3–4	79, 109, 166, 191
3:3	82, 103, 171
3:5–7	113	1:1	112
3:5–6	98, 116	1:3–8	197
3:5	106	1:5	63
3:7–8	166	1:6	33, 36, 50, 77
3:7	62, 169	1:7	57, 60, 113
3:8–11	197	1:9–23	43, 197, 199
3:8	52	1:9–20	197
3:9	169, 170, 182	1:9	33, 36, 50, 62
3:10	132	1:10	54
3:11	44	1:12	54, 62
3:12–14	31	1:13	42, 54, 69, 177
3:12	73, 75, 106, 114, 166	1:14	58
		1:15	52
3:13–14	64, 73, 51, 54	1:16	65, 81, 107, 113
3:13	62, 65, 106, 114	1:18	52, 67, 83
3:14	65	1:19	65

SCRIPTURE INDEX

Colossians (continued)

1:20	42, 58, 65, 78, 82
1:21–23	43
1:21–22	44
1:21	58, 70
1:22	43, 63, 74, 86
1:23	59, 60, 82
1:24–29	197
1:24	52, 62, 67, 86
1:25	59, 60
1:26	43, 56, 57, 107
1:27	61, 64
1:28	101
1:29	73
2:1–3	197
2:1	58, 79, 85, 86
2:2	61, 63, 79
2:3	62, 76, 107
2:5	44, 63, 76, 86, 134, 137, 169
2:6	54
2:7	50, 59
2:8	58, 77, 108
2:9	65
2:9–10	127
2:10–15	197
2:10	52
2:11	60, 74, 103
2:12	60
2:13	43, 70, 79
2:14	60, 69
2:15	60, 72, 77, 82, 98
2:17	54, 67
2:18–19	197
2:18	64, 79, 98
2:19	30, 52, 67, 82
2:20–22	187
2:20	70, 77, 161
2:21	188
2:23	79
3:1–2	182
3:1	56, 83
3:2	83, 84, 116
3:3–4	70
3:5–7	197
3:5	49, 69, 84, 116
3:6	53
3:7	54, 199
3:8	29, 65, 116
3:9–10	73
3:9	76
3:10	76
3:11	79, 85, 132
3:12	60, 116
3:13	34
3:14	42
3:15	52, 57, 127
3:16	42, 65, 79, 108, 127
3:18–22	112
3:18–21	195
3:22	57, 79, 62
3:24	62
3:25	106
4:2–4	197
4:2	25, 56, 196
4:3	76
4:5	54, 88
4:6	67
4:7	57, 113
4:8	79
4:10	113
4:12	57, 58
4:18	78, 79

1 Thessalonians

1:2–5	197
1:2	103
1:3	64
1:5	102, 108
1:8	39, 57, 87
1:12	32
2:1–10	12
2:2	72, 113
2:4	79
2:5	61, 157, 187
2:7–8	71
2:7	52, 65, 184
2:9	26, 65, 87, 108
2:10	26, 61, 197, 157
2:11–12	43
2:11	184
2:12	54, 108

2:13	116	5:6	70
2:14–16	197	5:7–8	68
2:14	32	5:7	106, 126, 134, 139
2:15	87, 92, 113	5:8	56, 69, 75
2:16	62	5:9	69
2:17	79, 83, 85, 187	5:10	109, 174
2:19	45, 51, 78, 80, 83, 88, 159, 187	5:11	59
		5:12–22	25, 196
2:20	80, 84	5:14–22	105
3:2	113	5:14	104, 105, 126
3:5	34, 41	5:15	106, 170
3:6–8	197	5:16–22	21, 127, 128, 134
3:6	33	5:16–18	105, 143, 145
3:7	26, 108	5:19	54
3:8	61	5:23	36, 113
3:9	64, 161	5:24	31, 88
3:10	41, 85, 87	5:27	157
3:11–12	94		
3:11	113	**2 Thessalonians**	
3:12	26, 33, 34, 35, 107		
3:13	36, 61, 64, 79	1:3–10	197
4:1	30, 54	1:4	108
4:3–7	197	1:6–7	152
4:3	61	1:7b–10	26
4:4	37, 51, 61, 85	1:8	155
4:5	88	1:9	37, 66, 85
4:7	37, 61	1:10	38, 155
4:8	106	1:11	115
4:9	31, 49, 191	1:12	81
4:10–12	191	2:2	55
4:11	86	2:3	53, 88
4:12	54, 88	2:4	27, 88, 191
4:13–5:10	109	2:5	159, 191
4:13–15	109	2:7	38, 40
4:13	32, 88	2:8–9	40
4:14	21, 35, 41	2:8	88, 155
4:15–17	132	2:9	26, 88, 107
5:1	26, 31, 107, 191	2:13–14	183
5:2–11	191	2:13	59, 60, 61, 69
5:2	184	2:15	61
5:3	69, 175, 184	2:16	108, 113
5:4–8	170	2:17	79
5:4–5	68	3:1	54
5:4	32, 33, 115, 184	3:2	92, 107
5:5	169	3:5	42
5:6–22	105	3:6	54
5:6–8	109	3:7	36, 92

2 Thessalonians *(continued)*

3:8	26, 41, 65, 85, 87, 108
3:9	114
3:11	54, 103
3:12	36, 85
3:15	171

1 Timothy

1:10	48
5:19	29
6:13	40
6:14	40

Philemon

2	21, 53, 61, 112
4–6	197
5	132
7	78
9	58
10–13	197
10	53, 56, 68, 78
11	92, 103, 170
12	78
13	58, 78
16	79
19	191
20	78
25	79

1 Peter

4:3	49

Revelation

7:1	39
9:4	39

Greco-Roman Writings

Aristobulus

fr. 2	90

Aristotle

Rhet.

1.1.1	13
1.1.2	13
1.15.13–17	156
3.1–12	10
3.2.6—3.12.4	3

Cicero

Att.

9.10.1	9

Fam.

9.21.1	9
15.21.4	9

Fin.

3.21	40, 198

Nat. d.

2.95	40

Off.

1.2	3, 47

Or.

1.3.12	13
1.23.107	13
1.23.109	13
1.32.146	13
1.142	1, 2
2.261	66
3.24.93	13
3.30.120—3.31.125	13
3.31.125	13
3.37	3
3.39	45
3.49	28, 45
3.52	22, 28, 45, 47, 48
3.100	48
3.104	22, 48
3.177	194
3.199	194
3.212	194

Quint. fratr.

1.1.45–46	9

Tusc.
1.28.68–70   40

Demetrius

Eloc.
190   9
225   9
229   9
235   9
240–304   194

Demosthenes

Ep.
1–4   9

Diogenes Laertius

Vit. phil.
7.59   3

Homer

Il.
1.249   2

Libanius

Epistolary Styles
48–49   9

Menander

Thais
187.1   188
218.1   188

Philo

Abr.
1.120   90

Aet.
46   90

Cher.
121   90

Conf.
27   90
4–6   90

Mut.
1.13   90

Post.
1.167–8   90

Prob.
43–44   90

Sacr.
1.101   90, 91
101   90

Somn.
1.229   90, 91

Spec.
1.19   90

Plato

Crat.
392b   90

Phaedr.
246a   90

Plutarch

Ep. 6.464   9
13.1012   9

Quintilian

Inst.
1.4–9   28
1.5.1   3
1.5.2   3
1.5.5   28
1.5.40   29
1.5.51   42
1.5.52   14, 29
2.13.9   93

Quintilian

Inst. (continued)

2.16.11	4
2.17.37	4
2.18.38	4
3.2.1	14
3.2.3	14
3.2.4	14
3.3.11	1, 2
3.6.66	81
5.4.40	30
5.11.42	156
6.1.33	156
8.1–11.1	3
8.1.1	2, 3
8.3.5	48
8.3—10.7	3
8.3.15–39	3
8.3.30–37	17, 48
8.3.15	3
8.3.40–89	3
8.3.50	30
8.3.53	29
8.4.1–4	87
8.6	3
8.6.1	49
8.6.4	49
8.6.5	50
8.6.24–27	90
8.6.36	87
8.6.44	66
9.1.11	93
9.2	3
9.3	3
9.3.11	29
9.3.58	114
9.4	3
9.4.19–20	9
9.4.41	200
9.4.42	199
9.4.126	196
9.4.128	197
9.4.136	197
9.4.138	195
11.1	3
12.10.49–51	10
18	29

Rhet. Her.

1.19	81
1.2.3	15
2.1.1	1, 2
4.11–16	194, 196
4.18	104, 200
4.46	66

Seneca

Ben.

2.34.3–4	90
2.35.2	90
5.12–17	90

Ep.

59.1	90
75.2	9

Seneca Maior

Contr.

2.3.21	29
7.pr.5	29

Suas.

2.13ff	29

Theon

Prog.

70	10

Early Christian Writings

Augustine

Doctr. chr.

4.3.4	14, 15
4.3.5	14
4.6.9—4.7.11	4
4.7.11	4
4.7.12–13	195
4.7.21	14
4.20/39–44	195

Did.

2:7	39
6:1	39

Eusebius

Praep. ev.
8.10.2 — 90, 91

Gregory of Nazianzus

Ep.
51.4 — 9
51.5–7 — 9

Ignatius

Phil.
6:3 — 39
7:1 — 44

Irenaeus

Haer.
3.7.1–2 — 4
3.7.2 — 40, 92
3.7.1 — 38

John Chrysostom

Laud. Paul.
4.10 — 4

Mart. Poly.
2:2 — 39
3:1 — 39
8:3 — 39

Origen

Comm. Jo.
4.2 — 4

www.ingramcontent.com/pod-product-compliance
Lightning Source LLC
Chambersburg PA
CBHW031809220426
43662CB00007B/581